Digital Cultures

Digital Cultures

Edited by
Glen Creeber and Royston Martin

Open University Press

Open University Press
McGraw-Hill Education
McGraw-Hill House
Shoppenhangers Road
Maidenhead
Berkshire
England
SL6 2QL

email: enquiries@openup.co.uk
world wide web: www.openup.co.uk

and Two Penn Plaza, New York, NY 10121—2289, USA

First published 2009
Reprinted 2011

A catalogue record of this book is available from the British Library

ISBN-13: 978-0-33-5221974 (pb) 978-0-33-5221981 (hb)
ISBN-10: 0335221971 (pb) 033522198X (hb)

Typeset by Kerrypress, Luton, Bedfordshire
Printed and bound in the UK by Ashford Colour Press Ltd., Gosport, Hants.

The *McGraw·Hill* Companies

For Tomas

Contents

Acknowledgements

With love and thanks to Katherine Porter and our children, Amelia, Martha and Orlando.

Royston Martin

For giving me faith in the future, I would like to thank Nicholas, Dan, Alex, Frankie, Marika and Orrin.

Glen Creeber

Contributors

Michael Allen is a Lecturer in Film and Electronic Media at Birkbeck College, University of London. His publications include the monographs *Family Secrets: The Feature Films of D.W. Griffith* (BFI 1999), *Contemporary US Cinema* (Pearson 2003) and the edited collection *Reading CSI: Crime Television Under the Microscope* (I.B. Tauris 2007). He has also published numerous articles on the history of media technologies, and is currently completing a book on the filming and televising of the Space Race.

David Bell is a Senior Lecturer in Critical Human Geography and leader of the Urban Cultures & Consumption research cluster in the School of Geography at the University of Leeds, UK. His most recent book is the second edition of *The Cybercultures Reader*, co-edited with Barbara Kennedy (Routledge 2008).

Alexander Clark is a Lecturer in Computer Science at Royal Holloway University in London. He has written a wealth of academic papers primarily concerned with unsupervised learning of natural language, and its relevance to first language acquisition. He won the Omphalos competition, and the Tenjinno competition, which were two grammatical inference competitions in learning context-free grammars and transductions, respectively. He is a participant in the PASCAL Network of Excellence.

Glen Creeber is a Senior Lecturer in Film and Television at Aberystwyth University. His publications include *Dennis Potter: Between Two Worlds, A Critical Reassessment* (Macmillan 1998), *Serial Television: Big Drama on the Small Screen* (BFI 2004) and *The Singing Detective: BFI Television Classics* (BFI 2007). He has also edited *The Television Genre Book* (2001, second edition 2008), *50 Key Television Programmes* (Edward Arnold 2004) and *Tele-Visions: An Introduction to Studying Television* (BFI 2006).

Sean Cubitt is Director of the Media and Communications Program at The University of Melbourne. He has published widely on media globalization, media arts and media history. His publications include *The Cinema Effect* (The MIT Press 2005), *EcoMedia* (Rodopi 2005) and *Digital Aesthetics* (Sage Publications 1998).

David Gauntlett is Professor of Media and Communications at the School of Media, Arts and Design, University of Westminster. He is the author of several books on media and identities, including *Moving Experiences* (1995, second edition 2005), *Web Studies* (2000, second edition 2004), *Media, Gender and Identity* (2002, second edition 2008) and *Creative Explorations: New Approaches to Identities and Audiences* (2007), which was shortlisted for the *Times Higher* Young Academic Author of the Year Award.

He produces the popular website about media and identities – www.Theory.org.uk, and has pioneered the use of creative and visual research methods, for which he has created the hub at www.ArtLab.org.uk.

Matt Hills is a Reader in Media and Cultural Studies in the School of Journalism, Media and Cultural Studies at Cardiff University. He is the author of books such as *Fan Cultures* (Routledge 2002) and *How to Do Things with Cultural Theory* (Hodder-Arnold 2005). Matt's current projects include a book on BBC Wales' *Doctor Who* for IB Tauris, and a study of the film *Blade Runner* for the Wallflower Press 'Cultographies' book series. He has published widely on cult film and television, and media fandom.

Michele Hilmes is Professor of Media and Cultural Studies and Director of the Wisconsin Center for Film and Theater Research at the University of Wisconsin-Madison. She is the author or editor of several books on media history, including: *Hollywood and Broadcasting: From Radio to Cable* (1990); *Radio Voices: American Broadcasting 1922–1952* (1997); *Only Connect: A Cultural History of Broadcasting in the United States,* 2nd edn (2006); *The Radio Reader: Essays in the Cultural History of Radio* (2001); *The Television History Book* (2003); and *NBC: America's Network* (2007). She is currently at work on a history of the flows of transatlantic influence between US and British broadcasters during radio and television's formative years, and their impact on the production of global culture.

Sebastian Kaempf is a postdoctoral fellow at the School of Political Science and International Studies at the University of Queensland, Australia. His general research interests include the relationship between ethics and the laws of war, critical security studies, American warfare (the regionalization of), peacekeeping, and the impact of New Media technology on contemporary security.

Gérard Kraus is a doctoral candidate at Aberystwyth University, Wales. He holds an MA in Science Fiction Studies from the University of Liverpool. His research interests include Japanese Visual Culture, Science Fiction and Fantasy in the Audio-visual Media and Gaming. His previous publications are on Luxembourg's films and national identity and the history of Science Fiction Film.

Royston Martin is an academic, journalist and documentary film-maker with research interests in the digital media, the role of journalism in mediating democracy and experimental factual film. His work has been broadcast by the BBC, NBC and CNN among many others. His recent academic study of Indymedia is published in *Making Our Media: Mapping Global Initiatives Toward a Democratic Public Sphere* (Hampton Press 2008).

Last Moyo is an Assistant Professor in the department of Media, Peace and Conflict Studies at Hankuk University of Foreign Studies in South Korea. He worked as a Graduate Teaching Assistant at Aberystwyth University, where he studied for his PhD and teaches in the dual MA programme with the UN University for Peace in Costa Rica. He has also lectured for three years in the Journalism and Media Studies Department at the National University of Science and Technology (NUST), specializing in media theory and print journalism courses.

Tim Pershing was the Electoral Analyst for the International Mission to Monitor Haitian Elections, a seven nation observation mission for the 2005/6 Haitian presidential and parliamentary elections, and has also worked for the International Crisis Group in Haiti. He has worked as a photojournalist and analyst since 1990 in Bosnia, Haiti and the USA. He is currently finishing his doctoral dissertation, 'The transnational dynamics of democratic development' through Brandeis University.

Jamie Sexton is a lecturer in film and television studies at Aberystwyth University. His publications include (as editor) *Music, Sound and Multimedia: From the Live to the Virtual* (Edinburgh University Press 2007), *Alternative Film Culture in Inter-War Britain* (University of Exeter Press 2008) and (with Ernest Mathijs), *Cult Cinema: an Introduction* (Blackwell Publishing, forthcoming).

Damien Steward has been an international television journalist for almost 25 years. After a long career with Reuters, he left in 1997 and has worked in the UK as a programme editor, reporter and director for ITN, Channel 5 News and Channel 4 News. He is currently Head of Features at ITV London and regularly appears as a reporter on a number of ITN programmes.

Introduction

Glen Creeber and Royston Martin

When this book was first conceived, one of our early discussions centred around whether or not to use the term 'New Media'. Among the key concerns was that the phrase was already dated, that there was actually very little 'new' about 'New Media' today. All media and technology have been at one time new and so the implicit meaning of 'New Media' is transient at best. We started to ask the question, if 'New Media' is old, then what should it be called? Although we may understand what we mean by 'New Media' today, its roots are clearly and inevitably located long in the past. But how far into the past should we go to understand it? Our seemingly modern concept of the digital can be traced back at least four thousand years to the Babylonians who first used the numerical value of zero. Without this number most of our computers would cease to work, or clunk along at speeds far too slow for today's information super highway. So how exactly recent is the media we now choose to call 'new'?

The term 'media' itself poses a similar problem. If we take media to mean ways in which we communicate with one another, then we must examine early cave paintings that date back at least ten thousand years. Although the precise meaning of the images of bison, lions, horses and human hands discovered at Lascaux in the Dordogne in France are not entirely clear, they do provide evidence that some humans produced 'media' as long ago as the last Ice Age. With such a long and complex history, when exactly did 'new' media begin? As this suggests, what actually counts as 'media' and what counts as 'new' is often highly debated and contested, and is dependent on the definitions used. The term 'New Media' could mean many things to many people.

Despite these problems, the editors did finally decide to use 'New Media' throughout this book, mainly because (rightly or wrongly) it has become the term which people most commonly use to refer to the profound changes in electronic communication that have taken place since the arrival of digital technology in the 1980s. This does not mean that we use it uncritically, only that it is a convenient label which many will instantly recognize, and one which we believe will simply help clarify and elucidate many of the issues and debates that currently take place around the contemporary media landscape. As we shall see, there are clearly problems and limitations associated with the term itself, but for the purposes of this book, it provides a general and accessible framework around which today's media-led issues can be clearly and coherently located and critically discussed.

What is New Media?

The free Internet-based encyclopaedia, Wikipedia (see Chapter 1), itself a product of New Media, defines New Media as the product of mediated communication technologies coming together with digital computers. Before the 1980s the media relied mainly on print and analogue models like newspapers, television, cinema and radio. Now we have digital radio, television and cinema, while even the printing press has been transformed by new digital technologies such as image manipulation software like Adobe Photoshop and desktop publishing tools. Some technologies we might therefore include as or associate with New Media are:

> The Internet and World Wide Web
> Digital Television
> Digital Cinema
> Personal Computers (PCs)
> DVDs (Digital Versatile Disc or Digital Video Disc)
> CDs (Compact Discs)
> Personal Computers (PCs)
> Portable Media Players (such as the MP3 Player)
> Mobile (or Cell) Phones
> Video (or Computer) Games
> Virtual Reality (VR)
> Artificial Intelligence (AI)

New Media might not be an ideal term for such a range of technologies, but it is one that is increasingly recognized internationally and one that is generally associated with the technological transformations in communication that have recently taken place. So, what are some of the major differences between digital and analogue media? First, digital media surpasses analogue technology in that it is easily transferable across distinctly different media platforms, it is easily manipulated and networked, it can be stored and remotely accessed or distributed and is more resilient to corruption during storage or transmission. Second, digital data is also easier to manipulate, and the end result can be reproduced indefinitely without any loss of quality. In short, digital material exceeds analogue systems in terms of speed, quality and performance.

At the heart of this cultural shift sits the Internet, the ultimate network of networks. With its roots in the 1950s and the 1960s, our Internet is not especially new itself. What is new is this interconnected series of computer networks tied together by satellite, wireless, fibre optic cable and wire which has enabled the traditional model of mass communication to be radically altered. Through keyword-driven Internet search engines like 'Yahoo!', 'Lycos', 'Ask Jeeves', 'Alta Vista' and 'Google', millions of people worldwide now have instant and easy access to a vast and diverse amount of information online. Compared to encyclopaedias and traditional libraries, the World Wide Web has enabled a sudden and extreme 'decentralization' of information (see Chapter 9). According to Internet World Stats (2007), as of 30 December, 2007, 1.319 billion people use the Internet (see www.internetworldstats.com/

stats.htm). This is a startling figure for a form of technology that only really became accessible to most people in the 1990s when personal computers first became affordable (see Appendix: New Media – a timeline).

Yet, while the Internet is usually identified with New Media, computers *per se* are not. Computers have been used to co-ordinate information in multiple locations since the early 1950s. This period is now generally known as the 'first generation' of computer technology which was mainly controlled through mechanical or electrome-chanical devices. In contrast, the 'second generation' of computers are usually linked with those that worked with the use of vacuum tubes. In those days, a computer with a memory of less than a megabyte would fill up a quarter of a soccer field. With the arrival of discrete transistors and SSI-, MSI-, LSI-integrated circuits in the 1970s so the 'third-generation' computer systems were produced which heralded more portable minicomputers. Inevitably, this generation was to also be supplanted by a 'fourth generation' which now currently use VLSI integrated circuits which produced the first personal or desktop computers (most commonly identified with current 'New Media'). Yet, this is clearly not the end of computer development; with a 'fifth generation' of computers (currently at the theoretical or experimental stage) likely to produce quantum computers, chemical computers, DNA computing, optical comput-ers and Spintronics-based computers (a form of magnetoelectronics which exploits the quantum spin states of electrons as well as making use of their charged state).

Meanwhile, although we could confidently argue that the Internet is a part of New Media, as the Internet itself changes so some critics argue that it is now also entering a new phase in its development, one that is distinctly different from its past. Indeed, some critics are now talking about 'Web 2.0'; that is, a second generation of web-based communities and hosted services that evolved after the 'dot.com crash' (the end of the dot.com boom which saw an ever increasing number of web-based businesses cease trading) of 2001. As one of the original creators of the term Tim O'Reilly explains:

> The concept of 'Web 2.0' began with a conference brainstorming session between O'Reilly and MediaLive International. Dale Dougherty, web pioneer and O'Reilly VP, noted that far from having 'crashed', the web was more important than ever, with exciting new applications and sites popping up with surprising regularity. What's more, the companies that had survived the collapse seemed to have some things in common. Could it be that the dot-com collapse marked some kind of turning point for the web, such that a call to action such as 'Web 2.0' might make sense? We agreed that it did ....

> (O'Reilly 2007)

This concept of Web 2.0 is distinct from Web 1.0 in that its websites allow users to do more than just retrieve information; it includes a social element where users generate and distribute content, often with freedom to share and reuse. Examples of this would include social-networking websites (such as YouTube, MySpace and Facebook – see Chapter 7), wikis (like WikiWikiWeb and Wikipedia – see Chapter 2) that allow users to create, edit and link web pages easily and folksonomies (such as Flickr and del.icio.us), which allow users to collaboratively create and manage tags to annotate and categorize content. In their initial brainstorming, O'Reilly and Media Live International formulated their sense of Web 2.0 (ibid.):

Web 1.0		Web 2.0
DoubleClick	->	Google AdSense
Ofoto	->	Flickr
Akamai	->	BitTorrent
mp3.com	->	Napster
Britannica Online	->	Wikipedia
personal websites	->	blogging
evite	->	upcoming.org and EVDB
domain name speculation	->	search engine optimization
page views	->	cost per click
screen scraping	->	web services
publishing	->	participation
content management systems	->	wikis
directories (taxonomy)	->	tagging ('folksonomy')
stickiness	->	syndication

Critics have since argued that given the lack of set standards as to what Web 2.0 actually means, it can suggest radically different things to different people. Tim Berners-Lee, the originator of the web, has questioned whether one can use the term in any meaningful way at all, since many of the technological components of Web 2.0 have existed since its early days. However, it is clear that the Internet is not a static entity and it is changing on a daily (if not, a minute-by-minute) basis. Would it not be strange, then, that sometimes these changes (however subtle) need to be given a new name or a title for us to recognize and understand their implications more fully? Today the Internet is different in terms of content, distribution and usability than when it was first made open to the public. As such, we now have a new (some would say improved) relationship that has increased participation, creativity and interactivy on the web as a whole.

Such complexities reveal some of the problems with using the rather loose label 'New Media', even for technologies often unproblematically associated with the term. In such an ever changing and unpredictable media landscape, is it not naive (perhaps even foolish) to try to pin technology down into one stable and distinctive period; particularly if that period is the 'here and now'?

Digital cultures

Whatever we define as being part of the New Media landscape, what is new about the media today is not confined to technological advances. What this book implicitly argues is that what is key to the phenomenon of New Media is our relationship to it. Citing Terry Flew, Matt Hills argues in Chapter 7 that rather than simply asking 'what are the New Media?' we should be asking, 'what's new *for society* about the New Media?' (Flew 2000: 10, emphasis added). What we are doing with New Media and what is New Media doing with us is at the heart of this book. As we can now represent, manipulate and communicate with the world in ways unimaginable a hundred years ago, so our lives and culture have inevitably changed in the process. New Media and the Digital Revolution is part of a global cultural transformation that is likely to have as great an effect on the world as the development of the printing press or electrification.

The 'Digital Revolution' is a recent term describing the effects of the rapid drop in cost and rapid expansion of power of digital devices such as computers and telecommunications. With the arrival of the digital media, the world was arguably altered and the way that we think of ourselves and the planet (indeed the universe) has conceivably changed forever. In particular, digital culture is associated with the speeding up of societal change, causing a number of technological and social transformations in a surprisingly short amount of time. As Charlie Gere has put it:

> The possibilities of convergence and integration that digital technology offers has lead to it to dominant technical developments in media and communications. Computers are ... the essential means by which the vast amounts of data that large techno-scientific projects require are managed and manipulated. The concurrent development of science, media and capital under the aegis of digital technology produces a kind of fast-forward effect in which everything appears to take place at an accelerated rate and to produce a dramatic change in a very short time.
>
> (Gere 2002: 10)

Increased and improved communication across the globe – through satellite technology, digital television, improved telephone links and the Internet – certainly means that we are now in touch with people and events internationally with a frequency, speed, quality and affordability never imaginable in the analogue age. This has seemingly resulted in an increasing 'globalization'; that is, the combination of economic, technological, socio-cultural and political forces by which the people of the world are gradually becoming interconnected. Although components of globalization are nothing new, the deployment of business and capital across borders have continued at an unprecedented pace since the arrival of New Media. This brings with it a different conception of the world we live in; altering our notions of time, space and identity and taking us ever nearer to realizing Marshall McLuhan's notion of a 'global village' (1962) (see Chapter 1).

For some critics, this tendency towards globalization produces a world of increased cultural diversity. Indeed, some argue that we are witnessing the birth of a more 'participatory culture', allowing audiences to become increasingly involved in the creation and dissemination of meaning – moving from a communication model of 'one-to-many' to a 'many-to-many' system which has radically changed traditional top-down models of communication and information distribution (see Chapter 7). As postmodern theorist Keith Bassett has put it:

> ... the rapid development of the New Media and computer technologies ... have the potential to transform the very nature of the public sphere and open up new channels of communication to a proliferation of new voices. The public intellectual of today must now be much more alive to the

possibilities for participating in what could become a new 'cyberspace democracy' – an expanded public sphere which is less academic and less elitist, and demands the use of more accessible forms of language and discourse than those which intellectuals have become used to.

(Bassett 1996: 519)

However, other critics argue that New Media is not only unequal in its geographical and social accessibility (see Chapter 8), but that it also encourages sameness and conformity, producing a 'Big Brother' state obsessed with personal surveillance, control and an obsession with triviality and consumerism. Rather than being seen as a symbol and facilitator of 'participatory culture', the Internet is regarded as a dangerous and out of control technology that allows pornography, extreme religious/political fanaticism and computer hackers/viruses to continually undermine civil society. Some countries have also been accused of turning the Internet into an instrument of repression. Officials from China, Iran and other nations have received criticism for censoring websites, spying on Internet users and persecuting bloggers. Information technology (IT) corporations like Google, Microsoft and Cisco Systems have consequently been made to defend their businesses in such countries, accused of ignoring civil rights in order to simply maximize profits. In the West, what may appear a free and liberated source of information may, in fact, be a heavily controlled site of ideological and commercial power. As John Hartley explains:

'Portals' – the points at which you begin to navigate yourself through the web (offering features such as search engines, databases, email and news) have techniques to encourage, if not direct, users to where they want to go. AOL's [America Online] walled garden strategy successfully directs their customers to remain within AOL confines for 85 per cent of their Internet usage.

(Hartley 2002: 125)

This book does not intend to promote one version of New Media over another. Hopefully, each chapter will give the reader a different and (sometimes even contradictory) account of a particular technology and its cultural impact. Indeed, what is important to keep in mind is that as the media itself changes so 'media studies' also needs to change in order to keep up with those technological and cultural developments (see Chapter 1). Some critics argue that we now need a new form of critical theory that will take on board such complex contradictions; that allow the arguments around New Media to be discussed within a critical framework that encourages such complexities to be fully understood and accounted for. For media critics like David Gauntlett, the arrival of the Web 2 concept means that we should now also start thinking about 'Media Studies 2'. What Gauntlett suggests by this is that as the media changes, so media studies also need to develop new ways of analysing it; of taking on board the cultural, social, political and technological developments that have so radically altered our sense of ourselves and the world around us.

For the purpose of this book, Gauntlett provided a brief but accessible account of 'Media Studies 1' and 'Media Studies 2' (see below). These two contrasting accounts clearly illustrate the differences between how the media was once studied and conceived and how it is generally studied and understood today. Notice how Web 2's tendency towards prioritizing and recognizing increased audience participation in the creation of meaning is now reflected in the way that we now understand and critically analyse the New Media landscape.

Media Studies 2.0

In an interview about the newly popular concept of 'Web 2.0', following a spate of mainstream media coverage of Second Life, Wikipedia, and other collaborative creative phenomena in autumn 2006, I found myself mentioning that we might consider a 'Media Studies 2.0', influenced by that approach. Although I would not like to be introducing a new bit of pointless jargon, the idea seemed like it might have some value, for highlighting a forward-looking slant which builds on what we have already – in the same way that the idea of 'Web 2.0' is useful, even though it does not describe any kind of sequel to the Web, but rather just an attitude towards it, and which in fact was precisely what the Web's inventor, Tim Berners-Lee, intended for it in the first place (for further information, see the introduction to Web 2.0 in the Wikipedia case study at the end of Chapter 2). I have subsequently fleshed out what Media Studies 2.0 means, in contrast to the still-popular traditional model, as follows. These points are not intended to suggest that we should throw away all previous perspectives and research; but that we need to take the best of previous approaches and rework them to fit a changing environment, and develop new tools as well (more on the origins of this approach, and examples, can be found at www.theory.org.uk/ mediastudies2).

Outline of Media Studies 1.0

This traditional approach to Media Studies, which is still dominant in a lot (but not all) of school and university teaching, and textbooks, is characterised by:

- A tendency to fetishise 'experts', whose readings of popular culture are seen as more significant than those of other audience members (with corresponding faith in faux-expert 'non-methods' such as semiotics);
- A tendency to celebrate certain key texts produced by powerful media industries and celebrated by well-known critics;
- The optional extra of giving attention to famous 'avant garde' works produced by artists recognized in the traditional sense, and which are seen as especially 'challenging';
- A belief that students should be taught how to 'read' the media in an appropriate 'critical' style;
- A focus on traditional media produced by major Western broadcasters, publishers, and movie studios, accompanied (ironically) by a critical resistance to big media institutions, such as Rupert Murdoch's News International, but no particular idea about what the alternatives might be;

- Vague recognition of the internet and new digital media, as an 'add on' to the traditional media (to be dealt with in one self-contained segment tacked on to a Media Studies teaching module, book or degree);
- A preference for conventional research methods where most people are treated as non-expert audience 'receivers', or, if they are part of the formal media industries, as expert 'producers'.

Outline of Media Studies 2.0

This emergent alternative to the traditional approach is characterised by a rejection of much of the above:

- The fetishization of 'expert' readings of media texts is replaced with a focus on the everyday meanings produced by the diverse array of audience members, accompanied by an interest in new qualitative research techniques (see Gauntlett 2007, 2008);
- The tendency to celebrate certain 'classic' conventional and/or 'avant-garde' texts, and the focus on traditional media in general, is replaced with – or at least joined by – an interest in the massive 'long tail' of independent media projects such as those found on YouTube and many other websites, mobile devices and other forms of DIY media;
- The focus on primarily Western media is replaced with an attempt to embrace the truly international dimensions of Media Studies – including a recognition not only of the processes of globalization, but also of the diverse perspectives on media and society being worked on around the world;
- The view of the Internet and new digital media as an 'optional extra' is correspondingly replaced with recognition that they have fundamentally changed the ways in which we engage with *all* media;
- The patronizing belief that students should be taught how to 'read' the media is replaced by the recognition that media audiences in general are already extremely capable interpreters of media content, with a critical eye and an understanding of contemporary media techniques, thanks in large part to the large amount of coverage of this in popular media itself;
- Conventional research methods are replaced – or at least supplemented – by new methods which recognize and make use of people's own creativity, and brush aside the outmoded notions of 'receiver' audiences and elite 'producers';
- Conventional concerns with power and politics are reworked in recognition of these points, so that the notion of super-powerful media industries invading the minds of a relatively passive population is compelled to recognize and address the context of more widespread creation and participation.

David Gauntlett

Digital Culture, then, is at the heart of this book, while the changes taking place within 'Media Studies 2' will also be apparent. So, how exactly will the book manage to clarify so many complex, intricate and confusing forms of technological, cultural and theoretical debates? Below is a brief guide to help explain this book's attempt to unravel the multifaceted components of multimedia.

How is this book structured?

The theoretical context of New Media is explored and discussed in the first chapter by Glen Creeber where he describes and accounts for 'digital theory'. Tracing the development of media analysis from the modernist period to the postmodern age, he argues that New Media now needs a new type of theory and critical methodology to understand the current media world. This opening section is followed by Sean Cubitt's analysis of 'digital aesthetics', an account of the digital characteristics of the contemporary world.

After this theoretical introduction, each chapter is devoted to particular technologies. Chapter 2 starts with an exploration of the World Wide Web by David Bell, with a case study on Wikipedia by David Gauntlett. A study of digital television written by Michele Hilmes follows in Chapter 3, with a case study on the dynamics concerning the making of digital television news by Damien Steward. Digital cinema is the focus of Chapter 4, Michael Allen providing both the main section and the case study on *Star Wars Episode II: Attack of the Clones* (Lucasfilm 2002). In Chapter 5, Gérard Kraus concentrates on video and computer games, providing a case study on the first-person shooter game, *Bioshock* (2007). In Chapter 6, Jamie Sexton concludes the focus on separate technologies by looking at the production, distribution and consumption of digital music, also supplying a unique and timely case study on the iPod.

The last chapters in the book will move away from actual technologies to look at issues, debates and current concerns around New Media. Matt Hills begins with a discussion of the new active media audiences in Chapter 7, examining issues of increased audience mobility and interactivity, focusing his case study on the changing face of self-identity developed by social networking sites like YouTube, MySpace and Facebook. This debate expands into the socio-political arena in Chapter 8 when Last Moyo will discuss the 'digital divide' and the nature of inequality at the heart of the global connections of New Media. This is followed by Sebastian Kaempf's account of the contemporary representation of war in 24-hour rolling news programming that, he argues, tends to turn the violent and ugly nature of global conflict into sanitized infotainment. In Chapter 9, Last Moyo returns to take an opposing view of such issues by looking at and accounting for the more 'democratic' potential of New Media. This is backed up with a case study by Tim Pershing that explores the development of digital electoral voting in the island of Haiti. The book concludes with a look towards the future, with Royston Martin providing an overview of possible future trends and a fascinating account of Natural Language Processing (NLP) by Alexander Clark.

In this way, it is hoped that these chapters offer an accessible introduction to New Media's most important technologies, issues and debates. The concept of a book itself may well be part of 'old media', but it is hoped that such a traditional conceptual tool may help explain and account for this 'brave new world'; with its new forms of media and with its new ideas, possibilities, problems and ambiguities. At the back of this volume is a brief timeline, included in the hope that it clarifies some of the most important dates and historical developments that have taken place in the production, distribution and consumption of 'New Media' since the end of the Second World War. This book does not aim to comprehensively cover every aspect of this historical trajectory, but it is hoped that it will aid readers in their endeavor to understand and critically interpret the changes in the media that are taking place around them and that they themselves are now increasingly part of. It may not remain new forever, but for now 'New Media' is an interesting and crucial example of the way that the (post)modern world is constantly changing and developing as it heads forcefully and inevitably into the future.

1 Digital theory: theorizing New Media

Glen Creeber

There is no set method or theoretical framework for studying New Media. As this book hopefully reveals, the field is a complex and diverse one and it would be naive to suggest that a methodological and theoretical approach could ever be drawn up and regarded as definitive. Indeed, as David Bell points out in the following chapter, the theoretical complexity that typifies New Media may even reflect the state of play in current Net and Web research, suggesting the openness of New Media to 'cut and paste' different methods and theoretical approaches together. However, although there may not actually be something as clearly discernible as 'digital theory', that should not prevent us from locating and exploring a new set of theoretical issues and methodologies which might better suit and reflect our current media age.

If we are to appreciate what these new theoretical approaches to New Media might be, it is crucial that we first outline the way the media has tended to be analysed and explained historically. This is because, rather than being a systematic overthrow of previous trends, these new theoretical approaches are inevitably a development and reaction to the way the media has been understood and theorized in the past. In order to clarify this historical debate, I will first discuss (old) media analysis within a largely 'modernist' context, and then move on to discuss the connections between postmodernism, post-structuralism and New Media.

Modernism and 'old media'

Beginning approximately at the end of the nineteenth century, modernism is the umbrella term we give to the way that human society responded to the changes that took place during the industrial revolution. With its roots in the Enlightenment period of the eighteenth century, modernism tended to challenge the theocratic and God-centred notion of the world that had helped define human society in the past. Ideas such as evolution in biology, communism in politics, the theory of relativity in physics and the emerging field of psychoanalysis attempted to explain the universe in scientific or quasi-scientific terms. In this way, modernism tended to challenge and revolutionize the religious mysticism of the pre-industrial world.

With its belief in the scientific inevitability of progress, many aspects of modernism tended to have an optimistic belief in the power of modernity to transform human life for the better. However, as the twentieth century progressed, so the brutal effects of science and industrialization on human life (particularly in both the First and Second World Wars) became increasingly evident. In particular, many modernists came to perceive industrialization as the enemy of free thought and individuality; producing an essentially cold and soulless universe. It was for this reason that modernism's reaction to modernity is often perceived as intensely paradoxical, offering both a celebration of the technological age and a savage condemnation of it (see Hall 1995: 17). Struggling with these contradictions, modernist artists attempted to reflect the chaos and dislocation at the heart of the modernization process. As the growth of technology and science transformed our conception of society and ourselves, so artists and intellectuals sought new ways to represent and articulate the fragmentation of this 'brave new world'. Surrealism vividly dramatized Freud's insights into the power of dreams and the unconscious, while the Futurists espoused a love for the machine, technology and speed. Yet, there was also a deep anxiety embedded in many of these artistic expressions; the schizophrenia of the modern experience seemed to be at the heart of the 'stream of consciousness' novel, while the paintings of the Abstract Expressionists seemed to articulate the chaotic, anarchic, idiosyncratic and nihilistic landscape of the modern world.

Implicit in these artistic movements was the modernist belief in the role of the artist, a romantic figure often regarded as a self-exiled hero whose genius was able to revolutionize and transcend both art and the world around us. As David Harvey puts it, the 'struggle to produce a *work of art*, a once and for all creation that could find a unique place in the market, had to be an individual effort forged under competitive circumstances' (emphasis in the original, 1990: 22). And it was partly modernism's belief in the power of art and the artist to transform the world that lay behind its overwhelming distrust and distaste for the sort of everyday culture to be found in pulp novels, the cinema, television, comics, newspapers, magazines and so on. As Andreas Huyssen points out, modernism was almost consistently 'relentless in its hostility to mass culture' (1986: 238), arguing that only 'high art' (particularly a strain of it known as the 'avant-garde') could sustain the role of social and aesthetic criticism. It was this tension between these two extremes (a 'mindless' mass culture versus an 'enlightened' avant-garde) that perhaps most explicitly defined modernism's reaction to the media's early development during the twentieth century.

There are many examples that reflect modernism's disdain for the media, but perhaps one of the most famous groups of intellectuals to take this ideological stance was 'The Frankfurt School'. Exiled from Germany to America during the Second World War, this group of European Marxists were struck how American mass culture shared many similarities with the products of mass production. In particular, The Frankfurt School liked to perceive the media as a standardized product of industrialization, frequently connecting mass culture with aspects of Fordism. Fordism was a term coined to describe Henry Ford's successes in the automobile industry, particularly his improvement of mass-production methods and the development of the assembly line by 1910. His use of mass-production techniques meant that cars could be made more cheaply and therefore became more accessible to ordinary American citizens. However, because they were mass-produced all his model T. Fords were exactly the same. When asked what colours his cars came in, Ford famously replied, 'any color – as long as it's black'.

For the Marxist theorists of The Frankfurt School, this 'Fordist' philosophy was also evident in all aspects of mass culture, where every television show, film, pulp novel, magazine, and so on were all identical. Their description of the 'Culture Industry' clearly reveals their distaste for these 'industrialized' products and their formulaic packaging. Instead of stimulating audiences, these media 'products' were designed to keep the masses deluded in their oppression by offering a form of homogenized and standardized culture. As Theodor W. Adorno explains with reference to popular music:

> *Structural Standardization Aims at Standardized Reactions*: Listening to popular music is manipulated not only by its promoters but, as it were, by the inherent nature of this music itself, into a system of response mechanisms wholly antagonistic to the idea of individuality in a free, liberal society ... This is how popular music divests the listener of his spontaneity and promotes conditional reflexes.

> (Adorno [1941] 1994: 205–6, emphasis in original)

Such anxieties about the media also came to inform some aspects of broadcasting policy. For example, the BBC's notion of 'public service broadcasting' was based on a number of cultural, political and theoretical ideals akin to modernism. In particular, its first director General, John Reith, argued that broadcasting should be used to defend 'high culture' against the degrading nature and influence of mass culture. This is one of the reasons why he argued so strongly that the BBC should be financed entirely by taxation, thereby avoiding the heavily commercialized nature of the American media. Although he would have been politically apposed to the Marxist beliefs of The Frankfurt School, Reith would have shared their concern for the corrupting influence of mass culture on a powerless and uneducated audience. 'It is occasionally indicated to us', he famously wrote, 'that we are apparently setting out to give the public what we think they need – and not what they want – but few know what they want and very few know what they need' (cited by Briggs 1961: 238).

This perception of a mass audience as generally passive and gullible was reflected in media analysis during the modernist period, particularly in the 'effects' model of audience research. Sometimes referred to as the 'hypodermic needle' model, this way of approaching audiences tended to conceive them as wholly defenceless and constantly 'injected' by media messages, as if it were some form of mind-altering narcotic. Audience research carried about by The Frankfurt School was clearly part of this 'effects' tradition, simply aiming to validate its pessimistic claims about media indoctrination. In terms of textual analysis the school pursued a similar trajectory, critiquing the means by which mass culture disseminated the dominant ideology of the bourgeoisie. Adorno's ([1941] 1994) work on popular music, Lowenthal's (1961) studies of popular literature and magazines and Hertog's (1941) studies of radio soap opera, all revealed similar preoccupations with the 'standardization' of mass culture and the media.

Despite the pessimistic approach of The Frankfurt School towards the media, it can still be praised for at least taking these new Media forms seriously and worthy of academic study. This project was continued and developed by the Structuralist movement which became increasingly popular in the 1950s and 1960s. Partly growing from a belief in the power of science and rationalism, structuralism argued that the individual is shaped by sociological, psychological and linguistic structures over which they have little control. This belief in the power of rational thought also informed a methodology that could be used to uncover these structures by using quasi-scientific methods of investigation. Semiotics played a central role in this endeavour, being applied to all manner of cultural texts from the cinema to advertising and from photography to comics. Based on Ferdinand de Saussure and Charles Sanders Peirce's work on linguistics, semiotics set out a clear and coherent methodology by which the meaning of any text could be read objectively as a system of 'signs'. By 'decoding' these 'signs', semioticians could gradually unravel the means by which an audience were being manipulated. As Daniel Chandler puts it, '[d]econstructing and contesting the realities of signs can reveal *whose* realities are privileged and whose are suppressed. Such a study involves investigating the construction and maintenance of reality by particular social groups' (emphasis in the original, 2004a: 15).

Roland Barthes's ([1957] 1973) hugely influential book *Mythologies* famously used structuralism and semiotics to analyse all forms of mass culture including wrestling matches, the Citroën car, Greta Garbo's face and soap-powder. Yet, as a Marxist, the conclusive nature of the textual readings supplied by the likes of Barthes left little doubt that structuralism still saw mass culture as primarily propagating the forces of a dominant and all-persuasive ideology. One of Barthes's most famous examples of this process at work was his semiotic analysis of the photo on the cover of a *Paris Match* magazine in 1955. Showing a young black soldier saluting the French flag, Barthes argued that this was an example of the media giving French Imperialism a positive image in a moment of national crisis. So while the quasi-scientific methods of structuralism helped to further legitimate the study of mass culture and the media after the war, its conclusions still tended to suggest that audiences were powerless to resist its hidden meanings (see Barthes 1977a).

In this way, then, we can begin to identify some of the major components by which the media and its audiences were conceived and analysed during the first half of the twentieth century. In particular, the context of modernism gives us a theoretical insight into the way in which the media was understood and the ideological impulses which inevitably influenced its critical theories. This type of theoretical approach generally distrusted the media, arguing that its audience needed to be protected from its standardized and debasing influence. It therefore differs profoundly from the theoretical ideas that have now come to define 'digital theory' and the role of New Media in the twenty-first century.

Postmodernism and New Media

Whereas modernism was generally associated with the early phase of the industrial revolution, postmodernism (first identified in architecture (see Jenks 1984) is more commonly associated with many of the changes that have taken place after the industrial revolution. A post-industrial (sometimes known as a post-Fordist) economy is one in which an economic transition has taken place from a manufacturing-based economy to a service-based economy. This society is typified by the rise of new information technologies, the globalization of financial markets, the growth of the service and the white-collar worker and the decline of heavy industry (see Bell 1976). Not surprisingly, it is seen that the culture and politics produced by a 'post-industrial' society will be markedly different to that which was dominated by the industrial context of modernism. These cultural changes can partly be understood as the inevitable by-product of a consumer society, where consumption and leisure now determine our experiences rather than work and production. This means that 'consumer culture' comes to dominate the cultural sphere; that the market determines the texture and experiences of our everyday lives. In this 'postmodern' world there is no point of reference beyond the commodity and any sense of technology itself as separate to experience is slowly disappearing.

These changes in post-industrial society have clearly influenced the way that critical theory now understands and conceives the role which the media currently plays in society. In particular, there has been a discernible shift away from the cultural pessimism that once defined the modernist approach to the media found in the likes of The Frankfurt School. Perhaps the first signs of such a critical shift can be detected in the work of McLuhan. While McLuhan shared many of the modernist anxieties about the ideological influence of the media on a gullible and powerless audience (see, for example, his early analysis of the detrimental effects of advertising in *The Mechanical Bride: Folklore of Industrial Man* (1951)), his work often betrayed an enthusiasm and excitement for the media that was seldom detected in modernist critical theory. Even his writing style seems steeped in the fragmented messages of the electronic media with famous aphorisms such as 'the medium is the message' appearing to mimic advertising slogans or sound bites. Indeed, his early use of the term 'surfing' (to refer to rapid, irregular and multi-directional movement through a body of documents), preceded the World Wide Web and multi-channel television by some 30 years. As Levinson (1999) points out in *Digital McLuhan*, much of his work anticipated the power of New Media to enhance an audience's interactivity with electronic information as a whole – transforming us all from 'voyeurs to participants' (pp. 65–79).

This theoretical shift in the conception of the media and its audience was later carried out by much of the work informed by post-structuralism. While structuralism generally reflected the modernist need to uncover the latent ideological meaning embedded in the media text, post-structuralism tends to take a less deterministic view about the nature of the media as a whole. Influenced by the work of theorists like Louis Althusser (1971) and Antonio Gramsci (1971), media analysis gradually began to acknowledge that ideology was more complex than first imagined, that media audiences could resist ideological meaning and that texts themselves could be 'polysemic', that is, consisting of multiple meanings (see Fiske 1998: 62–83). This inevitably meant that the modernist insistence that a media text could be stripped down to one ideological meaning became increasingly untenable. As Elen Seiter puts it:

> Post-structuralism emphasizes the slippage between signifier and signified – between one sign and the next, between one context and the next – while emphasizing that meaning is always situated, specific to a given context ... Theories of psychoanalysis and of ideology, under the influence of post-structuralism, focus on the gaps and fissures, the structuring absences and the incoherencies, in a text ....

> (Seiter 1992: 61)

The indeterminacy of meaning in a text is central to much of poststructuralist theory, changing the very means by which contemporary research not only understands the media but also its receiver or 'reader'. In particular, the influence of poststructuralist theory on media analysis means that current research has tended to put less emphasis on the way a text is *encoded* (by its producer) to the ways in which it is *decoded* (by its receivers) (see Hall 1973). Originally referred to as the 'Uses and Gratifications' tradition, new methods of media analysis have now produced a wealth of material that endeavours to show how complex the production of meaning between a text and its audience actually is (see Brooker and Jermyn 2003). This is a profound step away from the modernist and structuralist conception of the audience as passive cultural dupes, re-imagining them instead as active participants in the production of meaning.

As this suggests, crucial to both the postmodern and poststructuralist view of the world is the notion that meaning itself can never be entirely pinned down. Building on structuralism's understanding of culture through the structures of linguistics, post-structuralism argues that reality can only really be known through language and discourse. This means that rather than simply and innocently reflecting the real world, language actually *constructs* our view of ourselves and our notions of 'the real'. So, rather than looking for a deeper meaning which somehow magically exists beyond language and discourse, post-structuralism tends to analyse the discursive and practical conditions by which 'truth' is constructed (see, for example, Foucault 1991). So while modernism tended to search for meaning and truth among the chaos and fragmentation of the modern world, postmodernism appears to accept that the pursuit for such universal truth is futile.

This instability of 'truth' is linked to the postmodernist claim that by the end of the twentieth century people had gradually become more sceptical about utopian theories such as the Enlightenment and Marxism. Dismissing them as 'grand narratives', postmodern theorists tended to categorize these totalizing world views as nothing more than linguistic and narrative constructs. Although it may be difficult to conceive of such a theory in a world partly in the grip of religious fundamentalism, the belief in the utopian possibilities of modernism does appear to be contested by what many critics argue is an increasingly cynical Western world. As postmodern theorist Jean-François Lyotard puts it:

> In contemporary society and culture – postindustrial society, postmodern culture – ... The grand narrative has lost its credibility, regardless of what mode of unification it uses, regardless of whether it is speculative narrative or a narrative of emancipation ... Anytime we go searching for causes in this way we are bound to be disappointed.
>
> (Lyotard 1984: 37–8)

This distrust towards the revolutionary projects of modernity may help explain postmodernism's more relaxed attitude towards the media as a whole. While the media was generally dismissed by modernism as standardized, formulaic and shallow, postmodernism tends to celebrate popular culture generally for its implicit refusal to look for deep universal truths, tending instead to embrace image, surface and 'depthlessness'. This may help explain why postmodern aesthetics appear to indulge in increased levels of intertextuality, generic hybridity, self-reflexivity, pastiche, parody, recycling and sampling. Such characteristics may be seen as reflecting a world where traditional binary oppositions such as 'fact' and 'fiction', the 'real' and the 'unreal', the 'authentic' and the 'inauthentic' are less clear than they may have once seemed. This is perhaps why Andy Warhol's work is often conceived as intrinsically 'postmodern'. Warhol's 'Campbell's soup cans' (1962), for example, confuse and upset the very differences by which we have come to understand 'art' and the products of 'mass production'.

Indeed, some postmodern critics argue that it is now increasingly impossible to distinguish between the media 'image' and the 'real' – each 'pair has become so deeply intertwined that is difficult to draw the line between the two of them' (McRobbie 1994: 17). According to the philosopher Baudrillard (1994), in a contemporary society the simulated copy has now even superseded the original object. This phenomenon Baudrillard refers to as the 'third order of simulacra' which produces a state of '*hyperreality*'. It is not that simply the line between the media image and the real have become blurred; it is more that the media image and the real are now part of the same entity and are therefore now unable to be separated at all. As Best and Kellner puts it, '[r]eality and unreality are not mixed like oil and water; rather they are dissolved like two acids' (1997: 103). Some critics have even suggested that the differences between human and machine is now beginning to disappear, tending to eradicate the old 'human' versus 'technology' binary opposition upon which so much of the pessimistic theories of modernism were based. Although the idea of the cyborg (a hybrid of machine and organism) may still be in its scientific infancy, feminist critics like Donna Hathaway (1991) already use it as a metaphor for the power to deconstruct essentialist notions of gender and identity in a 'posthuman' world. As Mark Dery puts it:

> Our interaction with the world around us is increasingly mediated by computer technology, and that, bit by digital bit, we are being 'Borged', as devotees of *Star Trek: The Next Generation* would have it – transformed into

cyborgian hybrids of technology and biology through our ever-more-frequent interaction with machines, or with one another through techno-logical interfaces.

(Dery 1994: 6)

For some critics, then, such a theoretical framework gives us a new critical arena through which we can start to understand and account for various aspects of New Media. For example, the postructuralist and postmodernist distrust of a stable and fixed notion of the 'real' tends to reflect the landscape of New Media where such traditional definitions are increasingly becoming problematized by new technologies. With the arrival of artificial intelligence, cyberculture, virtual communities and virtual reality, our sense of what is 'real' and what is 'unreal' is clearly undergoing a dramatic transformation. For example, real existing companies now place advertise-ments in virtual worlds like Second Life, an artificial environment which affects real existing sales. So how can we separate the 'real' in this example from the 'virtual'? What part of this virtual world is 'real' and what part of it is not? Admittedly, this is an extreme example, but as the sociologist David Holmes points out, it is an illustration of the wider kinds of technological and cultural change that develop-ments in New Media are currently producing:

> Of the myriad technological and cultural transformations taking place today, one has emerged to provide perhaps the most tangible opportunity for understanding the political and ethical dilemma of contemporary society. The arrival of virtual reality and virtual communities, both as metaphors for broader cultural processes and as the material contexts which are beginning to enframe the human body and human communication …

(Holmes 1997: 1)

As this suggests, this problematizing of what we once recognized as 'real' will inevitably influence the very notion we may have of an 'authentic self', the conception of identity in a postmodern world becoming increasingly fluid and contestable. In particular, it has been argued that the increased interactivity of New Media generally allows audiences to play around with and make their own composite identities from various and sometimes even contradictory sources. This process is referred to by Hartley (1999: 177–85) as 'DIY citizenship', the notion that the media now allows us to all create our own complex, diverse and many faceted notions of personal identity. With so many different communities now open to us on the web, we can begin to simply pick and choose which identities we want to adopt and which ones we want to reject, allowing an individual to decide how they define themselves rather than simply having to stick to the narrow and limited number of choices that once defined the past. This is in stark contrast to a world where identity is primarily a matter of heritage.

This fluid notion of identity certainly appears to be in direct contrast to the concept of citizenship and identity that was propagated by the underpinnings that informed the roots of modernism, particularly a concept like public service broadcast-ing. John Reith's conception of 'culture' and 'Britishness', for example, now seems to be unforgivably narrow and restrictive in the transnational, multicultural world (what McLuhan (1962) famously described as the 'global village') that many now live in thanks to the arrival of email, satellites and global television. Postmodernist critics might argue that even the notion of 'broadcasting' itself is a totalizing concept which was never able to successfully reflect the sheer diversity of a nation or its people (see Creeber 2004). The phrase 'narrowcasting' – that is used to denote New Media's pronounced interest in addressing and catering for niche audiences – perhaps better encapsulates the role of television and radio in a world of multimedia (see Curtin 2003).

As we have seen, the increased interactivity of audiences in a New Media context is also articulated in poststructuralist theory whose tendency is to conceive the audience as *active* participators in the creation of meaning. Websites like YouTube, MySpace and Facebook appear to reflect this recent understanding of 'participatory culture'; not only creating virtual communities but also allowing audiences to become 'producers' as well as 'receivers' of the media. Theories of 'fandom' are important here with the Internet allowing the fans of different forms of culture to create virtual communities that add to the original understanding and even content of their chosen interests (see Chapter 7). For example, the rise of 'slash fiction' allows audiences to actively participate in the production of meaning by creating extra-textual material about their favourite television programmes (see Jenkins 2006b). Consequently, rather than being seen as essentially commercial and inactive, in a postmodern world consumption itself is now regarded as a positive and participatory act. As Mackay puts it, 'Rather than being a passive, secondary, determined activity, consumption … is seen increasingly as an activity with its own practices, tempo, significance and determination' (1997: 3–4). Such ideas have clearly informed David Gauntlett's notion of 'Media Studies 2', a theoretical embodiment of Tim O'Reilly's notion of Web 2, a world where users generate and distribute content, often with freedom to share, create, use and reuse (see Introduction and Chapter 2).

Indeed, John Reith's 'top-down' cultural 'uplift' seems particularly redundant in a world where audiences are increasingly determining their own choice of media and what they do with it. The hypertextual 'cut' and 'paste' culture of New Media – that seemingly encourages sampling, poaching and remixing – produces not only copy-right problems, it also further confuses the very means by which we conceive of the media and its relationship with its audience. Certainly, the idea that a media organization like the BBC could so rigidly dictate public tastes seems almost unimaginable now. As Lev Manovich points out, we may now require a completely new theory of authorship to help us understand the current relationship between the media and its audience, one which fits:

> perfectly with the logic of advanced industrial and post-industrial societies, where almost every practical act involves choosing from some menu, catalog, or databse. In fact … New Media is the best available expression of the logic of identity in these societies – choosing values from a number of preferred menus.

> (Manovich 2002: 128)

This increased interactivity among the New Media audience has also prompted some critics to suggest that there has even been an increased 'democratization' in the nature of New Media compared to old. 'Citizen Journalism' (where people use blogs, photos or phone footage to create and comment on the news of the day) is only one current example among many that postmodernists might select to illustrate the increased ability of 'ordinary' people to become actively involved in the very production of the media; moving power away from the 'author' into the hands of the 'audience' (see Chapter 7). Indeed, for theorists like Mark Poster (1997), the Internet provides a 'Habermasian public sphere' – a cyberdemocratic network for communicating information and points of view that will eventually transform into public opinion. As voting on the Internet becomes more widespread so it may increase our democratic rights even further (see Chapter 9).

The postmodern context I have outlined here tends to place New Media in a primarily positive light, as if technology itself is simply opening up increased levels of audience participation, creative involvement and democracy. However, other chapters in this book will clearly outline some of the more negative features of this New Media world, not least the 'digital divide' that currently enables only a small fraction of the planet to participate in this new digital culture (see Chapter 8). Even in the West, not all New Media participants are created equal. As Henry Jenkins explains, '[c]orporations – and even individuals within corporate media – still exert greater power than any individual consumer or even aggregate of consumers. And some consumers have greater abilities to participate in this emerging culture than others' (2006a: 3). Similarly, some critics refer to the 'myth of interactivity', arguing that the participatory nature of New Media has been over-inflated to such an extent that people now refuse to see its limitations. 'To declare a system interactive', Espen Aarseth warns us, 'is to endorse it with a magic power' (1997: 48).

Critics have also argued that a landscape of postmodernism and New Media are turning citizens of democracies into apolitical consumers, no longer able to distinguish between the simulated illusions of the media and the harsh realities of capitalist society that they implicitly conceal. Many critics argue that now even the political landscape is a triumph of image over substance, a terrifying symbol of McLuhan et al's (1967) aphorism that 'the medium is the message', that is, a world where *how* something is presented is actually more important than *what* is being presented. In particular, these critics tend to argue that the postmodern obsession with 'image' over 'depth' produces a superficial and artificial environment where little is taken seriously; that its predominantly 'camp' aesthetic has turned everything into entertainment. As Neil Postman puts it:

> Our television set keeps us in constant communication with the world, but it does so with a face whose smiling countenance is unalterable. The problem is not that television presents us with entertaining subject matter but that all subject matter is presented as entertaining ...

> (Postman 1985: 89)

Postman's nightmarish vision of a world where all information is packaged as entertainment is perhaps further facilitated by a form of New Media that appears to give us so much choice, but ultimately ends up by limiting *real* choice; reducing everything to exactly the same commodified and consumerist product. Critics argue that the avant-garde's revolutionary power has now also been reduced to sheer commercialism, modernism's radical forms and aesthetics used to sell alcohol and cigarettes in advertising (what David Harvey calls 'the official art of capitalism' [1989: 63]). Rather than increasing people's ability to play with various identities, critics have even argued that the globalization of the world (partly facilitated by New Media) may actually decrease cultural and national identities as we all become increasingly alike and culturally homogenous. This process has been provocatively described by one critic as the 'McDonaldization' of society (see Ritzer 2000).

The Internet has also been accused of narrowing people's choices down and encouraging obsessions with worthless and unimportant trivia such as bizarre hobbies and low-quality television shows (see McCracken 2003). As more and more virtual communities come into being so some critics argue that real relationships and communities are being neglected; the one-to-one human contact on which civilization was based becoming increasingly redundant (see Lister et al. 2003: 180–81). Meanwhile, the breakdown of the 'private' and 'public' sphere (people treating the public arena of cyberspace as if it were private) has serious implications on civil liberties that are only now being fully recognized. Recently, for example, it has come to light that many employers are surreptitiously using websites like MySpace to ascertain the online personality of a future employee (see Finder 2006). Similarly, it is still hard to conceive the democratization of the media actually taking place in a country like China where Google and Rupert Murdoch seem happy to cooperate with the strict censorship of a non-democratic government in order to gain access to the vast financial potential of the country.

Some critics of postmodernism also argue that if there has been a breakdown between the 'image' and the 'real', then we are entering an age of 'moral relativism' where little critical or moral judgement can be exercised and where theorists even discuss the 'reality' of the Gulf War (see Norris 1992; Chapter 8). Such thinking, it is argued, inevitably produces a dangerous and unregulated media, where endless hardcore pornography sits alongside chat rooms that prey on the young and the innocent or websites that give voice to extremist political forces (see Dean 2000). New Media may seem to offer a world of glossy images and limitless communication, but it is also important to keep in mind who and what is left out of its postmodern embrace. Technological utopianism might suggest that New Media will automatically improve our world for the better, but our future well-being clearly lies in how and what we do with the choices we now have on offer.

Conclusion

Whatever theoretical point of view you may take about New Media, it is difficult to argue that the media itself has not come under considerable change over the last 20 or 30 years. We therefore need a new theoretical framework which allows us to understand and appreciate both the positive and negative features of our current media age. This means that critical understanding of the field is essential if we are to produce a sophisticated theoretical approach. As I mentioned at the start of this section, it would be naive to suggest that a methodological and theoretical approach to New Media could ever be drawn up and regarded as definitive, but this section was simply intended to offer a framework through which a number of approaches can be more carefully contextualized and approached.

The theory of New Media is still in its early stages of development and there is much work to do to flesh out and expand some of the basic arguments set out here and elsewhere in the book. However, I hope that what is clear by now is that since its conception, the media has been analysed and examined through a whole plethora of diverse schools, theories and methodologies. I hope that by simply organizing some of these within their 'modernist' and 'postmodern' contexts, it has helped to clarify many of the major debates that have taken place in and around the field as a whole. Although other chapters in this book might not refer explicitly to modernism or postmodernism, they will clearly offer greater insight into some of the basic theoretical ideas introduced here. 'Digital theory' may not yet be discipline in its own right, but its presence will be felt throughout this book and the way that we conceive New Media long into the future.

Recommended reading

Gauntlett, David and Horsley, Ross (eds) (2000) *Web.Studies*, 2nd edn. London and New York: Arnold.

Jenkins, Henry (2006) *Convergence Culture: Where Old and New Media Collide*. New York and London: New York University Press.

Lister, Martin, Dovey, Jon, Giddens, Seth, Grant, Iain and Kelly, Kieran (2003) *New Media: A Critical Introduction*. London and New York: Routledge.

Manovich, Lev (2002) *The Language of New Media*. Cambridge, MA and London: The MIT Press.

Thompson, John B. (1995) *The Media and Modernity: A Social Theory of the Media*. Cambridge: Polity Press.

Case Study: Digital aesthetics

Sean Cubitt

Deriving from the Greek, the term 'aesthetics' refers to the study of sensory or sensori-emotional values. Originally, the term was primarily used in connection with nature; trying to identify the transcendent and timeless aspects of natural beauty. It was only in the eighteenth century that these notions of quality were transferred to the artistic value of art and culture as a whole. However, as judgements of taste and aesthetic quality are not only subjective but social value judgements, critics like Terry Eagleton have recently emphasized that such categories are 'inseparable from the construction of the dominant ideological forms of modern class society' (1990: 3). It is perhaps more accurate, therefore, to talk about certain *types* of aesthetics that either refer to a particular section of society (such as 'black' or 'middle-class' aesthetics), a political philosophy (such as 'feminist' or 'green' aesthetics) or an artistic movement (such as 'avant-garde' or 'postmodern' aesthetics), than making universal and essentializing claims about culture in its entirety.

Certain forms of media also share 'aesthetic' characteristics that differentiate them from other types of cultural form and expression. For example, critics like John Ellis (1982) have attempted to identify the particular aesthetics of television, distinguishing that medium's unique characteristics from the likes of radio, cinema and video. In this chapter I want to discuss 'digital' aesthetics, explaining and exploring how the digital representation of the world is aesthetically different from the one that was provided by analogue. I will start by giving a broad account of the digital landscape, offering insights into the means by which digital culture has transformed both our professional and personal lives. I will then move on to look at the textual dynamics and characteristics of digital technology in more detail, examining its form and finally asking whether or not such a unified 'digital' aesthetic even exists.

Defining the digital landscape

Our first question when defining the digital landscape is: What do digital media look, sound and feel like? The fundamental quality of digital media is that they are driven by minute, discrete electrical impulses, commonly characterized as 'on' and 'off'. So, one common aesthetic quality of digital equipment is a tangle of wires, and indeed some generating authorities are experimenting with 'smart electricity' which will supply network services through every socket in the home or office. Other applications like wireless networks and digital satellite television are transmitted through the air and are effectively invisible, inaudible and cannot be felt. This poses a first problem in digital aesthetics: many aspects of digital media simply cannot be sensed. In fact, as we shall see, what you *cannot* see is often the most significant thing about digital aesthetics.

Nonetheless, digital media normally require the support of some kind of physical device. Typically, these used to resemble small televisions with a typewriter in front of them: devices deriving from the 1930s and 1870s, respectively. Today, however, digital devices come in all shapes and sizes. The desktop machine has been the subject of a massive rethinking in design, from the beige boxes of the 1980s through Apple's successful translucent iMac design of the 1990s to the plethora of portable devices – laptops, personal digital assistants (PDAs), mobile phones, MP3 players – that we find everywhere in the 2000s. Most of these devices sport screens, and most of them have some kind of input device – mouse, stylus, keypad, click-wheel – but some have only one (e.g. the iPod Nano), and many other common digital gadgets like step counters, cameras and wristwatches have idiosyncratic combinations of screens, buttons and menus that bear little relation to the common image of the desktop computer. At the turn of the millennium, there was much talk in the industry of the convergence of all these widgets in one super widget, a portable device that would include a camera, MP3 player, mobile phone and personal assistant, that would link up with a master computer at home or work, but market trends seem to demonstrate that people like to have dedicated machines for each of these functions, even though many phones now come with the capacity to take videos and photos and play back music.

Unfortunately, many of our devices are incompatible. Each mobile phone company has its own proprietorial format for video, for example; few of which work with the standard computer formats. Texting and email work on very different principles, even though they appear to be very alike from the user's point of view. And synchronizing portable devices with domestic computers can be a high-risk activity (especially in multi-computer households, or where the blurring distinctions between work and home mean that an individual has two or three computers to work with). One problem here is the issue of software compatibility. All digital devices have as a basic design structure some kind of input device, a central processing unit, some memory and some kind of output. To make these work, the device requires a set of instructions: software. Typically, it will require an operating system (Windows, Mac OS, Linux ....), on top of which sit a layer of applications (word processing, image and sound manipulation and generation, spreadsheets, and so on). Though many manufacturers make applications for numerous operating systems, and try to maintain a similar look-and-feel to their operation regardless of what kind of machine they run on, under the bonnet there are substantial differences. These become especially apparent in networked processes, where a file has to be passed between users using different operating systems or even different versions of the same operating system.

As we have already suggested, digital media have inherited legacies from previous generations of media like the typewriter and the television. Television itself can be understood in a longer history beginning with the cinema, a public building for social viewing. Television, while also used extensively in public places like bars and youth clubs since the 1940s, has a much more domestic profile, and partly because of its size tended for several decades to be viewed in the family circle. Computers, however, moved the screen even closer: from the far end of a hall in cinema, to the corner of the living room with television, now computer screens sit a matter of inches from our faces, and 'third screen' devices like video iPods and mobile phones are even closer, more like clothing than familiar media. One source of this dynamic is the origin of ubiquitous computing in what is sometimes called the second office revolution. The first office revolution was accompanied by New Media and new devices: the typewriter, the adding machine, the filing cabinet, the rolodex and the slide-rule. The second digitized these, led by the aptly named company International Business Machines (IBM).

The typical office of both the first and second office revolutions looked much like the office inhabited by Bob Cratchett in Dickens's *Christmas Carol*: rows of desks facing a supervisor, and at each desk a clerk performing repetitive but intellectually demanding and skilled jobs. The skills of double-entry bookkeeping and copperplate handwriting were replaced swiftly with typescript and word processing, adding machines and spreadsheets. This rapid deskilling (see Braverman 1974) meant that office work could be less well paid, opening the doors to women workers, who were less likely to have high levels of education, less likely to unionize, and more likely to leave to bear children, meaning they had fewer expectations of a career structure. The other characteristic of the office is the division of the workforce, leading to the development of the individual workstation as a typical factor in computer design, further encouraging the individualization of public, domestic and now personal entertainment. Anyone who has attempted to work on a shared computer will recognize that they are not designed for multiple users or social use.

Deriving from this legacy of office provision, the typical screen interface for computers remains the desktop metaphor. That desks are not typical of everyone's working environment, and that folders and files and even trash cans are quite specific to the Western concept of a specific type of work, the major operating systems all evolved versions of this system, known variously as the GUI (Graphical User Interface) or, at one time, the WIMP (Window-Icon-Menu-Pointer) system. Such defining structures as file hierarchies seem to derive from exactly the same root. In this respect, as well as in terms of content, computing seems to follow the 'remediation' rule suggested by Bolter and Grusin (2000) that every new medium starts off imitating the medium before it. Thus, digital editing programs imitate film editing suites; image manipulation software mimics photographic darkrooms. It could also be argued that the design aesthetics of computers have followed slavishly the hierarchies and work discipline of the nineteenth-century office.

A key response to the desocializing aspect of computing has been the massive expansion in networked services, notably following the release of Mosaic, the first mass-release web browser, in 1993. While spreadsheets had been the 'killer app' that secured the office computer's place, email was the driver for the new generation of domestic as well as office users. Mosaic's replacement Netscape, released in 1994, provided a free, relatively simple email client in addition to its browser functions. The first generation of browsers borrowed their names from the idealistic vision of cyberspace as endless frontier (see Barlow [1996] 2001): Navigator, Explorer, Safari.

That these open-ended wanderings were on the one hand largely controlled by the most successful portals (in the early days AOL) and on the other perpetually framed by the browser window itself rarely seemed to matter. Skilled users could always escape the carefully marshalled shopfronts of their Internet service providers, and it was skilled users who tended to write the influential emails, articles and books. Software critique would have to wait almost a decade before it became a key part of the intellectual landscape (see Fuller 2003, 2005).

A critical if rather technical and therefore potentially baffling aspect of software aesthetics has become highly visible in the wake of the United Nations' World Summit on the Information Society. The Internet, which includes the World Wide Web, email services, bulletin boards (BBS), file-transfer services, many only partially public subscription services, and is in effect a network of networks, whence its name, is an iceberg: four-fifths of it or more lie hidden below the surface. A global network of telecommunications cables and satellites and switching stations, millions of computers, at least 15 major organizations charged with maintaining and developing technical standards and hundreds of other players working on everything from intellectual property rights to the protection of children are all involved in making decisions about how the system works. True to the Californian roots of much of the computer industry (see Barbrook and Cameron 1995), Internet governance has been a mixture of freewheeling innovation and entrepreneurship. But as the Internet becomes a key infrastructure for global commerce, politics and communication, those who have traditionally been excluded from the elite decision-making processes of computer and telecoms engineers, especially those outside the industrial West, have begun to demand a say. Meanwhile, the American government has been successfully lobbied by entertainment and software giants to prioritize the protection of intellectual property rights, convinced that as American manufacturing decays in the competition with Asia, films, television, music, games and software will replace it as the growth engine of the economy.

The current battleground is Internet Protocol version six (IPv6), the software that allows different computers to talk to each other. Without going into the technical details, it is worth mentioning Alex Galloway's (2004; see also Terranova 2004) thesis, derived from the work of French philosophers Foucault and Deleuze, that while modern societies were characteristically societies of discipline and postmodern societies of control, digital society is characterized by protocols, the invisible but ubiquitous codes which simultaneously enable and constrain what can and cannot be done in a given system, such as the Internet or indeed a given computer. Like Lawrence Lessig, campaigner against intellectual property enforcement and popularizer of the phrase 'Code is Law', Galloway argues that decisions concerning technical capabilities effectively shape the ways technologies perform, and the kinds of expectation we have of them, which in turn shapes our behaviours when we work with them. Far from the vistas of infinite freedom scented by Barlow and the Electronic Freedom Foundation, the Internet is rapidly becoming a highly and rigidly commercial domain.

Against this utopian vision are ranged some darker fears. David Lyon (1994) and Oscar Gandy (1993) are among the many warning of the rise of the surveillance state, although perhaps better founded fears are voiced by Greg Elmer (2004), for whom the key threat comes not from the state but from commercial surveillance, characterized by another invisible technology, cookies, small packets of software run by Internet applications on a user's computer which may report back on anything from what software you have to your browsing habits, without your knowledge, and with the collusion of browser manufacturers. Indeed, a great deal of the discourse about the web, in particular, and digital networks more generally, concerns the unresolved contradictions between the promise of freedom and plenty on the one hand, and fears for security breaches, theft, piracy, child abuse, pornography and, since 9/11, terrorism. Understanding how digital devices and networks work is thus more than a necessary step in forming an aesthetic appreciation: it is crucial in countering the ill-informed utopian/dystopian squabble that characterizes old media coverage of the new. This dialectic of excitement and trepidation over emergent media has a long history too: the digital media are being treated much as comics were in the 1950s, television in the 1940s, cinema was in the 1920s, and cheap newspapers and magazines were in the 1890s.

Digital characteristics

What then is new about New Media? Terry Flew (2002: 28) isolates some of the key qualities at the macro-scale of their articulation with major social changes: digitization and convergence; interactivity and networks; virtuality and globalization. From the much more restricted vantage point of the aesthetics of computers as experienced by the end-users of software, Lev Manovich (2002) identifies five characteristics:

1   numerical representation;
2   modularity (the principle of assembling larger units from smaller ones);
3   automation;
4   variability;
5   transcoding (the relationship between computing and everyday cultures).

In his account of 'visual digital culture', focused on the experience of viewing work made on digital devices, Andrew Darley (1999) emphasizes simulation, hyperrealism and spectacle, terms which suggest a divorce between the image and reality, a heightening of the quality of images to the point that they can substitute for reality, and the decline of narrative in favour of sheer visual pleasure. These approaches, and the many more that have been offered defining the distinguishing characteristics of digital aesthetics, offer highly recognizable facets of the phenomenon. We all recognize a digital animation by its sharply defined edges, lustre and spatial sophistication; we recognize computer graphics by their saturated colours, high gloss, use of mathematical and geometrical motifs; and we can mostly tell a digital special effect from a physical one like a real stunt. Everyone can recognize the digital sound of techno music, but some people swear they can tell the difference between a vinyl record and a digital CD, claiming that the older medium has more 'warmth'. Few amateurs, however, would be able to tell a digital from an analogue photo, or tell you whether a track had been recorded digitally or on old reel-to-reel machines. For his film *Princess Mononoke* (1997), Myazaki commissioned a new piece of software, Toonshader, which would give his digital animations the look of traditional hand-painted anime – increasingly, digital tools are used to disguise their own use. And since so much medical and scientific imagery, from ultrasound scans to Hubble Space Telescope images, are digitally gathered, treated and disseminated, the idea that the connection with reality has been broken is premature.

The problem can be put like this. Digital aesthetics, like any other form of aesthetics, has to respond to the material qualities of the media it investigates. An aesthetics of painting would look at brushwork, colour, depth and consistency of the paint and so on. But digital aesthetics has the uncomfortable job of looking at many things, from celnets to Internet governance, that simply cannot be seen or touched. And where products are produced digitally, we often have no clues left that they were made that way; and many digital tools, like the dozen or more computers in a contemporary car, are tucked away where the driver cannot see them. A second problem is that there is no single digital aesthetic, in the way one could imagine a single aesthetic of painting. Old school digital games like *Super Mario Bros* (1986) are different to the latest releases. Flash animations have one aesthetic, and locative media (the artistic use of mobile technologies in a defined geographical area) another one entirely. The aesthetic of electronic music is different to that of the digital engineers recording a classical quartet. The aesthetic appreciation of a clever text message bears little relation to our enjoyment of the latest Pixar animation or a particularly elegant piece of coding in open source.

What kinds of principle, then, can we bring to bear? Among those that have the longest track record is the aesthetic principle that a whole be more than the sum of its parts. This presents two difficulties for digital aesthetics. First, the digital domain is far too vast to ever be seen as a whole, even by whole populations, since much of it is person to person (digital phone calls, SMS, email) and much of it is privately owned and protected (bank accounts, whole areas of digital publishing). And second, Manovich's principle of modularity insists that the parts remain distinct from any larger whole into which they might be assembled. The nineteenth-century Romantic aesthetic of organic unity holds little more hope, partly because the metaphor of an organism seems mismatched to the complex technological infrastructure of the digital domain; and partly because our fragmented experience of modernity does not encourage faith in overarching unifications. The early twentieth-century principle of montage aesthetics looks a more likely candidate, but too easily slips from meaning-ful juxtapositions to meaningless jumble, and is in any case as characteristic of advertising as it is of fine art. Another twentieth-century aesthetic, this time from architecture and design, suggests 'truth to materials' as a guiding principle, but while this might be helpful in choosing how to use concrete, steel and glass, it is less so in choosing how to use invisible code. Gelernter (1998), a leading programmer who was also a victim of the Unabomber, proposes 'elegance' as a key value, a mathematical concept which describes formulae which are only as complicated as they need to be, but no more so. This is indeed a valuable principle, especially in a period in which built-in obsolescence and general bloat of operating systems and applications is almost universal, and where every program seems to offer what Critical Art Ensemble (1994) describe as 'redundant functionality', functions which users rarely if ever want from a particular application.

Other contenders offer themselves. Much of the utopian discourse about network media laid claim to a renewal of democracy, away from the orgy of voting followed by long periods of (mis)representation, and towards participation on a daily basis. While this falls outside the purview of this article, the principle of democracy has a place in aesthetics, notably in the composer Arnold Schönberg's principle of the equality of all notes in a composition. When every pixel in an image can be manipulated, every symbol rewritten, every note turned and stretched, when an iPod set on shuffle flicks from one end of the musical spectrum to the other without faltering, there seems to be apparent something more than endless jumble, something perhaps closer to the endlessness of mathematics discovered by the last great mathematical forerunner of computing, Kurt Gödel. This democratic aesthetic will make more sense, however, if we extend it beyond the human realm of social relations. In our dealings with machines since the beginning of history, human beings have enslaved technology, demanding that it do what we want. Increasingly artists and technologists are developing machines which have the capacity to evolve in their own ways, from game engines to robots. The digital aesthetics that emerge in the next century will have to involve both technologies and, as bio-computing becomes a reality, our eco-system in a democratic dialogue. In the end, there is no single or simple digital aesthetics, but there is or can be a digital ethics.

2 On the net: Navigating the World Wide Web

David Bell

> More than any other New Media technology, the Internet has represented the idea of change and newness within contemporary culture. A whole new vernacular has developed from its myriad forms that underline its pervasive influence and its normalization in our lives.
>
> (Marshall 2004: 45)

My aim in this chapter is to explore, in broad brush terms, the Internet and the World Wide Web as socio-technical phenomena integral to understanding New Media. I use the term 'socio-technical' to make explicit the complex commingling of society and technology; such that an object like a computer has to be seen as the product of, and occupying space within, particular socio-technical assemblages. This notion inevitably taps into long-running academic debates about the sociology of science and technology. I also use the term 'socio-technical' to foreground that the Internet and the World Wide Web are simultaneously technological *and* social artefacts – they bundle together in complex ways hardware, software, content, ideas, experiences and practices. These ideas are discussed below in order to untangle some of these 'bundles' and help us begin to understand how we might study the World Wide Web.

Screens, nets and webs

The Internet is best thought of as an interconnected, global network of computers (and other 'computational devices' such as personal digital assistants (PDAs), phones, and so on). In the late 1960s, various experiments in networked communication were being carried out, for various purposes, all driven by a shared enthusiasm to find new uses of emergent technologies in computation and telecommunications. Among these was ARPANET, an initially small network established by the US Department of Defense, connecting together a number of what were then considered supercomputers (see Abbate 2000). For some people, this particular strand of the origin story of the Internet, its implication in the DoD's Cold War strategizing – building a network of distributed nodes able to evade or withstand nuclear attack – means that to this day the Internet is at root a military–governmental project, and this origin can never be disentangled from its uses and meanings to this day (Edwards 1996). Yet, it is important not to overstate this part of the Internet's origin, and to remember too that its development is part of a number of other political, economic and technological projects, some more or less driven by the state, some by the computer industries, some by countercultures emerging from hobbyist and hacker groups interested in computing as a tool for democracy or revolution. These strands are often divergent in their aim, but share at root a belief in networked computers as a tool for progress (however that may have been configured).

Of course, the Internet is not just computers and phone lines (until recently the principal means of connection between the 'nodes' of the Internet). It is also software, in particular the protocols (with acronyms such as TCP, FTP, HTTP and IP) that enable data to pass along the network from node to node, to be 'sent' and 'received' in the right place at the right time, in the right way. Software also presents the Internet to us, in terms of the interface on the computer screen that visualizes the Internet in particular ways. These were once primarily textual, but are now truly multimedia, combining text, sound, still and moving images – in short, content. Now, some commentators would say that strictly speaking content isn't part of the Internet; it is the stuff carried by the Internet. But really, the Internet wouldn't be that useful and wellused if it didn't have all that content on it, so to me it makes little sense to disentangle the Internet from all that flows through it. And much of it flows to and from computers and screens – the interface is predominantly presented to us via a screen (on a computer, or increasingly a television, BlackBerry, PDA or mobile phone; note too that MP3 players usually also have a screen carrying information about the sound files they're storing).

Our experience of the Internet is, therefore, significantly mediated by screens, whether we're sending an email or browsing a virtual bookshop (see Harries 2002). Of course, there are times when we also experience the Internet as something more than or other than a screen – viruses remind us of its dense interconnectedness, crashes remind us of the (breakable) connecting routes, the varying speed of connection reminds us of the changing volume of users worldwide, and error messages remind many of us of how poorly we actually understand everything that is going on 'behind the scenes' or 'between the screens'. And the Internet is also an imaginative, even imaginary space, filled up with ideas and experiences, fear and excitement, banality and wonder. But, it is fair to say that most 'ordinary users' (see Bakardjieva 2005) connect with the Internet on screen, via an interface – most notably the World Wide Web.

The World Wide Web is, as David Gauntlett (2004: 5) neatly sums it up, 'a user-friendly interface onto the Internet'. The Web also has a well-known origin story, too: it was developed by Tim Berners-Lee, a scientist working in a mega-laboratory called CERN, where boffins collide miniscule bits of matter in an effort to uncover the ultimate building blocks of life, the universe and everything. Berners-Lee was working to solve some problems at CERN to do with scientists sharing and accessing information, and he ended up writing a program that turned the Internet into a publishing medium via, to reiterate Gauntlett, a user-friendly interface. The birth date of the World Wide Web is often cited as 6 August 1991, though it was a couple of years before this amazing innovation really took off, when Berners-Lee's idea was joined to a widely and freely available browser called Mosaic. The Web is a way of managing content on the Internet, based on shared protocols and standards. This means that all kinds of material is made available, can be stored on and accessed from any type of computer (providing it has the necessary computing power and connections), thanks to the use of a common computer language, Hypertext Markup Language or HTML. HTML is (or was) like the Esperanto of the Web, a way to 'translate' different kinds of data and move them around the Internet, where a browser can find them. But, there is a second key component to Berners-Lee's innovation: the hyperlink. This really powers the Web, in that it is a way of connecting collections of data, such as web pages, together. Hyperlinks, together with those door-openers' search engines, have given us the experience of moving through the World Wide Web, of navigating by clicking on links and being transported from page to page, site to site. So, the World Wide Web is a key way of accessing, managing, connecting, producing and consuming information over the Internet. While there are other significant uses of the Internet, notably email, most of the time most of us are using it to access the World Wide Web. But where is the World Wide Web, or the Internet – and where do we 'go' when we use it?

At one level, we aren't going anywhere: we're in front of a screen, our computational device connecting us to other devices, with data streaming between them. Yet, as I have argued before (see Bell 2001), we have to think about more nuts and bolts, wires and chips, bits and bytes: we have to think about the symbolic and experiential aspects of being online.

Cyberspace and Cyberculture are among the terms used to capture these additional dimensions of the Internet and the World Wide Web. The word cyberspace has yet another well-known story behind it; it is taken from a science fiction (sf) novel, a key text in a subgenre of sf called cyberpunk: *Neuromancer* (1984) by William Gibson. Gibson was captivated watching young people playing arcade computer games, marvelling at the level of immersion he saw – the way they were so involved in a game taking place on a screen, but experienced bodily. He used this observation to conjure a network of interconnected computers and databanks, which users entered by directly connecting their consciousness to the network or matrix – a process called 'jacking in'. Once inside, users could pass along the network and access the databanks, which ranged before them like skyscrapers. Much of this datascape was corporately owned, and Gibson's 'heroes' were hackers and other 'cowboys' who often illegally entered these banks (see Cavallaro 2000).

Gibson's vivid sf imagining had, some commentators argue, a powerful effect on how the Internet and the World Wide Web turned out; whether this is true or not, the key point is that symbolic resources such as sf novels, movies, and so on have an important role to play in shaping our understandings of and encounters with technologies. For a while, especially in the 1990s, cyberspace was a useful short-hand term to describe those understandings and encounters. Some academics – myself included – preferred a broader term, 'cyberculture', used to tag the ways in which things like the Net and the Web are at once shaping and shaped by culture – the Internet isn't just a technological artefact, it is a cultural phenomenon, and these two 'realms' cannot be disentangled. While other critics have argued that this term has lost its relevance, and should be jettisoned in favour of more new words – New Media, maybe, or digital culture – some of us stubbornly hang on to it, both for its breadth and for its sf resonance: it reminds us that we experience the Internet and the World Wide Web in complex and at times unpredictable ways, folding together that embodied, material experience (sitting at a computer, typing and gawping at a screen) with symbolic stories that circulate, such as those about the 'impacts' of new technologies (both positive and negative), and those such as sf which predict or conjecture possible futures (for more on this, see Bell 2001; for critical responses to cyberculture, see Gauntlett 2004; Silver 2004). But what kinds of experience are therefore produced and consumed? What, in short, are we doing when we are using the Net and the Web?

'Doing' the Internet

One way to answer this question is to focus on use: what do we use the Internet for? We can build a tidy list of actual and possible uses, though this is a notoriously time-sensitive list, as new uses pop up with amazing (or alarming) frequency. The Internet can be used to communicate from person to person, through text-based means such as email or 'chat' forums such as MSN; using audio, either via voice over IP phones (such as Skype) or through sound files (recorded messages); through audiovisual means, such as via webcams. It can be used to send and receive information in a number of formats, including text, still and moving images, and sound. It can be used to buy and sell things, to find new friends or lovers, to find out about practically anything, to tell other people about yourself and your world ... Already, as you can see, this list is getting pretty busy. And users have become very sophisticated in the way they use all the Internet has to offer, spinning new uses out all the time. Some of these uses are preset or configured into the Internet or its offshoots, but others are more or less unintended. Email was initially seen as little more than an add-on to the main work of the Internet, which was sharing access to computers to make more efficient use of their processing power; yet, email has become an almost ubiquitous communications medium – too ubiquitous, if tales of email overload and email addiction are anything to go by. Many of us now feel disconnected and ill at ease if we can't log on at least once a day and check our messages, but go back 20 years and our jobs and lives ticked over quite capably without email. Nevertheless, uses like email have become so stitched in to the fabric of everyday life for millions of users, making it commonplace to the point of banality.

But there is also a history to the uses of the Internet and the World Wide Web; or, rather, a set of histories: some are histories of power, others talk of resistance. From its early days in the military and scientific communities, the diffusion of the Internet has always been caught between these two trajectories; one towards greater openness and freedom, the other towards greater control and dominance. In the mid-1990s, for example, there was lots of talk about how the Internet was (1) freeing users from their 'real-life' identities and bodies, enabling them to remake themselves, for example on text-based interactive sites such as MUDs ('multi-user-dungeons, Domain or Dimension'), and (2) enabling new types of 'virtual community' to form, linking people with shared identities or interests, people who could now find a global, networked commonality (on the former, see Turkle 1995; on the latter, Rheingold 1993). Both arguments generated a lot of heat, as proponents suggested a new world was in the making, enabled by technology, while critics saw instead a withdrawal from 'real life' and a fracturing of society into endless tiny special interest groups.

This wave of debate was followed in the late 1990s by a period when many commentators feared that cyberspace was about to be taken over, colonized by corporate capitalism. The success of the Internet and the World Wide Web did cause a virtual land-grab, manifest in both the so-called 'dot.com boom', when a new generation of Internet entrepreneurs began to start up businesses trading online, and by the increasing presence of old-style corporations on the Internet – especially computer corporations such as Microsoft and media conglomerates such as the Murdoch Group. What's more, the migration online of previously offline activities such as shopping was seen by some critics as at once evacuating 'real life' (now people could shop from their homes), and as making cyberspace into a vast shopping mall, its users into passive shoppers. Around the turn of the millennium, David Gauntlett (2004: 9) writes, 'the capitalist obsession with the World Wide Web was so great that some Internet scholars felt that the creative potential of the global network had already been killed off by big business'. Of course, the dot.com bubble burst, slowing the rush to fill up cyberspace with shops and businesses; there was a (welcome) pause in the capital colonization of the Internet.

Then something else began to happen. Some online businesses carried doggedly on, weathered the dot.com crash, kept their faith and began to see their gamble pay off – Amazon (founded in 1994 but allegedly running at a considerable financial deficit for a good few years) is a classic case in point. Internet shopping has reshaped the high street and the shopping experience of many of us, for better or for worse (Zukin 2004). But alongside this, 'new' forms of trading online appeared, lessening the 'malling' of the Internet by also making it into a virtual jumble sale or swap-meet. Sites like eBay, founded in 1995, rose to prominence, and at times notoriety, as places where anything and everything could be bought and sold, and a paperclip could be traded for a house (Hillis et al. 2006). Such has been the success of sites like eBay that more straightforward commercial sites like Amazon have added eBay-like offshoots (in the form of Amazon Marketplace, but also by carrying themed 'lists' compiled by Amazonians, linked back to Amazon product).

At the same time, a new generation of innovators was looking for killer applications for extant and emerging technologies. In 1999, a site called Napster was created by Shawn Fanning to enable his fellow students to share music recorded as audio files stored on their PC hard drives. Such informal sharing was labelled peer-to-peer (P2P) to indicate the lack of commercial involvement. Napster quickly caught on, and was equally quickly attacked by the music industry for infringement of copyright. The site shut down, to later reopen as a 'legal' subscription file-sharing site. Yet Napster and other sites like it had already changed for ever the way recorded music is distributed, kick-starting music downloading and setting the scene for the iconic iPod and the attendant new cultures of music acquisition, distribution and sharing – Napster had picked up on a long-running ethical debate running through the Internet: who owns information? Why not share things for free (as Berners-Lee had done, after all, with the World Wide Web)? At the same time, sites like Napster weren't only interested in swapping songs; they also connected people, through their shared love of particular musics. Trading sites like eBay, too, began to take on this broader social function, sometimes referred to there as 'friending'. The passive web surfer, who for a while resembled a shopping zombie, had turned into someone new: someone who was not just after a bargain, or some free tunes to download, but who wanted to build social spaces around these activities.

Which brings us to the latest buzz around the Internet: the rise (or return) of social networking online. Activities such as blogging sites like MySpace and Facebook have been heralded as transforming what we 'do' in cyberspace, in crafting new forms of social interaction mediated by the Internet and the World Wide Web, but not contained within. Now, Gauntlett (2004: 12) archly remarks about debates around blogging that 'the most striking thing about these recent debates is that it's all so ... 1996!' – and he's right. Debates from the mid-1990s about virtual community are strangely absent from the current social media hype – a hype epitomized when *Time* magazine used a mirrored cover to display its person of the year for 2006. That person is ... you. Or, rather, the 'you' that is currently 'revolutionizing' the Internet by producing streams of 'user-generated content', such as blogs, wikis, vlogs, moblogs, and so on. As John Quiggin (2006) describes, these platforms are together forming a new 'creative commons', a shared space of self-expression and social interaction that radically alters what it means to write (and read), who can produce (and consume) web content, creating a parallel universe, the blogosphere, where – crucially for our discussion here – flows of media content are disrupted, redirected, upset and, to use a phrase from within these emerging scenes, mashed up.

New Media/me media

Sites like MySpace, YouTube or Blogger have each in their own ways changed the ways users make use of the Internet and the World Wide Web. They are part of some broader transformations in the overall New Media landscape; transformations such as convergence and multi-platform intertextuality (see Harries 2002). We might say that the Internet and the World Wide Web have become 'new-mediatized' – they have become a central part of a new way of 'doing media' (and 'thinking media', too); one that unsettles or refuses age-old differentiations, such as those between producer and consumer, amateur and professional, reality and fiction, as well as between 'old media' platforms such as film, television, radio and the Internet (Marshall 2004).

Convergence refers to bits of media becoming indistinguishable – whether those bits are bits of content, bits of the industry or whatever. Convergence happens when media hybridize and recombine, as when movies are distributed over the Internet to download, or podcasts of radio shows can be listened to on an MP3 player or via a PC. So, there is convergence in terms of delivery and devices, in terms of the tools and places we use to access content – such that watching a film on a computer screen is no longer considered weird. But there is convergence in the content itself, for example via the cross-platform intertextuality that binds a computer game to a movie to a soundtrack to a commercial. Like the hyperlinks connecting web pages, these intertexutal links form a complex web of associations of content (Harries 2002).

A site like YouTube (founded in 2005) is a perfect illustration of this content convergence. Started as a site to share homemade video clips, YouTube's millions of clips now include user-generated content of virtually every imaginable type, perhaps most famously 'leaked' clips of current television shows and homemade remakes of film scenes, but also including seemingly random bits of webcam tomfoolery, home video and found footage. So the site now offers clips of all kinds, with all sorts of origin, without distinguishing on the basis of genre, production values, platform, whatever. YouTube evidences new forms of content creation, novel ways of distribution, and changing patterns of media consumption. Clips of television shows appear on YouTube, officially and unofficially, as well as countless parodies and remakes, but clips from YouTube also appear on television and regularly make the news (as well as circulating over email in those endless 'Have you seen this???!!!' messages forwarded worldwide). Searching earlier for catch-up information for a new television series that I have so far missed, *Primeval*, I clicked between the station's 'official' website, various 'unofficial' and fan sites, links to clips on YouTube, screenshots of key scenes, and off into the labyrinth of more or less connected sites and pages. I could watch clips of previous and future episodes, view interviews with the cast, watch spoofs and read earnest discussions of what's wrong with the science behind the science fiction. It didn't matter who had made what or whether sites were 'official' or not; all that mattered was whether they grabbed my attention and answered my questions. And there were countless opportunities for me to have my say, to comment, to link up with other fans of the show or any of the actors in it. Mass media has become New Media or, to use another current term, 'me media'.

Convergence and cross-platform interextuality is also changing our experience of media spaces, making a nonsense of any lingering distinction between the 'real' and the 'virtual'. Experiments in ambient or ubiquitous computing, for example, project the virtual onto the real, so that we encounter the Internet, say, not just on a computer screen but on a street corner (Galloway 2004). And as access to the Internet and the World Wide Web becomes more mobile, untied from the desktop, so we can begin to experience and encounter cyberspace literally all over the place. Charting the changing roles, meanings and experiences of what she refers to as 'mobile digital devices', for example, Adriana de Souza e Silva (2006) describes a key transformation to the 'interfacing' capacity of such technologies: where the interface once mediated between the user and the machine – as in the graphic user interface that we see on a PC screen – mobile digital devices mediate a 'social interface' between users, and also between users and the 'hybrid' (at once 'physical' and 'virtual') spaces they move through. As she defines this new space, 'hybrid spaces are mobile spaces, created by the constant movement of users who carry portable devices continuously connected to the Internet and to other users' (Souza e Silva 2006: 262). So, convergence in terms of devices (Web-linked phones) also brings divergence in terms of media (or cyber) spaces, and in terms of reconnecting users via the interface. As with arguments about other forms of social media, here we see a story of connectivity between users enabled by new technology.

Crucially, these new devices make it possible to be constantly connected both to networks such as the Internet and to other (human) users while moving through (hybrid) space, thereby enfolding remote and promixal contexts and contacts: rather than disembedding the user, as PCs have been thought to do when users enter cyberspace, users can now 'carry' cyberspace through physical space. Moreover, emerging patterns of use suggest that 'mobile interfaces are used primarily inside social public spaces' (Souza e Silva 2006: 268) – yet, rather than privatizing those spaces, these devices 'enfold' space, remixing public and private, physical and virtual. New gaming applications illustrate this enfolding especially vividly, layering physical and virtual landscapes for players.

Ultimately, for Souza e Silva (2006: 274), these new technologies 'recreate urban spaces as multi-user environments'. Clearly, therefore, there are profound implications for the multiple users of these environments. As with earlier transformations brought about by digital technologies, such as the shift from one-to-many to many-to-many (as in peer-to-peer) broadcasting that characterizes the 'me media' aspects of the Internet and which subverts the 'old media' relationship between producer and consumer, this new hybrid space potentially rewrites forms and experiences of technologically mediated sociality. Such arguments demand new language to describe hybrid spaces and subject positions (in the last day, reading for this chapter, I have seen 'viewser' used to combine user and viewer in order to capture the screenic experience of the Internet, and 'prosumer' used to mix producer and consumer of media content) and new theories and methods to uncover what goes on in these cross-platform, convergent New Media cultures.

(Re)Thinking social media

As scholars begin to write not only the histories of the Internet and the World Wide Web but also the histories of academic study of the Internet and the World Wide Web, so they begin to discern patterns, phases, hot topics and fads. David Silver (2000) wrote a useful summary of the ways of thinking about the Internet and the World Wide Web up to the turn of the millennium, distinguishing between 'popular cyberculture', 'cyberculture studies' and 'critical cyberculture studies'. The first strand includes journalistic accounts of experiences online, branched into utopian and dystopian forms. The former is best exemplified by the establishment of new magazines discussing cyberspace, such as *Wired*, while the latter often took the form of populist books offering portents of doom about the digital age. This first bloom of publishing overlaps in Silver's account with the second phase, in which journalistic or popular accounts rub shoulders with academic work engaging with bodies of theory, and with key interests in online identity, community and communication – mapping the *social effects* of cyberspace. The third stage is marked by the more systematic development and deployment of 'theory', and by a broadening out of focus as more and more academics and commentators set their sights on cyberspace. We are arguably largely still in this third stage, though the terrain has been complicated both by trends in the technologies and their uses, and by internal debates about what to name this thing of ours (and therefore how to go about thinking about it).

Running alongside Silver's typology is a second story; this time a story about research methods: how is the Internet to be understood empirically, what tools do we have and what works? Nina Wakeford notes that 'there is no standard technique for studying the World Wide Web. Rather, it is a case of plundering existing research for emerging methodological ideas developed in the course of diverse research projects, and weighing up whether they can be used and adopted for our own purposes' (2004: 34) (see also Chapter 1). While this might seem a bit casual, it rightly reflects the current state of play in net and web research: an openness to trying different techniques, to mixing methods, rather than a desire to fix a gold standard. Such research practice, Wakeford continues, means 'moving back and forth between long-standing debates in methodology and the distinctive challenges posed by new electronically mediated research' (Wakeford 2004: 36). It seems likely, nonetheless, that the close attention to detail shown in ethnographic studies of Internet use, such as that carried our by Bakardjieva (2005), will continue to prove popular and fruitful. Yet, the current alleged demassification and resocialization of 'Web 2.0' (see Case Study below), the rise of me media and 'new' social networking media, will inevitably challenge again our methodological choices. In particular, it seems to me we will need to find ways to explore the processes of 'writing' and 'reading' 'me media' texts such as blogs (see Curtain 2007), and new ways to research how users interact in and with those hybrid spaces that Souza e Silva (2006) talked about. New theories and new methods can, in fact, together fittingly form a new agenda for research into New Media as socio-technical assemblage: Media Studies 2.0 (see Case Study below).

Recommended reading

Abbate, Janet (2000) *Inventing the Internet*. Cambridge, MA: The MIT Press.

Bakardjieva, Maria (2005) *Internet Society: The Internet in Everyday Life*. London: Sage Publications.

Bell, David and Kennedy, Barbara (eds) (2007) *The Cybercultures Reader*, 2nd edn. London: Routledge.

Burnett, Robert and Marshall, P. David (2003) *Web Theory: An Introduction*. London: Routledge.

Gauntlett, David and Horsley, Ross (eds) (2004) *Web.Studies*, 2nd edn. London: Edward Arnold.

Marshall, P. David (2004) *New Media Cultures*. London: Edward Arnold.

Case Study: Wikipedia

David Gauntlett

Wikipedia is the world's biggest collaborative project, and excitingly highlights some significant differences between traditional and new approaches to knowledge, and the authority of 'experts', which have been energized by the digital revolution. Wikipedia embodies the essence of 'Web 2.0', and is a quintessentially 'Web 2.0' project, and so first of all we need to take a step back and consider what 'Web 2.0' is.

The origins of Web 2.0

When Tim Berners-Lee created the World Wide Web in 1990, he thought of it as a place where people could collaborate to share and build knowledge. He even considered calling it 'The Information Mine', which would have meant that instead of visiting the 'WWW' sites which we are now so familiar with, we would all now be looking at 'TIM' sites instead – though he rejected this attempt to immortalize his own name as rather self-indulgent.

He intended that every web browser would be able to *edit* pages, not just read them. When I read about this idea in his book *Weaving the Web*, in 1999, it seemed nice, but rather naïve, and I had no idea how it could possibly work. Those of us who made our own web pages back in those days spent a lot of time and effort perfecting them in terms of both design and content. So, why on earth would we want *other people* to come along and muck up our work? It seemed like a bizarre prospect.

This was the dominant attitude for almost a decade, and was matched by the fact that nobody had really worked out how web browsers could be used to edit other people's web pages. More recently, however, there has been considerable excitement about 'Web 2.0' – not actually a sequel to the World Wide Web that we know and love, but rather a way of using existing systems in a 'new' way: to bring people together creatively. Tim O'Reilly, who coined the phrase 'Web 2.0' in 2004, has described it as 'harnessing collective intelligence'. The principle has also been summarized by Eric Schmidt, Google's Chief Executive Officer, as 'Don't fight the internet' – which may sound strange at first: after all, who wants to fight the Internet? But the point is spot on: what he means is 'Don't resist the *network*', which is what we were doing when we didn't want *other people* messing up our websites. In other words, individuals should open themselves to collaborative projects instead of seeking to make and protect their 'own' material. (Sometimes, of course, you might want to make your own perfectly crafted, personal thing, and that's fine too, but 'Web 2.0' reminds us that the possibility of collaboration with the millions of other people out there can be great.)

Wikipedia

The best-known and probably most remarkable embodiment of the 'Web 2.0' ethos is Wikipedia, succinctly described on its main page as 'The free encyclopaedia that anyone can edit' (www.wikipedia.org). A wiki is a website that any visitor can add to, and amend, using a normal web browser. Wikipedia did not invent the concept, and was not the first wiki, but within a few months of its launch in 2001, it was by far the most widely recognized wiki in the world. Alongside each wiki page, there is a discussion page, and a history of all edits, so that its development is transparent. If a page is vandalized – or amended in a way you happen to disagree with – it can be restored to a former version, via the history page.

Wikipedia grew out of Nupedia (2000–03), a free online encyclopaedia written by experts, set up by Jimmy Wales and Larry Sanger. This had the open-source, free licensed content ethos of its successor, but as Wales recalls (Jimmy Wales interviewed in Marks 2007: 44), '[Nupedia] was no fun for the volunteer writers because we had a lot of academic peer review committees who would criticise articles and give feedback. It was like handing in an essay at grad school, and basically intimidating to participate in.'

Frustration with this process led Sanger to suggest they set up a wiki as an extra feature for Nupedia, a proposal that Wales quickly warmed to. (The 'History of Wikipedia' article at Wikipedia gives the full story, naturally.) Wales says:

> Our idea was very radical: that every person on the planet would have access to an open-source, free online work that was the sum of all human knowledge. Within about two weeks I knew it was going to work. By that time we already had more articles online than we had in nearly two years with Nupedia.

> (Marks 2007: 44)

In 2003, Wales founded the Wikimedia Foundation, a non-profit charitable organization, and donated Wikipedia to it; an act intended to secure its non-commercial future. In doing so, Wales surrendered the opportunity to sell Wikipedia, potentially losing out on an estimated $3 billion (!).

When I first drafted this article in February 2007, Wikipedia had over six million articles in 250 languages, including 1.6 million in the English edition. Over 75,000 people had made more than five edits during the previous month, January 2007, while many thousands more will have been less frequent contributors. By April 2008, Wikipedia had expanded to over *ten million* articles in 253 languages, including 2.3 million in the English edition, and Wikipedia had moved up to number nine in the global website rankings (www.alexa.com). By this point Wikipedia seems to be so big that some of the automated statistics systems are no longer able to calculate some of its growth (but check www.en.wikipedia.org/wiki/Wikipedia:Statistics). In any case, it is one of the obvious flaws of print publishing that these figures will be out of date by the time you read this. Happily, and unsurprisingly, Wikipedia itself contains a good selection of articles about itself, including 'Wikipedia', 'Wikipedia: About', and in particular 'Wikipedia: Replies to common objections', which I recommend you read for up-to-date facts and viewpoints.

Wikipedia greatly benefits from the passion and expertise of enthusiasts in thousands of scientific, technical, hobby, craft and pop culture topics. It is a good example of the 'long tail' phenomenon (Anderson 2004, 2006): both Wikipedia and the *Encyclopaedia Britannica* will include articles on key topics in art, science, geography and history, but only Wikipedia will have detailed articles on new or not very popular rock bands, individual railway stations, obscure computing issues, movies and television series, Scottish Renaissance poetry, Muppet characters, knitting techniques, and anything else that some people are into but which there wouldn't be room for in a published encyclopaedia. Because communities of enthusiasts collaborate to create encyclopaedia-style factual articles about their area of interest, a kind of frenzy of friendly but competitive fascination tends to generate precise and carefully composed articles on every subject.

Don't fear the wiki

Students from various schools and colleges often tell me that their tutors have informed them that Wikipedia is an unreliable source of information which should not be referred to – and this seems to be common (see, for example, Jaschik 2007). This is clearly the opposite of Web 2.0 thinking – it is '*Do* fear the Internet!'. However the notion that any statement that anybody has ever managed to get into a book or article is going to be *inherently* better than Wikipedia content clearly doesn't make sense, especially as Wikipedia is subject to continuous checking and updating – precisely *unlike* anything in print. It is now a long time (in terms of Wikipedia's growth) since a study published in the science journal *Nature* compared Wikipedia and *Encyclopaedia Britannica* and found that – and I quote – 'Wikipedia comes close to *Britannica* in terms of the accuracy of its science entries' (Giles 2005: 900): 'The exercise revealed numerous errors in both encyclopaedias, but among 42 entries tested, the difference in accuracy was not particularly great: the average science entry in Wikipedia contained around four inaccuracies; Britannica, about three'.

Furthermore, unlike its rival, Wikipedia gets substantially better every month, and we can reasonably expect that it is now far better than it was in 2005.

Some of the concern about Wikipedia seems to be that its information cannot be attributed to a particular 'expert' author (although it *can* be attributed to a specific version of an article, which remains fixed and stored under the 'History' tab, with details of all changes and their contributors). This sweet faith in singular 'experts' is wholly overturned by the assumptions of Wikipedia. In the online collaborative process which generates every Wikipedia article, people with varying degrees of expertise (who may include traditional experts, as well as students, amateurs and enthusiasts) engage in a dialogue from which the 'ideal' form of an article evolves.

Therefore, trust needs to be placed in this *process*, rather than in, say, the formal qualifications of individuals, as Shirky suggests (Shirky 2006; see also Shirky 2008):

> A former editor-in-chief of *Encyclopaedia Britannica* has likened Wikipedia to a public toilet, in an attempt to say 'there's no source of authority here; we have a source of authority, whereas they don't'. In fact what Wikipedia presages is a change in the *nature* of authority. Prior to *Britannica*, most encyclopaedias derived their authority from the *author*. *Britannica* came along and made the relatively radical assertion that you could vest authority in an *institution*. You trust *Britannica*, and then *we* in turn go out and get the people to write the articles. What Wikipedia suggests is that you can vest authority in a visible *process*. As long as you can see how Wikipedia's working, and can see that the results are acceptable, you can come over time to trust that. And that is a really profound challenge to our notions of what it means to be an institution, what it means to trust something, what it means to have authority in this society.
>
> (Shirky 2006:)

For those who feel that society has become fundamentally decadent, antisocial, selfish and doomed, the flourishing world of Wikipedia offers a strong suggestion that this may not be the case. Instead, here we see people spending many hours collaborating on building an accessible resource for others, for very little personal reward.

Certainly, some people may gain a sense of not purely altruistic well-being from having the opportunity to show off their knowledge, but Wikipedia contributors get nothing more than occasional kudos from other contributors. Of course, contributing to the site may also fulfil the basic human need to feel a part of a community, and provide a sense of belonging. The authors of books and articles, such as this one, are incredibly vain and isolated by comparison. (Fancy putting your *name* on it!). Wikipedia embodies an *optimistic* ethos which, to the dismay of committed cynics, actually seems to work.

So, perhaps you're thinking that this all sounds nice in *theory*, but aren't there lots of problems with it in practice? Well, let's consider some common arguments about Wikipedia.

Don't people always mess it up?

Well no, on the whole, they just *don't*. At any particular moment, there may be an instance of vandalism happening somewhere within the millions of articles, but these are usually soon corrected by others. Some articles are 'protected' (cannot be edited) or 'semi-protected' (cannot be edited by new users), due to high levels of vandalism, but there are surprisingly few of these. (See 'Wikipedia: list of protected pages'.) The encyclopaedia always aspires to have articles unprotected. Currently, fully protected articles include passive smoking, Steffi Graf and surrealism (!). The semi-protected list includes more predictable targets such as George W. Bush, alongside Paris Hilton,

Adolf Hitler, oral sex and Jesus. On the whole, though, an incredible majority of Internet users seem to respect the Wikipedia project, and either do not have – or manage to resist – the unhelpful urge to spoil it.

Straightforward vandalism is easily spotted. A greater concern is *subtle* vandalism – the addition of biased statements, harsh interpretations or convincing-looking 'facts' which are simply wrong – as well as partisan contributions. But, as with many criticisms of Wikipedia, the answer is simply that over time these things are corrected or balanced. Controversial topics attract people with axes to grind, but then those people are forced into dialogue with others, and a balanced presentation of different viewpoints is arrived at. (This does not mean that controversial views are *excluded*, but rather that they may end up with whole articles of their own: as in the case of the detailed articles on, for example, 9/11 conspiracy theories, and holocaust denial.)

Isn't it just the opinions of people who are not experts?

As we saw above, Wikipedia certainly challenges the traditional idea of the 'expert'. Ultimately, it comes down to whether you want to trust one person, who appears to be an expert because of their education and experience, and has written a book or article for some reason – perhaps to advance their career, and/or make money (these are common reasons); or a whole community of people who have an active passion for a subject, and contribute to Wikipedia articles just because they're interested. You may feel there's not a clear-cut answer to this. There's nothing *wrong* with the individual expert. But the passionate collective sounds like quite a good bet too.

Isn't Wikipedia a juggernaut – like McDonalds?

It might seem to be a worry that Wikipedia is one big, singular, successful thing. If it's so great, this worry goes, how come there's just one of it? Doesn't that make it like other big, monolithic corporations like McDonalds and Microsoft? The answer to this is a strong no, because of the fundamental difference in nature between a profit-making corporation with a small set of elite owners and shareholders, versus a collaborative non-commercial encyclopaedia produced by everybody.

The more people use and contribute to Wikipedia, the better it gets. And it's highly *convenient* that it has become such a widely recognized single repository for knowledge – as long as it continues to be managed fairly – for the same reason. If there were 25 reasonably good wiki-based encyclopaedias, the situation would be frustrating because you wouldn't know which one to turn to, and potential contributors wouldn't know which ones to work on. So, unusually, this is a case where it's good to have just one identifiable superstar in the field, so that we can all just work to make this one the best that it can be.

Wikipedia and the public sphere

The German social theorist, Jürgen Habermas, famously outlined the notion of the 'public sphere' as a forum for rational critical discussion, such as that which took place in eighteenth-century salons and coffee houses – apparently (Habermas 1989). This has been taken up by scholars as a kind of ideal model of how the media should work in society, fostering valuable social discussion and keeping a check on the power of the state. Previously, however, this argument had to be focused on news media and journalism, and there was not really much sign of it happening. The public sphere was a useful concept as an 'ideal type' – something we might aspire towards – but there was not really any sign that the mass media was fostering the kind of informed discussion, leading to consensus, that Habermas favoured. On the contrary, rivalry between politicians and political parties, along with competition between journalists and media companies, meant that the public sphere was characterized by unresolved conflict, rather than consensus, on the levels of both big social issues and trivial personality clashes.

Then in the 1990s, the Internet became incredibly popular, and Habermas's ideas seemed to be revitalized: here was a place where open, rational discussion could take place freely, where individuals of all points of view could come together as equals, not bound by association to particular media companies, to discuss ideas. However, again, this didn't really seem to happen in practice. Sure, the 'free' debate happened, but was still characterized by partisan hostility and 'flame wars' (increasingly abusive battles fought by people hiding behind the anonymity of text on screen). The Internet could bring people together in a discussion which they otherwise might not have had, but (unsurprisingly, perhaps) did not seem to be able to steer them towards any kind of agreement.

Wikipedia, however, may offer a solution. The very *process* of collaboratively producing an article on a topic with a 'neutral point of view' seems to force those with different viewpoints to acknowledge and deal with their conflicting arguments in a relatively mature manner. The article 'Wikipedia: replies to common objections' states:

> Wikipedia has fairly decent, balanced articles about [for example] war, propaganda, abortion, Scientology, and prostitution. Wikipedia is actually notable as a means of coming to agree on controversy, and has been studied by some researchers for its ability to neutralize the often noxious debates on such topics. [...] Partisans from both sides try to push their views on Wikipedia. An example of this is the Cornwall page in which the difficulties over Cornwall's legal status and its relationship to England have over time been worked into what is a largely acceptable form of words to all parties. (The corollary of this particular debate is that the article is far more complete than it would otherwise have been, and certainly makes the point far more accurately than certain other encyclopaedias we could mention).
>
> (Wikipedia 2007)

This suggests that the site where thousands of people come together to collaboratively build an online encyclopaedia may have produced, for the first time, an electronically enabled version of the public sphere that Habermas was talking about (see Chapter 9).

Wikipedia and Media Studies 2.0

Thinking about all these issues prompted me to develop the 'Media Studies 2.0' argument, which is presented in the Introduction of this book. This is just one example of the kind of transformation that Wikipedia is suggesting to people in a number of fields. Ultimately, as we have seen, Tim Berners-Lee, creator of the World Wide Web, can take the credit for this, as his vision for creative and collaborative communication has shaken up so much: not simply making the Internet into a powerful tool, but setting off an earthquake with powerful effects across all of art, media, science, society and communication.

3 Digital television: high definitions

Michele Hilmes

Two threads stitch together the global media scene in the twenty-first century. They are the dispersal of digital media – from computers to cell phones to digital television to the Internet – and the convergence of formerly separate media brought about by the digital revolution. Both of these are important factors in the development of digital television. The term *'digital'* simply means that information is broken down into a series of 1s and 0s and put into a form that can be easily manipulated by the ever-speedier microchips that lie at the heart of every digital device. This distinguishes computers and their many subsequent offspring from older *analogue* media like film, radio, television and audio/video recordings as we knew them prior to 2000. Analogue media rely on a physical replica (or analogue) of a physical phenomenon, like sound or pictures, that can be transmitted or preserved through some kind of physical medium; whether it is magnetic signals on a tape, electronic waves transmitted through the spectrum, or chemical changes on a strip of celluloid.

Digitization – in production, distribution and reception – transformed traditional media, starting in the mid-1990s: in satellite communications, in recording technology, in a new generation of television sets, in cable television, in radio and television broadcasting, and many more. Industrial convergence soon followed. From compact discs (CDs) to digital audiotape (DAT) to digital video discs (DVDs) and smart VCRs (DVR and TiVo), from high-definition television (HDTV) to multiplexed digital television (DTV) to direct broadcast satellite (DBS) to YouTube, from video cell phones to iPods to satellite radio (XM, Sirius) – all these draw on various forms of industry convergence as well as digital technology. They threaten to break down the borders of older media, and challenge old structures of ownership, control, content and audience uses as well. They make some things easier – like sharing various forms of media across national and intellectual property barriers, and some things harder – like protecting privacy and figuring out who will pay. This chapter discusses these histories, technologies and debates in turn, beginning with the origins of digital television.

Origins

The story of digital television begins in the 1980s with the development of what looked like the next big thing in television technology: *high-definition television*, or

HDTV. This was a technology developed in Japan that promised to greatly improve the quality of the television image by increasing the *definition*, or number of scanning lines, of the picture, using analogue methods. It also rearranged the *aspect ratio* of the screen, from the boxy 4 to 3 ratio of traditional television to a more cinemascope-like 16 to 9, allowing movies to be shown on home television sets in their usual proportions, without cropping the picture or having to letterbox it. Japan became the first country to initiate regular HDTV broadcasts in 1992.

The prospect of HDTV made a particular impact in the USA, which has always had a poorer quality television standard (NTSC) than most of the rest of the world, having settled for a 525-line picture – each television image is electronically scanned, back and forth, 525 times top to bottom – instead of the higher quality 625-line PAL standard prevalent elsewhere. But transmitting the Japanese MUSE standard high-definition picture (up to 1,080 lines) required far more bandwidth than its NTSC equivalent – six times more than the standard US broadcasting frequency. This meant that HDTV could not be broadcast over the television channels now assigned to US broadcasters; they would need a new, bigger frequency in order to successfully broadcast HDTV to the public. The public, meanwhile, would have to invest in new HDTV sets in order to receive such an image.

By some reports, the interest of US broadcasters in HDTV technology was spurred by the prospect of the Federal Communication Commission's plan in 1986 to auction off a large chunk of the valuable UHF spectrum (never fully utilized by broadcasters) to mobile telephone companies. The National Association of Broadcasters, the leading industry trade group, appealed to the Federal Communications Commission (FCC) to hold off on letting the spectrum space go, since it would be needed if HDTV were to have a chance in this country. The US government, worried about Japanese domination of the electronics manufacturing industry, wanted to encourage the development of homegrown US high-definition technology, rather than becoming dependent on Japan. It agreed to reserve the UHF frequencies for television, if US broadcasters and manufacturers could come up with a workable competitive technology (Hilmes 2002).

But as US companies struggled to design their own HDTV device, the digital revolution overtook them. With new digital technology – homegrown in Silicon Valley – a much higher definition television picture could be produced, as good or better than the Japanese MUSE technology that had started the whole thing off. By 1993, US manufacturers had come up with the strategic Grand Alliance standard, representing a technical compromise between the competing needs of different industry segments that could handle a variety of digital high-definition formats with varying degrees of resolution, pixel density, frame rates and scanning methods. However, a funny thing happened on the way to the Grand Alliance: it dawned on everyone that, with digital technology, you can do many more things with that spectrum space than simply provide beautifully clear pictures. One advantage of digital is that its signals can be compressed, so that it is possible to transmit up to six standard definition television signals (SDTV) in an existing broadcast frequency, all of them with as good or better clarity than existing television images (a single cable channel could carry 12 or more!). This was called *multiplexing*. Only if broadcasters wanted to opt for the highest density, richest definition picture possible did they need the spectrum capacity that the old HDTV systems had required; otherwise, the owner of a license to broadcast now in effect controlled six channels rather than one, an enormously profitable prospect.

The US Telecommunications Act of 1996 laid out a plan to introduce HDTV (or multiplexed DTV) across the country over the next decade. Each holder of an existing television license was given, free of charge, a new channel assignment on the UHF spectrum large enough to be used for fully fledged HDTV. They would also be allowed to keep their old channels in the VHF band and continue broadcasting in analogue, since the transition to digital television would take a while; for many years, some consumers would only be able to receive old-fashioned, standard broadcast signals on their old sets. In return, broadcasters agreed to begin terrestrial digital broadcasting in 1998. By 2006 – by which time, it was assumed, HDTV sets would have reached 85 per cent penetration of US homes (an overly optimistic projection, it turned out) – broadcasters would have to return their old frequencies in the VHF or UHF spectrum to the federal government (to be auctioned off to fill treasury coffers). This was called 'digital switchover'. Many predicted that 2006 was far too early a deadline for television to convert entirely to digital, especially since consumer prices for HDTV sets in 2000 remained in the $4,000 range. But the big US networks, and several cable channels, began limited high-definition digital broadcasting as scheduled in 1998, and by the end of 1999 those in the top 30 markets had gone partially digital, even though few consumers had the ability to receive the signals. Cable television seized its broadband advantage and introduced digital cable in 1998, though mostly in multiplexed form – high-definition television would take longer. Satellite television (DBS) had begun transmitting digitally in 1994 and initiated high definition in 1998. Currently, the date for digital switchover in the USA is set for midnight on 17 February, 2009 (FCC).

Digital television launched across western Europe in 1998 as well, both by satellite and by terrestrial (land-based antenna) distribution. Rupert Murdoch's Sky Digital satellite channels began transmitting that year, on top of its analogue DBS in existence since 1989. By 2001 it discontinued analogue and signed up its five millionth subscriber. Terrestrial digital television rolled out in the UK in 1998, with six multiplexed services allocated by the Independent Television Commission to six different companies, including the BBC's Freeview service. Currently, over 50 channels serve the British public, most of them at no extra cost and many of them with interactive capacities. In the next few years most European countries would introduce the new technology and formats, spreading eventually around the world. Luxembourg became the first country to complete digital switchover, in 2006, with many others planned for 2007 and 2008. Digital switchover in the UK is planned for 2012.

Production, distribution and reception

Digital media share one characteristic that differentiates them profoundly from older analogue forms: each copy of a digital text is not only perfectly reproduced but also perfectly reproducible, unlike the imperfections and degradation involved in copying older forms like audio and videotape. Their equally easy transmission through various digital means, like the web or digital disc, means that each time a song or a film or a television show is downloaded as an MP-3 file or burned or purchased, it essentially produces another original (Vaidyanathan 2003). This has led to the incendiary battles over *file sharing* – the transmission of digital files from one individual to another – starting with Napster in 1999 and moving on to various other venues. The USA, one of the biggest producers of media distributed – often illegally – around the world, passed the Digital Millennium Copyright Act in 1998 in an attempt to control unauthorized downloading of intellectual property. In 2001 the European Union (EU) crafted the EU Copyright Directive along similar lines. Many other nations also adopted such legislation, but in some areas of the world, most notably China, digital piracy continues with abandon.

Digital media also permit a higher degree of *interactivity* than possible with analogue media. Digital television allows a much greater range of 'on demand' services, whereby viewers can select individual programs from a menu and watch them whenever they choose, unimpeded by the rigid scheduling of streaming television broadcasts of the past. DVDs permit viewers to modify their viewing experience in all manner of ways, from selecting different languages to substituting director or other creative commentary on the soundtrack. Digital video recorders (DVRs), like TiVo, encourage not only detachment from the television schedule but from the very economics of commercial media, as viewers blithely skip past the advertisements. Web-based video, though still in its infancy, allows viewers to become producers and distributors, posting their own or acquired video on sites such as YouTube, or downloading (often illegally distributed) television programmes and films through services such as BitTorrent.

These qualities of reproducibility and interactivity have made their mark on every aspect of television: production, transmission and reception. The rest of this chapter discusses these in turn, focusing on the ways that digital television shifts the boundaries that applied to analogue media, creating convergence not only among applications and industries, but across cultures as well.

Production

Digital video production can be traced back to professional formats in the mid-1980s, notably the Sony Digital Betcam, which made its debut in 1986. Consumer digital production became possible only in the early 1990s, as Apple debuted its Quick Time architecture and MPEG-1 and MPEG-2 playback standards were developed. With the launch of inexpensive and relatively easy-to-use digital linear editing systems in the late 1990s, such as AVID, Final Cut Pro, Adobe Premiere, and the like, along with digital Mini-DV camcorders, digital video production slipped the bounds of professional studios and moved into the living rooms, bedrooms, backyards and offices of the general population. The concept of 'digital cinematography' as a growing practice both in the industry and by individuals had gained sufficient ground by 2002 that *Star Wars II: Attack of the Clones* (Lucas 2002) was produced entirely on digital video (see Chapter 4). Animation practices have been completely transformed by the possibilities inherent in digital production.

Combined with digital recording and playback technologies like the DVD, independent and low-budget film-making has experienced an enormous renaissance; it is estimated that the cost of making a fully digital feature film amounts to one-tenth or less of the costs of a 35mm production. Of course, currently most theatres are not yet equipped with digital projection, so that feature films for mainstream theatrical release must still be transferred to 35mm film before they can be distributed. There is still much dispute over the quality of sound and image in digital video as opposed to traditional film. However, as digital media are increasingly transmitted via the web and wireless, image quality takes on a different meaning, especially when the screen of the future is the one on your cell phone or iPod.

Distribution

Thanks to the enormous transformation of connectivity brought about by the Internet and World Wide Web, it is in the area of distribution that digital technology has most affected television. From a medium originally sent out from a few fixed analogue transmitters mounted high above the ground on antennas, to the advent of coaxial cable and, later, fibre-optic cable that took the television signal through fat wires into the home, to satellite signals caught by, at first, dishes big enough to block the sunlight, or, beginning in the 1980s, via bulky videotapes, television has become a medium that can be broken up into bits, streamed and captured by virtually anyone to virtually anyone. Digital television is, effectively, digitally *transmitted* television, no matter what form it originated in or what form it ultimately takes at the reception end.

Satellites

Digital satellite services, the first to debut globally, brought multiple channels of existing television programming and channels with material uniquely developed for satellite and cable directly into the living rooms of people around the world. Satellite television works by beaming signals from a ground station up to a satellite in geostationary orbit, 2,300 miles above the earth's surface. In this position they are just at the right point in the earth's gravitational pull to rotate at the same speed as the earth, keeping them in a fixed position relative to points on the ground. A mix of government and privately owned satellites occupy the geostationary band; there are so many now that the band is getting crowded. Signals are relayed by the satellites transponders operating in the *KU band* of frequencies back down to earth, where they are received by satellite dishes, placed either on individual roofs or balconies, or in a satellite array set up by companies who retransmit their signals in another form (like cable or broadcast). Satellite 'feeds' stream into news-producing organizations from all points of the globe day and night, transforming news operations and opening up a million new eyes on the world.

In the USA, DirectTV, launched in 1994, and Echo Star's Dish Network, launched in 1996, are the two primary providers of digital DBS. They carry most of the regular US terrestrial and cable channels, but also provide a host of channels from other parts of the world, available in special subscription packages. These are particularly important for diasporic populations, in the USA and around the globe, who keep in touch with home cultures and languages via satellite television. In the UK Rupert Murdoch's BSkyB brought some of the first satellite offerings into British and European airspace, challenging the hegemony of public service broadcasters and threatening another wave of Americanization of culture, since so many of the channels carried US-originated programming. These fears have abated somewhat, however, by the many indigenous channels that have sprung up, along with transnational cooperative ventures like Arte, a joint venture between France and Germany; the Euronews and Eurosports channels; the US-based but internationally programmed Discovery Channels; Azteca, based in Mexico but serving all of South and Central America; and the pan-Arab news channel Al-Jazeera.

Cable

Cable television in its analogue version is almost as old as television itself. Coaxial (meaning many-wired) cables were strung from poles and buried underground throughout many countries in the 1940s, 1950s and 1960s as a simple way to get television signals to communities with poor or nonexistent transmission from terrestrial broadcasters. Not until the advent of the broadcast satellite in the late 1970s did cable begin to come into its own as a medium that originated its own programming; in the USA one of the first successful cable-only channels was Home Box Office (HBO) which began beaming major sports events and uncut theatrical films up to a satellite and then down to cable operators across the country. Cable took off in the USA in the 1980s; by the late 1990s over 85 per cent of the US audience received its television via cable or DBS. Digital cable was introduced in the late 1990s; the average digital cable home can receive over 100 channels with many further pay per view and on-demand options.

In countries with strong central public broadcasters, cable was slower to develop. There are some exceptions: the Netherlands remains one of the most heavily cabled European countries since only by low power stations linked by cable could the small nation surrounded by larger neighbours find the transmission space to have multiple national channels. Elsewhere, cable sometimes sprang up illegally in countries where access to television was limited or highly political; in Taiwan, pirate cable operators helped to bring about a liberalization movement in the 1980s, in politics as well as media policy. Cable operators in Canada thrived on offering US channels unavailable over the air. Now digital cable is becoming a popular way to receive the Internet service, and the provision of telephone service via cable is not far behind as cable television and traditional telecommunications companies converge.

Web-based digital television

The Internet itself, whether delivered via cable, modem or wireless, has become a medium of television distribution in its own right. From sites like BitTorrent, a peer-to-peer file-sharing site specializing in films and television along with music and games, to the popular iTunes which allows authorized TV downloads for a fee, to the rapidly growing YouTube with its user-generated videos, the Internet has made a new kind of access to formerly heavily controlled programming possible. Most major television-producing institutions have added a significant Internet presence to their offerings, not only distributing programmes themselves via their owned and operated websites, but providing a wealth of additional information and entertainment in an online form. Yet such venues pose a considerable threat to the economic and public service functions of established broadcasters.

In the USA, where *monetizing,* or figuring out how to make money from, web-based television remains the highest priority, networks and cable channels first experimented with digital downloads via Apple's iTunes service. For fees in the range of $1.99 an episode, viewers could download episodes of prime time television programmes a few hours after their initial broadcast, to be viewed on iPod or computer, or for the technologically sophisticated, relayed to the digital television set. In the summer of 2007 the NBC network broke off from iTunes to start its own web distribution service via Amazon's Unbox, which will allow both temporary downloads for low prices and purchase by download for a higher fee (Barnes 2007 chapter 1). The BBC initiated its own video on demand digital download service in 2005 to operate in conjunction with the Interactive Media Player, a type of digital video recorder. ITV began experimenting with special 'mobisodes' of *Coronation Street* (ITV 1960–) clips sent to cell phones in 2006. 'Entertainment is no longer linear,' said Jana Bennett, BBC Director of Television. 'You have to think in terms of a broader life cycle of a show – how it will play on TV or computer, in a game, on a phone – and you have to embrace a new kind of creative partnership with your audience' (cited by Foroohar 2005: 48).

DVD

One area of digital distribution that seemed to take the television industry by surprise was the sale of television series on DVD (Digital Video Discs), particularly whole seasons in *box-set* format. The videocassette, an analogue technology, had an enormous impact on the film business but much less on television. Videotapes were bulky and possessed a small recording capacity; they worked fine for feature films but a whole season of a television programme would have weighed quite a bit and have taken up an entire shelf! But DVDs presented a whole new set of possibilities. Not only could five or six television episodes fit on a single disc, the discs were lightweight and could be packaged four or five together in a compact box, enough room even for a US-style 26-episode series – and commentary and extra features besides. It took a while for the television industry to recognize the potential of this additional market for their goods; only the success of a few popular programs on DVD beginning in 2005 – *The Sopranos* (HBO 1999–2007), *Sex and the City* (HBO 1998–2004), *Buffy the Vampire Slayer* (Warner Brothers 1997–2003) – began to open eyes to the potential in both sales and rental. The BBC was not slow to follow up on this market, especially for past hits like *Monty Python* (1969–1974) and *Blackadder* (1983–1989), along with more traditional offerings such as *The BBC TV Shakespeare Collection* (2005).

A market for DVD sales across national and linguistic boundaries has sprung up, thanks in part to the storage capacity that allowed subtitling in several different languages to exist on one disc, easily selected by the viewer. Entrepreneur distributors like Koch Entertainment in the USA began to offer not only British series but television programmes from France, Germany and Italy, and large distributors like Amazon.com expanded their international offerings in 2005 and 2006. However, as the advent of new high-definition DVD, in two competing formats – Blu-Ray and HD-DVD – threatened to raise prices and make old players obsolete, many began to wonder if the increase in Internet speed would not give downloads the advantage in coming years. DVD sales of independent and smaller productions stalled in 2007, due to an abundance of releases and concentration at the retail level, with less-known productions getting squeezed out. As one distributor put it, 'We're all drowning in a sea of DVDs. Five or six years ago maybe a hundred titles a week would come out. Now we're fighting 200 or 300 titles every Tuesday' (cited by Reesman 2007).

Reception

We have already noted that digital television's capacities blur the distinction between production and reception common to analogue media, but it is worth noting a few aspects of what users or viewers can do with their new digital options when it comes to putting digital technology to use. It turns out that, though regularly scheduled television programmes still retain their popularity, the ability to shift programmes to more convenient times and to view them in time-compacted blocks (not doled out week by week) have become increasingly popular. DVRs, including the popular TiVo, were introduced in the USA in 2004; by 2007 nearly 20 per cent of US homes owned at least one DVR and used them for an ever-increasing proportion of their television viewing, as did viewers in the UK, where both Sky and the BBC introduced DVRs in 2005, far ahead of most other countries. Fast-forwarding through the advertisements seems to be especially cherished, to the alarm of many in the television industry. One US cable company, Time Warner, announced in 2007 that it would make a DVR available to its customers that would allow programme shifting but would specifically not be able to fast forward through the advertisements.

Combine DVDs, DVRs, iTunes, BitTorrent and YouTube with the ever-growing array of on-demand options available on digital distributions systems and, as Derek Kompare points out, television as a medium seems well on its way to a shift away from its traditional configuration as a service to the mass public, streaming a continuous flow of common communication strictly regulated in its availability, to a model more closely analogous to publishing or to the film industry (Kompare 2006). Individuals make selections from an expanding inventory of offerings available from a number of sources at different times, across formerly policed barriers of time, space, nation, language and format.

Conclusion

Television screens have both expanded and shrunk dramatically, from the increasingly theatre-like flat screens, now part of home entertainment centres, to the tiny windows on cell phones and iPods. The computer screen becomes a television, while television screens hook up with computers. Many former couch potatoes now use their television screens only for playing video games. New programme forms debut from 'mobisodes' and 'webisodes' – television material only available on cell phones or websites – to increasingly interactive formats that allow viewers to affect the narrative, as in voting for the next Pop Idol or calling in questions to be discussed on air. If we do not like such changes, YouTube and digital production technologies allow us to make our own television. Clearly, the digital revolution is still in progress, and television remains one of its main battlefields.

Recommended reading

Boddy, William (2004) *New Media and Popular Imagination: Launching Radio, Television, and Digital Media in the United States* (Oxford Television Studies). Oxford: Oxford University Press.

Brown, Alan and Picard, Robert G. (eds) (2005) *Digital Terrestrial Television in Europe*. Mahwah, NJ: Lawrence Earlbaum Associates.

Castaneda, Mari (2007) The complicated transition to digital television in the United States, *Television and New Media,* 8(2): 91–106.

Hilmes, Michele (2002) Cable, satellite and digital technologies, in Dan Harries (ed.) *The New Media Book*. London: British Film Institute.

Nicholas, Kyle (2006) Post TV?: the future of television, in Glen Creeber (ed.) *Tele-Visions: An Introduction to Studying Television*. London: British Film Insitute.

Case Study: Making television news in the digital age

Damien Steward

Television news is about change. Its novelty and its immediacy are among the things that have always clearly distinguished it from newspapers. Television news is now changing more quickly then ever before. Changes in philosophy, burgeoning competition and ownership have all played their part. But perhaps the most powerful agent of change in contemporary television journalism is technology, the methods and machinery which actually bring the latest pictures to our screens. And those same methods and machinery have also made it possible for non-professionals (those outside the magic circles of the industry) to influence as well as be influenced by this most powerful of mediums.

Since the late 1990s all the UK's major television news operations have been experimenting with digital technology in order to better manage the thousands of hours of footage which stream into their newsrooms every week. News managers saw the advent of affordable server technology, where huge amounts of moving pictures can be electronically stored, as an opportunity to improve their journalism and cut costs.

There was little change in the way news footage was managed from the early 1980s for more than a decade. Then, footage was shot on cameras using the beta tape format and physically returned to the newsroom. The footage was then edited 'tape to tape', requiring the use of bulky and expensive editing machinery and the skills of a professional craft tape editor. It was a system that worked well enough, but one that had obvious drawbacks. Apart from the cost of the infrastructure, the potential for tapes to go missing and for massive bottlenecks to slow the production process were constant problems. The advent of server-based technology and desktop editing has changed all that. Sky News's technical manager James Weeks (interview with author, 2007) says:

> It used to be the case that a producer would tie up a £250,000 edit suite for five minutes just to cut an eight second opening shot. Now they can browse pictures on their desktop, pick the shot they want, add audio to accurately represent the sense of the story they want to publish. It allows them to take responsibility and ownership of a chunk of output. In terms of job satisfaction and the ability to react to breaking stories that's a huge leap.

In theory, such desktop systems mean that the craft editors can be used just for the stories, the features, the specials, and so on, where their skills are most useful. But the reality is that the people in charge of the purse strings at the broadcasters also see the new technology as an opportunity to cut the headcount and with it the proportion of the budget spent on people rather than machinery.

The new technology has also started to make serious inroads into the business of getting the pictures back to the newsroom. From the late 1970s onwards television news companies relied on satellite transmission from overseas, and then increasingly at home, to ensure footage got to them as quickly as possible. The price of such transmissions has fallen precipitously in the last decade and a half. But now the broadcasters find that pictures can be sent from the field via a laptop computer. The quality of these transmissions is still not the best but new software, particularly the Flash-based P2 system that Sky has pioneered in the UK, is narrowing the gap almost by the month.

Peter Barron, editor of BBC's *Newsnight* (BBC 1980–) has a more intriguing, even perhaps romantic, view of television technology's march into the future (interview with author, 2007):

> In my view, what's going on with digital media industry is not unlike what happened in the music industry in the late 70s. In those days making a record was a multi-million pound, months in the recording studio, undertaking that only the huge bands like Led Zeppelin and Genesis knew how to do. For them in the TV industry, read the likes of the BBC and ITV. Then in the late 70s the technology came along so that almost anyone could make a record for a couple of hundred quid or less, and many did. Most of it was of course rubbish – just the same way that most blogs are rubbish – but in the mass of material some gems rose to the top, and very quickly bands like the Undertones made the old order look like lumbering dinosaurs. So what happened? Some of the dinosaurs died out (read *Top of the Pops* and *Grandstand*), but the big record companies – threatened by the likes of independent labels like Small Wonder and Rough Trade – simply adapted, copied them by pretending to be small labels themselves and eventually bought them out. So, the big media players would in my view be mad not to adapt to the changing digital landscape or say that's not what we do. If they do that they're going out of business, but I think it's far more likely they'll adapt and survive, with a few casualties along the way.

But despite the pace of change, Barron believes that there is still some resistance to the new way of doing things (ibid.):

> I think it's quite surprising, however, how slowly big organisations adapt to change – in parts of the TV industry but also in the NHS and elsewhere. Why is it that individuals in their private lives embrace change very readily – no-one for example insists on maintaining a pantry now that we all have fridges, or hardly anyone has a butler but lots of people employ Polish cleaners – but in big organisations you often hear people saying the TV or NHS equivalent of 'we can't let the butler go, who will keep the pantry properly stocked?'

Some of that resistance is based on more than just an attachment to the old ways, and desire among technical staff, not least craft editors, understandably anxious to keep their jobs. The recent signing of a £250 million six-year deal between ITV and ITN for news coverage was predicated on a large proportion of that money being spent on new technology, with a resulting 64 jobs losses, virtually all of them among the technical ranks. And the move from employing craft editors for almost all tasks to passing on all but the most complex editing jobs to journalists is one that makes some significant assumptions about the very nature of journalism. Television journalists today are a highly trained group. All new recruits to the business now are graduates, the vast majority with a post-graduate journalism qualification. The days of a reporter from a local or national newspaper crossing disciplines, or even somebody from the administrative grades, are over. But this new generation of television journalists, even though most will have had some desktop editing training during their education, want to be exactly that – journalists. Even those who prove competent at the technical end of the job do not always enjoy the task. As an understandably anonymous journalist at a major television news company told me:

> The new way of doing things looks very impressive at first, you go out with a cameraman, you see what's shot, you go back to the newsroom, sit at your computer and cut away. You're under complete control. But that's part of the problem. Everything I, or anybody else, writes for one of our bulletins is read and probably re-written at least once, sometimes twice. And if the news-reader is serious about their job, three times. But the pressure of work is now so intense that most of the stuff that I edit goes straight to air without being seen by anybody else at all. It's not ideal, and even though I'm reasonably competent on the desktop there are still quite a few people, excellent journalists otherwise, who genuinely struggle with the system. I'd say the number of technical faults with the average programme, missing audio, mistaken shot choices, has definitely gone up since we moved to the new system. And I don't think there's a single colleague of mine who wouldn't prefer to work with a professional editor. I wouldn't expect them to do my job, though I suspect many of them are more than capable. So why should I do theirs? Why should I want to?

> (anonymous interview, 2007)

It is a problem with journalists self-editing on a desktop that many of the more thoughtful senior journalists are conscious of. Julie Hulme is a senior programme editor at Channel 4 News where the new Avid-based system, Newscutter, is installed. As she explained shortly before it became operational:

> Once we finish transfer in October [2007], everyone in the newsroom including correspondents, programme editors, producers and presenters will be able to see material, work through rushes and cut pictures to create packages. One of the drawbacks of the current system is the need to visit a VT suite to add sound. Now everyone can do that at his or her desktop. As a

programme editor I'll have to put together stories yet I'll try and strike a balance so that our journalists remain journalists and don't become technicians

The introduction of server-based technology has had one unexpected, and quite strange, consequence. In the pre-digital age any tape containing an item that simply had to go on air immediately could simply be rushed into the newsroom, inserted into a player and broadcast immediately. It is a scene that many older television news people remember with a mixture of excitement and dread. But today that tape would have to be downloaded into a server before it could be transmitted. Only the latest machinery operates at anything faster than real time. Meaning a 30-minute tape takes 30 minutes before it can be edited or broadcast. So when the last tape machine is finally removed from the last gallery or play-out area, likely to happen sooner rather than later, the technology has actually slowed the process of putting important material onto the public's screens.

It is in the area of archive and library access that server technology perhaps offers the greatest promise. At the moment the major television news providers are compelled to store huge numbers of tapes which have to be physically tracked down by a librarian every time a particular image or story is required. The problem is compounded by the fact that, for example at ITN, the archive they manage, which stretches back to the late nineteenth century, is stored on a number of different formats, including beta, u-matic and even film. They now have an ambitious plan to digitize 100,000 hours of pictures. They will then be available not only to journalists at their computers but also to sales and marketing, an increasingly important source of income for the company. But this process will have to be very carefully managed to provide the editorial benefits ITN hope to achieve. Not least, they need to ensure that each story is uniquely tagged. The almost complete disappearance of professional library researchers from some television newsrooms has already proved the difficulty of tracking down the right pictures without skilled help. It is another skill set many journalists would prefer not to have to acquire.

In the medium term though, it became clear that the technology that is really changing television news is not that in the hands of the broadcasters but in the hands of the public. The ubiquity of camera-equipped mobile phones, highbandwidth broadband connections and, perhaps most importantly, the public's lack of deference towards the broadcasters, means that so-called 'citizen journalism' is seen as a vital part of the television news universe. Why, ask the major television news organizations, allow companies like YouTube and MySpace to be the only big fish swimming in the ocean of video now being created by ordinary people? As an internal ITN memo I received in July 2007 put it:

> Over recent weeks, User Generated Content (UGC) has once again been the mainstay of most TV News programmes. The burning car at Glasgow Airport, the smoldering terrorist brought down by the public, the M6 arrests. We've all been in UGC Utopia, the pictures just seemed to roll-in, as our unspoken contract with the public delivered in spades. You film it – we'll broadcast it.

The above was not written by YouTube's PR agency but by Deborah Turness, ITN's editor – the person in charge of all news programming on ITV. The BBC set up an entire team to deal with user-generated content as a pilot in 2005. In the wake of the 7/7 bombings in London and the Buncefield oil fire, the team's importance was realized and the group was expanded. In the wake of the Buncefield fire the BBC received over 5,000 photos from viewers. The BBC does not normally pay for content generated by its viewers. However, if they were to be handed an exclusive like the 21/7 arrests it is hard to see how they could resist opening their wallet.

In 2006 CNN launched iReport, a project designed to bring user-generated news content to the once internationally dominant CNN. Sky News has perhaps been the most aggressive in seeking pictures from the public, with regular on-air appeals for pictures from its viewers. There is also no doubt that the 'always on the air' nature of the products from Sky, BBC World and CNN, not to mention smaller players like al-Jazeera means there is at times a desperation simply just to fill air time.

User Generated Content has already proved its worth to ITN. In July 2005 they bought footage of the arrest of the would-be 21/7 bombers from a neighbour. They paid him £60,000, perhaps the largest sum ever handed over to a member of the public by a television news company for footage. It proved to be a shrewd investment; not only did the material provide ITN with a stunning exclusive, the cash laid out was recouped in days by sales to other broadcasters, newspapers and agencies. Turness told me that she sees UGC as 'exploiting more of what the "users" have got to offer. It's about understanding the contribution that ordinary people can make to our programmes, and the editorial, commercial and strategic value they can bring to us' (interview with author, June 2007).

ITN think that they have spotted a gap in the market which could make their future, clouded by ownership issues, a little more secure. So at the end of July 2007 they launched a service called 'Uploaded'. ITN hope the service will mean they will have a whole network of 'citizen journalists', bringing new types of stories to the network and its associated services on the net and on mobile phones. ITN believe that aside from the potential editorial value, there is a clear commercial argument for connecting with engaged, motivated, individuals – individuals who increasingly get their news from non-traditional television and web sources.

The service will allow every viewer who has signed up to submit their views – via mobile phone, webcam or whatever device they have – on the story of the day (which, we should note, will still be chosen by a senior group of ITN journalists). The very best of the clips will run on the Lunchtime News, Evening News and the News at Ten Thirty. ITN insist that this material will not replace the work of ITV News reporters and correspondents. Viewers will then be encouraged to go online, view more clips and add their own views. For ITN it seems to make all kinds of sense, particularly marketing and commercial sense. They call it 'the virtuous circle of promotion' – people are permanently propelled forward from television to online and back to television again.

This, of course, poses all sorts of questions about how this content will be regulated. One only has to think about how various Radio 4 polls for personality of year, for example, have regularly been manipulated by well-organized pressure groups with an agenda that perhaps the editorial teams felt were less than appropriate. The most extreme case against, muttered by many a journalist foot soldier in many a newsroom, is that the end result of the growing use of UGC will be news programmes where the agenda is set by what the public sends in, with news executives simply holding the ring while the journalists themselves do simply end up as over-educated technicians.

That is of course, a pessimistic view, a talent free wasteland of shaky pictures from unskilled 'reporters', in which the broadcasters desperately try to shore up earnings and profits by selling pictures online and down the phone. For their part the people who are in charge of the major television newsrooms insist that they know, and research bears out, what attracts viewers. That means major investment in foreign bureaus, field reporting and undercover investigations. And that is high-quality reporting, backed up by a true understanding of the stories and issues, none of which is cheap. And it is surely foolish to think that the television news makers could ever turn their backs on technology which allows them so much flexibility, in the field as well as the newsroom, and at the same time offers the viewer an ever-growing number of news sources. Baron Reuter's pigeons were no doubt incensed when they lost their jobs through the laying of undersea telegraph tables.

Perhaps what is different today is pace of technological change. The editor who spliced together the moving film of Queen Victoria's Golden Jubilee in 1897 would have easily recognized the machinery used by his descendants in the newsrooms of the 1960s and 1970s. The major British news organizations of the early twentieth century are using their fourth or fifth new electronic editing system in a decade. This means that most television journalists would argue that they have less time to think about what they want to say and how to say it and that much more is consumed by the process of actually getting it, whatever it is, to air. Journalism has never really been sure whether it is a calling, a profession or a trade. It still is not, but there is little doubt that the artisanal aspects are currently getting the upper hand. The last decades have proved a boom time for the designers, makers and sellers of television hardware and software alike. Whether the next decades also prove to be a boom time for journalists and television journalism is altogether another matter.

4 Digital cinema: virtual screens

Michael Allen

Film director George Lucas has been famously quoted as saying that film is a nineteenth-century medium, developed out of photography through both media using celluloid strips for capturing and recording their images. This technology formed the basis for films, film-making and cinema for around one hundred years, from its first developments, referred to by Lucas, at the end of the nineteenth century, to the end of the twentieth century. Lucas's comment, in its denigration of the 'ancient history' of celluloid, indicates a new reality, a replacement for celluloid; a new beginning for film-making and cinema: digital cinema. In the past 20 or so years, digital technologies, techniques and visual aesthetics have had a massive effect on all phases of film-making and distribution process. '[D]igital cinema is above all a concept, a complete system, covering the entire movie production chain from the acquisition with digital cameras to post-production to distribution to exhibition, all with bits and bytes instead of 35mm reels' (Michel 2003). This chapter offers an overview of these changes, explaining the basic working of the technology and mapping the range of practices that had been affected as a result of the appearance of the digital.

Digital production and post production

Until recently, the actual filming process of a movie production has been done using traditional 35mm or 70mm film cameras using canisters of celluloid. The image quality produced by digital cameras was felt to be significantly lower than film, and so, while the film footage was increasingly being fed into computers for post-production manipulation, the production process itself remained celluloid-based. Digital filming began, in theory, in the late 1980s, when Sony came up with the marketing concept of 'electronic cinematography'. The initiative failed to take off with professionals and public alike, and it was only at the end of the 1990s, with the introduction of HDCAM recorders and a renaming of the process to 'digital cinematography', that making films using digital cameras and related equipment finally began to take hold.

George Lucas was instrumental in engendering this shift, when, in 2001–2 he shot the 'Attack of the Clones' episode of his *Star Wars* saga digitally, using Sony HDW-F900 HDCAM camcorders fitted with high-end Panavision lenses (the French feature *Vidocq* (Pitof 2001) was actually the first shot with the Sony camera). While capable of shooting conventional American standard 30-frame/second interlaced pictures, the cameras could also shoot at 24-frames/second, the standard for film cameras, and also progressive video, video made up of complete frames rather than interlaced fields.

High-end cameras use a single sensor which is the same size as a 35mm film frame, and allows the same shallow depth of field as conventional film cameras. Moreover, shooting in progressive HDTV format gives an image size of 720 or even 1080 pixels. The result is a 'filmic' rather than a 'televisual' look to the captured image.

By the mid-1990s, the Sony DCR-VX1000 MiniDV format camera promised an image quality such that, while still not as good as film, was good enough for low-budget film-makers to begin shooting their features digitally and editing them on relatively inexpensive desktop software programs. The high-end cameras use minimal or no compression processes to reduce file size, whereas the MiniDV systems typically employ high compression rates, reducing image quality in the interests of storage size.

Because of the lower dynamic range of digital cameras, the correcting of poorly exposed footage is harder to perform in post-production. A partial solution to this problem is the addition of complex video-assist technology during the shooting process. This might 'simply' consist of a high-performance video monitor which allows the cinematographer to see what is being recorded and to make any broad adjustments necessary. At its most complex, however, it will include monitors displaying precise waveforms and colour analysis so that the cinematographer and his assistants can make minute adjustments to every component of the image. Such high-technology solutions are, not surprisingly, only at the disposal of the biggest budget productions.

The increase in the use of digital technologies and processes in the production of feature films has also affected the logistics of film production, enabling real locations to be partially or, increasingly, fully replaced by digitally created ones. This replacement can be wide ranging. At its simplest, it can just be the augmenting of an ostensibly real space, where small objects or parts of a scene are digitally added to the original footage. More extensively, digitally created scenery can be substantially added to real 3-D spaces, as was the case with the Coliseum scene in *Gladiator* (Scott 2000). At the current furthest extreme, digital images can form the wholesale replacement of a real-world diegesis with a digitally created one, such as in *Sky Captain and the World of Tomorrow* (Conran 2004) where the actors are virtually the only non-digitally created elements in the film.

A further advantage of the digital creation of sets and locations, especially in an age of increasing film serials, sequels and franchises, is that the virtual sets, once created in the computer and stored as data, can be easily regenerated for future film productions, making those lucrative sequels and franchises easier to establish and to make. Economies of scale in digital processes are therefore employed to offset the increasingly spiralling costs of modern feature film production. An interesting reversal of this trend, perhaps, is that this virtual replacement of real locations places an increasing premium on the now recognizably expensive productions which still go to the real geographical location in order to shoot their footage. The James Bond franchise, for example, is still sold on the exotic and expensive fact that the production *actually* still films its actors in far-flung locations rather than having them stand in front of a green screen with footage of the locations added later in post-production.

The consequence of this increasing use of computer-imaging techniques in the making of films is that the balance between production (the filming of the scenes which will constitute the narrative of the finished film) and post-production (the cleaning-up of the images captured during the production stage and the adding of analogue, and now digital effects to those basic images) has been significantly altered. In contemporary feature film-making, the post-production period is now generally far longer than production period, with most of what will constitute the final image seen on screen being the result of work done in the CGI (computer-generated imagery) and editing suites rather than on-set or on-location. While CGI effects, especially in the largest blockbuster movies, are complex, expensive and time consuming, the latter two are consistently decreasing and are far more attractive to film-makers than the risks and costs often incurred on live location shooting.

Other aspects of the modern film-making process are also feeling the effects of increasing digitization. Editing used to be a rather delicate process of handling strips of celluloid, physically cut and stuck together in hard-to-reverse operations. In such conditions, editing decisions were performed only after long and careful thought. In the digital age, such physical processes have been dispensed with. The 'film' images have, until recently, been stored on tape, but are now increasingly 'tapeless,' recorded as data files on hard disk or flash memory. These are then downloaded into an editing system employing RAID (Redundant Array of Inexpensive/independent Drives/disks). Different versions of edits can be performed with the change of a few settings on the editing console; the sequence being compiled 'virtually', in the computer's memory, rather than as a physically tangible thing. A wide range of effects can be tried out easily and quickly, without the physical restrictions posed by conventional cut-and-stick editing.

A downside of this increased efficiency has, however, been noted by a number of practitioners. The speed and ease of modern digital editing processes threatens to give editors and their directors, if not an embarrassment of choice then at least a confusion of options. The careful forethought that came before a physical edit of celluloid has been replaced by a 'try-it-and-see' philosophy which can result, in undisciplined hands, in a chaotic range of barely separable choices, potentially making the editing process lengthier rather than shorter. But with the editing process on many effects-heavy productions now inextricably intertwined with the complex combination with live action footage with computer-generated images across a lengthy post-production period, this potential slowing of the editing process becomes both less critical and less easy to identify as a separate part of the production.

Digital cinema aesthetics

Digital imaging has impacted to varying degrees on the ways in which scenes in a film are built up shot by shot, and the pacing of sequences of images in such scenes.

Historically, this has partly been due to the crude image quality of early CGI; a certain unrealistic artificial quality to CGIs which appeared far different visually from the images of real-world objects and people that had been photographed chemically onto celluloid in the traditional way.

There were some significant consequences of this different visual quality. One was that images containing significant amounts of CGI work usually appeared on screen for shorter durations than 'real-world' images; the logic being that the CGI images would not be on screen long enough for audiences to register their artificiality, thereby threatening to break the suspension of disbelief necessary for a spectator to believe the world of the film appearing on screen in front of him/her. And a consequence of this was that genres which favoured this kind of 'snippet-viewing' – horror, action; genres which involved hiding and then spectacularly revealing objects and people for maximum shock value – tended to be favoured over more genres which relied more on complex human emotional interaction, where longer shot lengths and an absolute believability in the reality of the characters mitigated against artificially created images.

Editing patterns – the cutting back and forth between people, objects and spaces in the building of a believable three-dimensional screen space – thereby became conditioned by the need to invisibly incorporate the CGI elements into the reality of the film's world. Character point of view, traditionally used to cue the next image as something that a character was looking at, came to be used as a means of convincing the spectator that the thing looked at – often a CGI object or creature – was actually inhabiting the same diegetic space as the live humans. But the gap in image quality between the CGI and the real images necessitated the two largely being kept in separate shots – the character first looking off-screen and then the CGI object/ creature being looked at.

The cohabiting of the two in the same frame became one of the 'resistances' in building scenes shot by shot using the combination of photographed and CGI-created screen elements. When it was attempted, the result was usually dangerously contradictory; think of Ja-Ja Binks, Liam Neeson and Ewan McGregor uncomfortably sharing the same shot in *Star Wars: The Phantom Menace* (Lucas 1999). The widely differing visual qualities brought to the image by human and CGI figures threaten to dismantle its illusion of believability. And also, the difficulty of combining CGI with the photographed human meant that the two elements had to be kept separate in different parts of the frame, with no intermingling or one crossing in front of or behind the other. This lent a certain static frontality to such images, similar to the stationary frontal camera used in the earliest films of the late nineteenth and early twentieth centuries. The Lucas aphorism quoted at the beginning of this chapter is therefore incomplete. Film may be a nineteenth-century invention, but early CGI also displayed a nineteenth-century aesthetic; frontal camera, lateral movement and non-penetration of scenic space.

But, by dint of that, the 'coming of age' of CGI thereby became both the attaining of a photo-realistic quality to the CGI and the ability of the camera to seem to enter the 3-D space of the CGI scene, moving around it as a traditional film camera would a physical set or location. Such complex interaction between photographed actors and CGI creature was first seen, fleetingly, in action scenes in films such as *The Abyss* (Cameron 1989; when the water creature first visits the crew) and *Terminator 2: Judgement Day* (Cameron 1991; most notably in the fight scenes between the two terminators), but in both the overwhelming majority of images showing both real actors and CGI elements together still kept the two in separate parts of the frame, with only occasional overlaps. It was *Jurassic Park* (Spielberg 1993) which first showed the intermingling of actors and CGI creatures in the first sighting of the brontosaurus by Sam Neill and Laura Dern's characters, when the two actors walk in front of the dinosaur in a travelling camera shot held for nineteen seconds; more than enough time for a scrutinizing spectator to spot the artifice and break the illusion. The impact and impressiveness of the shot comes from both its length and its camera movement; the latter keeping actors and dinosaur in perfect registration as it tracks left to right, triumphantly announcing the full integration of the photographed and the computer-generated. However, the camera, for all its movement, remains frontal to the action.

It would take several years more, most notably in *Gladiator*, in the scene depicting the entry of the gladiators into the Coliseum, where the camera follows the men into the arena and then sweeps around them in a 360° circle as they look up at the crowd in the multiple tiers of the building; most of both being digitally created to save production costs. The sweeping camera, keeping gladiators and background tiers in exact registration as it explores the supposed 3-D space of the arena, confirms in the complexity of its movement the existence of what does not exist in reality: the crowd in the upper tiers of the Coliseum. With the development of such sophisticated techniques and images, CGI finally became invisible; no longer a foregrounded spectacular effect intended to impress its audience but a fully integrated part of the image-creation tools at the disposal of the film-makers.

Digital divides? Mainstream, independent and minority film-making

The focus of critical studies into the use of CGI and digital technologies in film-making has tended to be of a large-scale, mainstream feature production: the special effects-laden 'blockbusters'. There are, however, two other areas of film production that are worthy of consideration in this respect: low-budget independent and Third World.

An immediate reaction to the idea of using CGI in independent film production might be that the glossy, artificial look of CGIs might be antithetical to the gritty realist aesthetic conventionally assumed of low-budget indie work. But the independent sector is now so large and diverse that such restrictive definitions are increasingly outdated. Indeed, many independent film-makers are interested in using the particular look and visual aesthetic of CGI for specific purposes, to make their films stand out from the crowd of features released each year. Wes Anderson's *The Life Aquatic With Steve Zissou* (2004), for example, used computer imaging to add a whimsical, cartoon-like quality to the film, both to echo the quirky comedy and play in opposition to the moments of pathos delivered in the narrative. Richard Linklater, for his substantially lower-budget *Waking Life* (2001), shot the live-action footage very quickly, using digital camcorders, before manipulating the images digitally on computer, using a technique called 'rotoscoping' (a technique in which animators trace over live-action film movement). Both examples are of independent film-makers actively seeking new digital techniques to lend their films a distinctive and striking visual quality.

The other interesting use of digital film technology is in the service of enabling national cinemas to produce films specific to their cultures in ways that the more restrictive structures and economics of traditional film-making prevented. Cheap cameras and computer-based editing software have increasingly enabled films to be produced for virtually zero budgets. The capability of digital cameras to allow film-makers to shoot endless footage without wasting expensive celluloid has transformed film production in some Third World countries:

> Of course digital cameras have all the advantages that everyone knows about: you don't waste time changing film, you get as many takes as you need and you are flexible ... On *Yizo Yizo* we were shooting about 23 set ups a day and getting eight to nine minutes of material.

> (Markgraff 2005)

And digital distribution, whether in DVD format or in cinemas with digital projection, enables easy and cheap distribution exhibition, getting the films out quickly to local audiences for maximum impact. DVD releases are of the order of hundreds of thousands of copies, while special initiatives are striving to set up networks of digitally equipped cinemas. In September 2005, for example, South Africa created 20 digital cinemas for showing indigenous product alongside foreign features.

In Nigeria, film production, labelled 'Nollywood' (after its Holly- and Bolly-counterparts), is a multi-billion-dollar-a-year industry. Two hundred digitally shot features are produced annually, making Nigeria the third biggest producer of features behind Hollywood and Bollywood. The production of feature films using digital technologies is not seen simply as a quick and easy money-making initiative. There is a serious political aspect to the phenomenon; a means of bypassing the cultural blockage created by a glut of Western film products which fails to relate to the reality of life in Africa:

> With digital technology, it becomes possible to boost creativity, to produce more without sacrificing quality, to inquire again about African memory and enrich it. A new world opens up for cinema: capturing and re-mapping the image of Africa by reducing the high expense of analogue technology. But an African director still needs to know what he is doing and needs to have a story to tell in order not to suppress his song, his part of African history.

> (Bakupa-Kaninda 2003)

But the ease of access and use of digital equipment for producing feature films cheaply and quickly is seen as having a downside. Some critics see access to cheap digital film-making technologies as potentially damaging, allowing inexperienced producers to 'saturate the market with popular cheap productions, overshadow the efforts of serious directors. Filmed in a hurry, their stories lack basic narrative structure' (ibid.).

Digital distribution and exhibition

Digital distribution, projection and exhibition is obviously not only to the advantage of minority and Third World film concerns. For the mainstream film industry, the electronic downloading of films in digital format, from central servers to servers in cinema projection booths, is a cheap method of distributing copies of latest releases to the large number of cinema screens demanded by modern saturation-release strategies. There is a substantial saving on print costs in such cases: at a minimum cost per print of $1200–2000, the cost of conventional celluloid print production is between $5–8 million per film. With several thousand releases a year, the potential savings offered by digital distribution and projection are over $1 billion.

Distribution currently takes a variety of formats: a series of DVDs (typically 8–10 per feature), deliverable hard drives or via satellite. As an obvious security measure, the data contained on any of these delivery platforms will be encrypted to prevent piracy and cloning. At the moment, individual cinemas organize their own screenings through one of these methods, but eventually it is planned that cinema chains will be digitally networked, allowing a central mainframe server to simultaneously play out a feature film to a number of cinema screens.

The ease and cheapness, together with the ability to hold on to a film rather than having to send a print on to the next cinema, allows a wider range of films to be screened and viewed by the public; minority and small-budget films that would not otherwise get such a release. Certainly, this has been the aim behind the UK Film Council's 250-screen digital projection initiative, designed to enable specialized films to get wider distribution in UK cinemas. It is also easier to 'scale up' with extra digital copies if a small film achieves surprising box office success. Worldwide release for major films such as *The Da Vinci Code* (Howard 2006) and *Mission Impossible III* (Abrams 2004) is replacing staggered global release strategies. The latter allowed for the too easily pirated copying of initial release prints such that later releases were forced to directly compete with, or even be pre-empted by, pirate copies. In contrast, digital distribution enables the low-cost simultaneous global release rather than the same block of prints being slowly circulated in staggered markets.

As with the previous phase of audiovisual technology (early sound systems, videotape formats, etc.), certain incompatibilities between compression and server systems mean that films currently have to be distributed in a range of formats. However, in March 2002, 'Digital Cinema Initiatives' was formed by the major studios – Disney, Fox, MGM, Paramount, Sony Pictures, Universal and Warners – to develop an open architecture technical specification for digital cinema which could be taken up by all industry parties. Version 1.1 was released in April 2007. Another initiative, 'Digital Cinema Implementation Partners' (DCIP), formed by the AMC, Cinemark and Regal cinema chains, is planning to use digital projectors and servers in all its cinemas from 2008.

The cost of converting cinemas from celluloid to digital projection is high; over $150,000 per screen. As in the days of conversion to synch sound at the end of the 1920s, the exhibition sector has been resistant to pressures for it to fund this conversion. But as digital processes become ever more ubiquitous in all phases of the film industry, and as the convenience and flexibility of digital distribution have become evident, exhibitors are acquiescing to the inevitable. Some early predictions estimated that conversion to digital exhibition will be complete by 2012, although the slowing of take-up rates in recent years has cast a question mark over that date.

Conclusion

At the end of the 1990s, just as digital cinema was taking hold on the modern film-making and exhibition landscape, Thomas Elsaesser prophetically announced that cinema 'will remain the same and it will be utterly different' (1998: 204). One way of interpreting this statement is that digital processes and technologies, while they have fundamentally transformed the material base of cinema – from individual photographic frames on strips of celluloid to pixels and bytes – and modified the various stages of the film-making process, from first idea to finished film, have not radically altered either that production process itself or the viewing of the finished product. Films are still scripted, logistically planned, captured and stored as images during a production shoot, and assembled as combinations of originally shot and artificially created images, composited and edited together to form, usually, 100 to 120-minute feature films. These are then watched by people assembled together in darkened auditoria to form attentive audiences who sit motionless through the run-time of the feature until its end credits roll. Many, if not most, of those watching a digitally projected feature are no doubt oblivious to the 'revolution' taking place before their eyes.

Similarly, the *kind* of image that may be seen on screen might be noticeably different to those seen in pre-digital times – with a brighter palette, a harder, artificial edge and yet less substantial weight to them – but artificial imagery has been the stuff of cinema since its inception, from Melies's artificially constructed scenes to Ray Harryhausen's stop-motion skeletons. Difference and continuity are the pall-bearers to the supposed death of cinema; an entertainment form that, partly because of the exciting new (and digitally replicated) techniques on offer to its practitioners and the economies of scale which allow digital copies of films to reach their audiences far more cheaply, will ensure the continued existence of that mass public pleasure for the foreseeable future.

Recommended reading

Elsaesser, Thomas and Hoffmann, Kay (eds) (1998) *Cinema Futures: Cain, Abel or Cable? The Screen Arts in the Digital Age*. Amsterdam: Amsterdam University Press.

Keane, Stephen (2007) *CineTech: Convergence, Film and New Media*. Basingstoke: Palgrave Macmillan.

King, Geoff (2000) *Spectacular Narratives: Contemporary Hollywood and Frontier Mythology*. London: I.B. Tauris.

Pierson, Michelle (2002) *Special Effects: Still in Search of Wonder*. New York and Chichester: Columbia University Press.

Willis, Holly (2005) *New Digital Cinema: Reinventing the Moving Image*. London: Wallflower Press.

Case Study: Star Wars Episode II: *Attack of the Clones*

Michael Allen

From the very outset of his preparations for the fifth film in his *Star Wars* saga, George Lucas determined to make the entire production using digital technologies. Computer-based production equipment, whether animation software or non-linear editing systems, had been employed on previous episodes in the series, but with *Attack of the Clones*, Lucas's intention was to capture all elements of the film, including live action sequences, digitally.

The decision to shoot the film digitally, rather than using conventional celluloid film, was a controversial one, and Lucas received a lot of adverse criticism. For example, Victor Kemper (2005), President of the American Society of Cinematographers, interviewed for a web documentary, commented that 'The quality of an image that's captured on a digital camera does not stand up against the same image that would be captured on a piece of motion picture film'. Lucas's firm intention was to prove such detractors wrong.

In 1996 Sony and Panavision began to develop cutting-edge cameras and lenses capable of capturing high-definition progressive scan digital images which would be indistinguishable from traditional 35mm celluloid. The sensitivity of the camera and the precision of the lenses, which were computer-designed, worked together to produce the required sharpness and clarity of the captured images. As Fred Meyers, an engineer with Industrial Light and Magic, commented during the same web documentary:

> [t]he actual chips that are in the camera are smaller than a 35mm film image. That meant that the performance of the lens actually had to be better than a 35mm lens since you were using a smaller area to image the entire high-resolution frame on.

> (Meyers 2005)

It was hoped that the cameras would be ready for filming *Star Wars Episode I: The Phantom Menace*, which was released in mid-1999 but, in the event, Sony was unable to perfect them in time. The cameras that eventually arrived for Lucas to use on the filming of Episode II shot at a frame rate of 24 frames per second, the same as traditional film.

But before the cameras rolled on the production itself, an extensive period of what Lucas has termed 'previsualization' took place. Previsualization, based on Lucas's script and rough storyboard drawings, consisted of two main operations – videomatics and animatics. With videomatics, members of the crew acted out scenes from the film in front of 'green screen' and then added crudely detailed vehicles, backgrounds and sets using computer graphics. These were then sent to Lucas for approval and feedback. The animatics that were then produced were a finer version of the videomatics, with digital figures replacing the crew members and more detailed CGI backgrounds.

Both operations enabled Lucas and his crew, before any real filming had taken place, to see how the finished film would fit together in terms of shot-to-shot transitions, pacing of action sequences, and so on. This had a real-world economic pragmatism to it, as Rick McCallum (2005), one of the film's producers explained in a documentary on the making of the film: 'The cost of making a movie, and the cost of marketing a movie, are so intense that we have to look for ways that make us much more cost efficient, that allows us to express ourselves in this huge world'.

It also allowed those who were then involved in the filming process itself, cast and crew, to be able to visualize what the scene they were creating would look like in the finished film; an important aid when they were acting and operating camera equipment in a virtually empty film set largely dominated by green screens. Without this visual aid, actors found it extremely hard to react convincingly to characters, actions and events that would be added to the raw footage weeks or months later. With digital techniques being increasingly employed across the film industry, such strategies will undoubtedly become the norm in helping actors and crew perform their tasks in the virtual world of contemporary film-making.

Lucas has commented that the possibilities offered by digital equipment and techniques have radically changed the way the production period of a film is conceived and executed. Conventional film production up to recent years has traditionally comprised a relatively short pre-production planning period, followed by a longer filming period, followed by a post-production period in which the raw footage shot during the production period was edited and visual effects added. Any shot or scene found to be unsatisfactory would often require costly re-shoots involving the reassembling of cast and crews who may well be far away or involved in new productions. The speed and flexibility of digital, on the other hand, offer a very different process now. As Lucas explains:

> I've refined the process of working more visually; I shoot for a period of time, about 60 days or so, and then I stop and work on the film for a while. Then I come back and shoot for another 10 days or so, and then I stop and go back and work on the film, rewrite and change things, and then I come back and shoot for another week. I do it in pieces rather than in one long shoot. That way I can actually look at what I'm doing, cut it and study it. The previsualisation process [allows me to] put scenes together without having to shoot them, see how they fit in the movie and then, if they work, I can cut them in and actually go out and shoot them. There's a lot of freedom and malleability that didn't exist before. It's easy to move things around in the frame, to change various visual aspects of the film, which just wasn't possible before.
>
> (Lucasfilm 2002)

In addition, shooting on high-definition digital cameras allowed large monitors to be available on set for playback of a shot as soon as it had been taken. Any errors or technical problems could therefore be identified immediately, rather than hours or days later, and the shot retaken then and there, saving considerable time and money.

Placing every element of the film – actors, sets, spacecraft, and so on – into the digital realm from the outset makes them fully malleable, such that they can be easily moved around the frame, and have their physical values (light, texture, colour) changed at will. Lucas has referred to this on many occasions as being more like painting than film-making and editing, in the traditional sense of the term:

> You pick up pieces of shots rather than shots as a whole, and then you construct the shot later ...... You're able to collect bits and pieces that go into the images separately, sometimes a year apart, and just stick them in. It's a very different way to approaching the medium ... I'd much rather go around and put things together and look at them and move them around again and look at them until I get them the way I like them ... And that's a huge change in the movie process, because it allows the artist to have much more control over the image and the type of image. You don't have to go out and sit on a mountain for three months waiting for the lighting to get just right. You can actually create it and make it to be just right, the way you want it in your mind's eye.
>
> (Lucus, 2005a)

As I have noted elsewhere, early CGI sequences, partly due to the mix of celluloid and digital media, were forced to keep their photographic elements and their CGI elements in separate parts of the composed frame; the CGI object being composited with the photographed one on the filmstrip. With all elements, live actors and CGI, now beginning the process in digital form, the two can be wholly intermingled within the virtual diegetic space. We see this everywhere in *Attack of the Clones*. In the early scene of the Chancellor's Meeting, a digitally created Yoda (the result of a great deal of discussion by the film-makers, who were worried the CGI character would not sufficiently resemble the old hand-operated puppet of the earlier films) is seen sitting at the end of the row of characters. At first he is positioned in a discrete part of the frame, without overlapping any person or object in the scene. But as Padmé (Natalie Portman) enters, he stands and walks behind Mace Windu (Samuel L. Jackson) and later is surrounded and partly hidden by several characters as they stand talking together. Later, when Obi Wan Kenobi (Ewan McGregor) visits the alien creature Dex in his diner, they appear to physically hug one another across two separate shots. Obviously, such total integration of live and CGI elements goes a long way in convincing spectators of the reality of the scene they are witnessing.

Together, these various advantages have taken a lot of the unpredictability out of the creation of a feature film. Some might say that they also take some of the spontaneity out of the creation too. Previsualization tends to foreground action over characterizsation, and separately shot actors are forced to perform their lines and gestures in an emotional vacuum, as it were, against green screen rather than other responsive actors. The result, as can be witnessed at times during *Attack of the Clones*, can be a certain lifelessness and awkward delivery of dialogue in an actor's perform-ance, such as when Ewen McGregor struggles to look interested when inspecting the clone factory early in the film, or does not produce quite the right believable facial reactions when supposedly talking to his digitally created alien friend in Dex's Diner.

Interestingly, having the actors' performances in the digital realm from the outset allows Lucas to change and manipulate them:

> [A]fter converting their performances to digital video, he tweaks line readings and interchanges facial expressions from scene to scene or slows the synch in a performance in order to slip a cut around an eyeblink. With ILM artists implementing his ideas at their keyboards, 'I would say that at least a third of the shots in *[Clones]* have been manipulated in that way,' Lucas said.
>
> (Prince 2004: 25)

One fairly explicit example of this comes when Anakin (Hayden Christensen) and Padmé stand together overlooking a lake on Naboo. The frontal shot of the two actors standing side by side originally showed Hayden Christensen with his hands together in front of him. The following framing, behind them, shows his hand caressing her back; a movement that was deemed to be too sudden without his hand being shown to reach out to touch hers just before the cut. His hand was therefore digitally moved from its real position in the first shot, and made to touch hers so that the caress that follows in the second shot becomes a continuation of that move.

In this way, one of the markers of a film's 'reality effect' – that there are real people being watched performing real actions, reaction and gestures in response to one another – is lost, or at the very least compromised. But with so many characters appearing on screen being wholly digitally created, it is perhaps inevitable that the human actors would be similarly closely manipulated. The subtitle of the film forming the present case study – *Attack of the Clones* – becomes eerily prescient for the film industry as well as the fictional narrative.

And yet, as I have argued elsewhere, the presence of living human actors in films in which digital imagery is used extensively helps to anchor the potentially unconvincing world created through CGI. Seeing real people seemingly inhabit these virtual spaces, and being unable to discern the artifice, helps convince us that the world of the film really exists. In this sense, the physical reality of the actors is extremely important. But if we are then made aware (through advertising or making documentaries about the film) that the actors' performances are similarly computer-generated, then the grounding of the virtual is undermined. The end point of such a trajectory, obviously, will be wholly computer-generated characters as well as settings; a move that will make all films into animated features.

It is therefore significant that in spite of the world(s) depicted in *Attack of the Clones* being predominantly created in the computer, there are strategic scenes which have been filmed in real locations. Partly, this is a simple pragmatism by the film's producers, as Lucas (2005b) has admitted, 'Almost any location I've shot, I've been able to get material that I just couldn't get in a studio or would take a very long time to recreate digitally'. However, having captured that location material, he consciously manipulates it to make it into something else: 'All the environments we're shooting I've always intended to digitally change so they don't look quite like they do in real life' (ibid.).

So, taking the scene of Anakin and Padmé by the lake just described above as an example; it is a real lake of great natural beauty: Lake Como in Italy. That Anakin and Padmé begin to fall in love in such a setting helps strengthen the emotions that are being generated in the scene, in a way that having the scene played out in front of green screen, with a CGI lake and mountains added afterwards, would not. This is still the case even, as Lucas admits, details of the image are then altered digitally. The image's reality as a real physical place lays the foundation upon which the digital artifice can be laid. Gavin Bocquet (2005), the film's production designer, is right when he comments, 'The more real things you can get in your image the more believable those images are, and you just have to tweak them on set or in post-production'.

This effect does not work only within scenes but also across them, with location reality and CGI replication interacting across their juxtaposition. For example, another location-based scene has Anakin and Padmé continuing to fall in love while sitting in an open landscape in front of a range of spectacular waterfalls. The tangible reality of the waterfalls is acknowledged in the audio commentary to the DVD of the film, in which it is noted, by visual effects supervisor Pablo Helman (2005), that when the scene was filmed, the roar of the cascading water drowned out the dialogue of the actors, which had to be replaced in post-production, as did a quieter replication of the sound of the waterfalls. (In a further case of 'is it real or is it digital?' Helman also notes that the location was plagued with gnats, which buzzed around Christensen and Portman as they performed the scene, and which had to be individually digitally painted out in post-production.)

The visually spectacular waterfalls are allowed to register with the viewer before the scene closes in on the two characters and their bantering conversation, before showing them again towards the end of the scene. When the scene then changes to a computer-generated sea from which a gigantic winged creature rises, the water, on one level patently artificial (confirmed by the impossible creature emerging from it), is lent a certain degree of verisimilitude from the recently witnessed real water of the waterfalls in the previous scene. Indeed, this is an explicit example of what Stephen Prince (2004) has termed the 'correspondence effect', which CGI images often demand that we employ in reading them. Essentially, when looking at an image we know to be artificially created, in our present context by computer software, we bring to mind a similar real-world image and use it to compare the accuracy of the CGI one. We compare a dinosaur's hide in *Jurassic Park*, for example, with that of an elephant and decide if the CGI dinosaur hide passes the believability test. Similarly, and far more consciously, the CGI sea in *Attack of the Clones* is explicitly compared by us to the recently seen waterfalls and the latter used to confirm the former.

George Lucas's dream of a revolution in cinema was that all stages of the process of getting a film from initial idea through to exhibition in a cinema would be performed digitally. The use of digital projection to screen the films to audiences was an important part of that vision, especially as it would allow him to avoid the rather retrograde step, which has always been necessary for all films employing digitally created images, of transferring the finished work back onto celluloid for distribution and exhibition. Although the film was screened using a Barco digital projector at the 2002 Cannes Film Festival, Lucas was unable to persuade more than a handful of commercial cinemas to equip themselves with hugely expensive digital projectors.

But times change. As of July 2007, the USA has around 1,400 digitally projected screens, while Europe has around 300. The future of digital cinema is now assured, with total conversion from celluloid to digital film-making and projection anticipated in the next few years. *Star Wars Episode II: Attack of the Clones* was the proof of concept for an industrial revolution the like of which cinema has not witnessed since the coming of sound in the late 1920s. And George Lucas, again ahead of his time in 2002, has had to wait for the rest of the film industry to catch up with him.

5 Video games: platforms, programmes and players

Gérard Kraus

The 'video' in 'video game' traditionally refers to a raster display device. In computer graphics, a raster graphics image, digital image or bitmap, is a data structure representing a generally rectangular grid of pixels viewable via a display monitor. However, as the term 'video game' has come into general use, it now refers to all types of games whether they use raster graphics or not. The electronic systems used to play video games are known as 'platforms', examples of which include arcade machines, PCs, game consoles, DVDs, hand-held devices and mobile phones. As such, the term 'video game' is now simply used as a way of differentiating this type of gaming from the more traditional type of board or card games which do not need a visual display unit of any sort.

'Video games' are increasingly becoming a part of everyday life and items that we now perceive as common within our digital culture are often spliced with them. Flat-screen televisions or digital receivers (set-top boxes) are sometimes shipped out with 'video games' integrated on their circuit boards, easily accessible via the remote control. The circulation of mini-games in offices and more importantly through viral advertising is also on the rise. The current generation of game consoles such as the Nintendo Wii offer integrated services from online communities, to shops, download-able video and audio content as well as the possibility to access games that are not available outside cyberspace. So while the term 'video game' is not always technically accurate, it is a phrase that we have all come to recognize as part of the landscape of digital culture. This chapter proposes to look at how these games have evolved, analysing both their historical/cultural development and examining their gradual academic development as a subject of study in their own right.

Origins

One of the earliest examples of the 'video game' was produced in 1947 when the idea for a 'cathode ray tube amusement device' was conceived by Thomas T. Goldsmith Jr. and Estle Ray Mann. The game consisted of an analog transmitter that allowed a user to control a dot on the screen to simulate a missile being fired at targets. A few years later in 1952, Douglas Alexander created a game of *Tic-Tac-Toe* (also known as *Noughts and Crosses* or *Three-in-a-Row*) which ran on Cambridge University's EDSAC computer.

It was a version of the game usually played on paper, involving two players trying to align three of their symbols (Os or Xs) in a 3 × 3 grid. It was a logical choice for the early computer as it involved a finite amount of possibilities. Meanwhile, William Higginbotham's *Tennis for Two* appeared in 1958 and ran on an oscilloscope (a type of electronic test equipment that allows signal voltages to be viewed, usually as a two-dimensional graph) at the Brookhaven National Laboratory. Higginbotham, a nuclear physicist, who had worked on the first nuclear bomb, devised this game in which players would use a button to hit the ball and a knob to determine the angle to hit the ball at.

Like much of today's digital technology, video games really came out of the technological race at the heart of the cold war. Governments on both sides of the Iron Curtain decided to rely on the newly emergent power of computers to simulate scenarios of attack and defence. The developing space race between the Americans and the Russians (as well as science fiction in the form of Doc Smith's *Lensmen* series) was clearly the inspiration behind Martin Graetz, Steve Russell and Wayne Wiitanen's *Spacewar* in 1962. In it, two players control two spaceships through a makeshift control board that enabled them to shoot 'torpedoes' at each other while trying not to hit a planet or a star located on the screen. The fact that *Spacewar* was programmed for a 'microcomputer' (still the size as a large fridge) that was popular with institutions also meant that its makers were able to pass on the code for the program to others, resulting in this being the first game that was actually distributed. Many of its basic ideas would also lay down the blueprint for the action simulation genre that, through the likes of *Asteroids* (1979) and *Space Invaders* (1978), would remain popular to this day.

1967 saw the launch of ADVENT (which had its name truncheoned because the computer could only handle six letters), which was the first text-based game in which the player controlled the fate of a character whose surroundings were explained purely through text. Meanwhile, 1971 saw the arrival of *Computer Space*, the first commercially sold, coin-operated video game. Created by Nolan Bushnell and Ted Dabney, it used a standard television- and game-generated video signal for display. Though not commercially sold, the coin-operated minicomputer-driven *Galaxy Game* preceded it by two months, located solely at Stanford University.

It was the launch of the Magnavox Odyssey in 1972 which finally put Video Gaming on the map. For the first time, the Odyssey put the control over television content into the consumers' hands and sparked a whole new industry. Invented by Ralph Baer, the console sold about 100,000 units in one year and could play seven games. In the same year the makers of *Computer Space* founded Atari, a name that is still associated with digital games all over the world. The first offering from Atari would be the *Pong* arcade game. Surprisingly similar to a game on the Odyssey (it actually resulted in a successful patent infringement lawsuit against the company), *Pong* was based on table tennis or 'ping pong'. Although the game merely involved hitting a dot between two players from either side of the screen, it was enormously popular.

In the wake of the Odyssey many electronics companies decided to launch their own game consoles into the newly emerging video game market. Over the period between 1972 and 1984 hundreds of models appeared that imitated the Odyssey's controls and games (for a non-exhaustive list of these, see Wolf and Perron 2003: 303–14). In 1977 Atari launched its own Video Computing System (VCS) 2600 which would be one of the keystones to modern console gaming. It featured a wealth of game cartridges that were sold separately and made Atari money through loyalties and licensing fees, allowing them to sell the main console at a loss. In particular, the 2600 is credited with being the console that popularized the use of programmable cartridges. The VCS was updated with the 5200 in 1982 and the 7800 in 1986.

On the arcade front, the Japanese game industry provided the world with iconic games in the form of *Space Invaders* (1978) and *Pac-Man* (1980), introducing what can now be seen as the first 'golden age' of video games. The consoles were also continuing to bring simple game concepts to the home, while the arcades were slowly but surely pushing the creative boundaries of what could be done creatively. However, the saturation of the console market combined with a series of disappointing high-profile releases (the most popular example being the *E.T.* (1983) game and a poor version of *Pac-Man*) created a downward spiral that would bankrupt a large number of game companies during the early 1980s. In addition to this, PCs were becoming more affordable and more versatile, allowing for word processing and other applications to be run as well as games. PCs also meant that games could be copied from cassette or floppy discs. PC game developing is not regulated by manufacturers' licences and thus allows any user with programming skills to contribute, enhancing possibilities of interactivity. Early games on these machines were adventures that used the premise originally set up by the purely text based ADVENT, but expanded upon it by adding graphics and sound. One of the most prolific early developers was Sierra On-line and their *King's Quest* (1984–1994) and *Space Quest* games (1986–1996).

After the North-American video game crisis of the 1980s, the US console market was crippled. However, a Japanese game card and toy manufacturer would ring in a new era in the video game business. Nintendo had produced game cards and toys from 1889, but in the early 1970s they acquired the distribution rights to the Magnavox Odyssey in Japan and went on to release their TV-Game 6 and 15 in 1976 and 1977, respectively. In 1981, after Nintendo had to quickly come up with a new game design, Shigeru Miyamoto created *Donkey Kong*, which 'starred' a plumber character that would forevermore be associated with Nintendo and digital games in general. Until *Pac-Man*, video games had been devoid of identifiable heroes, but Mario was the first human-like hero that players could control.

In 1983 Nintendo went on to release the Famicom in Japan; two years later it made it into the recently cleared video game shelves in the USA as the Nintendo Entertainment System (NES). The NES bundle included Miyamoto's next game *Super Mario Brothers* (1986), revolutionary in its construction and development. In particular, the game set a distinctive goal, getting from the start to the finish of a level, starting from the left and going to the right and involved a captured princess story, ushering in basic characters and narrative content. Also premiering on the NES, was Miyamoto's long running *Zelda* series (1986–), which were inspired by a pen-and-paper fantasy role-playing game systems like *Dungeons and Dragons* (TSR 1976). The NES also created a new digital game hype that spread to the mainstream and even inspired children's cartoons (*Super Mario Bros. Super Show* (1989), *Captain N* (1989–91), *The Legend of Zelda* (as part of the *Super Mario Bros. Super Show*, etc.). It was followed, in 1989, by the hand-held Game Boy allowing for digital gaming to finally move away from the television set at home.

Games for the NES were licensed, meaning that Nintendo had to give the go-ahead to any game published for the console as well as asking for a licensing fee from any developer. This meant that video gaming was now a hugely successful global business, with profits overtaking traditional industrial businesses such as car manufacturing. As David Sheff explains:

> The money earned from its video games and the NES system that played them transformed Nintendo into one of the world's most profitable companies. By 1991 Nintendo had supplanted Toyota as Japan's most successful company, based on the indices of growth potential, profitability, penetration of foreign and domestic markets, and stock performance. Nintendo made more for its shareholders and paid higher dividends between 1988 and 1992 than any other company traded on the Tokyo stock exchange.
>
> (Sheff 1994: 5)

The Japanese company Sega (originally founded in 1940 by Martin Bromely, Irving Bromberg, and James Humpert to provide coin-operated amusements for US servicemen on military bases) finally entered the home console market with its Master System in 1986, unsuccessfully challenging Nintendo on the portable platform market with its Game Gear. Sega had moved to 16-bit in 1989 with the Genesis or Megadrive, which also introduced its own trademark mascot, a blue hedgehog (*Sonic the Hedgehog* (1991)). With the Megadrive, Sega managed to speak to a more mature consumer, the players that had grown up on console and arcade games that found more adult-oriented games which matched their grown-up tastes.

In the 1990s PC gaming was mainly focused on areas that the consoles did not seem to cover. So-called 'point and click' adventure games (like LucasArts's *Monkey Island* series, 1990–2000) and the early First Person Shooters (*Wolfenstein 3D* (1992), *Doom*, (1993)) made their debut on the PC. The sequel to the *Dune* adventure game (1992), *Dune 2* (1993) invented the contemporary real-time strategy games that *Command and Conquer* (1995–present) and the *Star/Warcraft* series (1994–2003/1998–present) popularized. The openness of the PCs allowed developers to become more creative, fuelled by the development of 3D accelerators (processors dedicated to handling the calculation of graphics) and the ability to upgrade other elements of a PC without having to buy a whole new machine. Foremost among these are the first-person shooter (FPS) titles like *Unreal* (1998) and *Halflife* (1998) which relied heavily on highly defined graphics and high frame rates (30 frames per second and above).

Another added advantage of the PC was the relatively early availability of online play. The first online games can be seen in the form of the text-based multi-user-dungeons (MUDs) in which players would adventure (role-playing style) through dungeons programmed in advance – the possibility to join other players in common quests and talk to them in 'taverns' clearly added to their allure. The FPS phenomenon also spawned a culture of players meeting for LAN parties (local area network) in which they connected their computers to a network and compete in FPS and real-time strategy games. Later, 'massively multiplayer online role-playing games' (MMORPGs) (*Ultima Online* (1997), *Everquest* (1999), *World of Warcraft* (2004)) merely added advanced 3D graphics to this idea. *World of Warcraft* was particularly able to draw on the popularity of the line of real-time strategy games and combined them with the new popularity of MMORPGs to pierce the mainstream and gain a widespread user base (over eight million subscribers worldwide in May 2007)).

Not to be overtaken by PCs, home game consoles also continued to develop during the 1990s. The Super Nintendo Entertainment System (SNES) was first released in 1990 and the Atari's Jaguar in 1993. However, it was not until Sony's PlayStation was produced in 1994 that the game console finally became a ubiquitous piece of everyday technology. Playstation presented a hi-fi component look-a-like console that could play music CDs and featured the (in terms of space) superior CD-ROM technology which allowed for more game content, higher-quality video and CD-quality audio. It went on to dominate the market in the years after 1996 with the capability to make game worlds larger and stories more compelling than had been possible before. By 2005, PlayStation and Playstation Portable (PSP) had shipped a combined total of 102.49 million units, becoming the first video game console to reach the 100 million mark.

The added processing power and increased storage space that the generations of consoles after Playstation offered have been used to full effect to now create more cinematic, story-driven and realistic-looking games. *Final Fantasy VII* (1997), *Resident Evil* (1996) and *Lara Croft: Tomb Raider* (1996) are among a plethora of titles that were hugely popular on these consoles. Sony updated to Playstation 2 (PS2) in 2000 and continued its market dominance almost unrivalled until Microsoft entered the business with Xbox a year later. PS2 relied on the same mature content and featured a DVD player which added appeal as the price for DVD players was still relatively high at the time of release. *Grand Theft Auto III* (2001) gave rise to a vast number of so-called 'sandbox games' which combined elements of driving games, shooters and others in a 3D environment which let the player choose which, if any, goals he wanted to accomplish or just roam an environment interacting with the artificially intelligent occupants of the later.

The dominance of Sony's Playstation brand was finally challenged with the arrival of the Nintendo Wii in 2006, becoming the world's fastest selling console in 2007. What was revolutionary about this product was that unlike existing game consoles (which were based on a controller held with two hands which required buttons to be pushed), its controls were able to sense motion, depth and positioning dictated simply by the acceleration and direction of the controller – arguably producing a more intuitive and realistic gaming experience than was possible before. A direct successor to the Nintendo GameCube, it was aimed at a broader demographic than that of Microsoft's Xbox 360 and Sony's PlayStation 3 (PS3), but it was also meant to compete with both as part of the seventh generation of video game consoles.

Video games now have the opportunity to change media consumption. The current generation consoles, PS3, Xbox360 and Wii, as well as their hand-held counterparts, are all capable of accessing the Internet and deliver non-game information through a medium that was considered purely a toy in the mid-1980s. For example, the Wii's News Channel delivers headlines on a plethora of subjects from all over the world. PS3 comes with an Internet browser that allows the World Wide Web to be surfed in one's living room. The PS3, through the Playstation Network, fuelled by Sony's media empire, also adds the opportunity to download film trailers, game content and other multimedia content. It should not take too long before films and video on demand join downloadable games and music.

As this very brief history suggests (see Kent 2002 and Wolf 2007 for more details), gaming has come a long way since its early origins with primitive video games like *Tic-Tac-Toe*, *Tennis for Two* and *Pong*. Modern digital gaming now contains a unique synthesis of 3D art, CGI special effects, architecture, artificial intelligence, sound effects, dramatic performances, music and storytelling to create whole new virtual worlds. This is perhaps why gaming is now attracting so much critical attention. Although departments of computer science have been studying the technical aspects of video games for many years, theories that examine games as an artistic medium are now being developed and are increasingly becoming part of the media studies curriculum, both at school and university. I will trace and account for this critical tradition below.

Studying video games

Much of the critical reception of video games has historically centred on their most controversial aspects, notably their depiction of graphic violence. In particular, FPS games have attracted a great deal of media attention as they were seen to be immersive and non-ethical in their depiction and handling of killing within the games (see Anderson et al. 2007). Over the years the use of sex and profanity in gaming has also proved problematic. Controversy was generated recently with the discovery of a downloadable modification that unlocked a sex-driven mini-game in the highly popular *Grand Theft Auto: San Andreas* (2004). However, I do not want to dwell on such issues here as I believe these controversial debates are a diversion which often prevents the wider impact of these games being taken seriously. Some critics, for example, argue that video games are actually a source of enormous educational potential and such sensational debates devalue and obscure the larger social and cultural value that gaming now has to offer (see Gee 2003). That is not to say that such issues are not relevant, but that in order for this area of study to develop into a serious academic discipline in its own right, I believe it needs to move away from this simplistic moral conception of the field to create a more complex and sophisticated understanding of the subject as a whole.

As film studies emerged from literary and cultural studies and later developed its own approaches, so has video game scholarship emerged from a number of different fields and disciplines. It should not take long for video games criticism to develop their own unique tools; in fact, many scholars are busy with this task (Wolf and

Perron 2003). Indeed, Espen Aarseth, in his essential *Cybertext: Perspectives on Ergodic Literature*, claims that the study of digital games must establish its own techniques from fear of 'theoretical imperialism' from other branches of the arts (1997: 16). However, I will look at a number of approaches (both from within and without video games studies) in order to give a broad understanding of the field as it stands currently.

In their introduction to their *Video Game Theory Reader*, Wolf and Perron determine a number of elements that are at the heart of what makes the video game a unique medium, and need to be addressed in any discussion of them. The most fundamental of these elements are: 'an algorithm, player activity, interface, and graphics' (2007: 14). In order to understand this more clearly, I first define each factor separately:

- *Graphics* can be understood as the visual element of video games. They are the predominant way in which the game transmits the information (through the images, videos, icons and written information); the player needs to make informed decisions as to what to do next. Some games can include multiple screens or display capabilities on the interface which are mostly designed to increase immersion and the realism of interaction.
- *Interface* is made up of any element of the hard or software of the game that allows the player to input their decisions. These come mostly in the shape of joysticks and control pads or mouse and keyboard setups, but also include on-screen buttons and control bars as well as more elaborate devices.
- *Player activity* is what makes a video game interactive. Without the player, the game is likely to stand still or will become a mere simulation devoid of the variable and consistent player input that it is programmed to react to. In particular, player activity describes what a user does to achieve a desired effect within the game. Both the way in which the player interacts with the interface and the results on-screen are taken into consideration and termed extra-diegetic and diegetic activities.
- The *'algorithm'* is a term used in mathematics, computing, linguistics and related disciplines, which refers to a definite list of well-defined instructions for completing a task. In terms of gaming, it is deemed responsible for representation, responses, rules and randomness within the game. It is the program itself, the heart of the game if you like.

These four tasks are then subsequently defined as:

- *Representation* is the regrouping of all the algorithms' various outputs ranging from the visual on-screen, the aural (music, effects, speech, etc.) on speakers or headphones, as well as the added sensual experiences that games offer through vibration in control devices and seats or wind and lighting effects from additional devices.
- *Responses* are the reaction that player input (and the resulting actions and situations) trigger within the game. This includes the actions of the Avatar (like shooting when the fire button is pressed), other characters in the game

(ducking behind cover when shot at), as well as environment interaction (projectiles impacting a wall or ground).

- *Rules* are the guiding structures behind the algorithm; they define the possibilities the player has as well as the limits the player can go to. They also delineate the 'responses and game play' (Wolf and Perron 2003: 17).
- *Randomness* adds elements of unexpectedness to games; making sure that no two games played are exactly the same. Randomness fulfils the role that the dice plays in most analogue games (board games, gambling and role-playing games).

These basic elements are but the starting block to any inquiry into video games. The emerging field of video game studies, by its very nature, still hold opposing views on some issues; some are likely to be resolved through compromise, while other debates will form the core of different paradigms.

From a literary studies perspective games are interesting as they are works of fiction, and therefore abide to many of the fundamental rules of story-telling such as genre and narrative. Even so-called historical games are akin to 'what if?' scenarios, allowing players to explore what it would possibly have taken to change the outcome of battles or events. In this way, literary studies can be used to approach the narrative of a story-driven-based game in much the same way that the narrative of a book or filmic text would be studied. However, the problem with applying literary studies to gaming is that a remarkable number of games make little to no use of a strictly narrative world. Early games were even lacking a fictional world altogether. *Pac-Man* (1980), for example, was trapped in a labyrinth, chased by ghosts that he could only defeat with the few power pellets strewn across the playing field. Meanwhile, sport simulation games do not have a narrative structure that literary theorists would understand – at least in the traditional manner.

Despite these limitations, literary studies has still tried to uncover the narrative working of video games. Kücklich (2006: 101–03) highlights the fact that most video games will adopt two basic genres: one will be the genre that is based on iconography and thereby based on the long-standing genre traditions within literature and film studies; the other will be one that is based on the way in which the player interacts with the game or what options he/she has. For example, what both fields would identify as adhering to the conventions of the 'war genre' would be war iconography and a first-person shooter in which the player is a soldier reliving the battles of World War II like the popular *Medal of Honor* (1999–present) and *Call of Duty* (2003–2007) series or a strategy game as in the *Close Combat* series (1996–2000). Similar examples can be found for the 'science fiction', 'horror' and 'fantasy' genres among others (for an in-depth analysis and proposed genre definitions see Wolf 2001: 113–34).

The video game industry also matches the outlines that the Frankfurt School revision of Marxist theory saw applied to popular culture as a whole. The economics of digital games are such that games are created for a mass market. Small games destined for niches are almost never distributed openly and 'art', 'alternative' and 'avant-garde' games are restricted to a dedicated website underground. A commercially successful game type, most prominently first-person shooters, become formulaic and standardized as the industry continues to churn out carbon copies of what has gone before (Crawford and Rutter 2006). This is not to say that creativity is sidelined, for the alternative developers' industry is alive and popular even constrained to its niche, and every so often game distributors take a risk and release a less 'formulaic' game.

The visual nature of video games also makes them easily connected to a film studies approach. Both media share a strong dependence on visual stimuli and similar codes are apparent. The impression of a coherent fictional game world on screen is now created through audiovisual features such as the framing of images, *mise-en-scène*, shifts in time and space, and the use of sound effects and music. The manipulation of these qualities is what provides orientation for the player, establishes meaningful contexts and resonances within which gameplay occurs, and contributes to the creation of emotional states – such as fear and suspense in horror and some action-based games. Thus, video games now borrow techniques that film has tried and tested over many years.

Not surprisingly, then, critics like King and Krzywinska (2006: 118–21) propose that *mise-en-scène*, iconography and sound (all used in film analysis) can also be helpful in the analysis of gaming. They further introduce the notion that narrative in video games can be compared to contemporary film narrative in that they both seem to provide moments of spectacle that halt narrative to give way to special effects – for films – or heightened player interaction – for games. This seems to be in exact opposition to each other as narrative cut scenes (the true moment of spectacle in video games) are most often moments of narrative progress where contexts and elements of the story are revealed while the player watches. In contrast, the actual gameplay is often most concerned with getting the player characters from point A to B and have him shoot, jump or solve riddles along the way, with elements of story featuring minimally. This does point to the problematic nature of narrative in video games and the need for a theoretical approach that is fully inclusive of the differences from film and literature that video games represent. As Espen Aarseth put it in his editorial in the first issue of the journal *Game Studies*:

> Games are both object and process; they can't be read as texts or listened to as music, they must be played. Playing is integral, not coincidental like the appreciative reader or listener. The creative involvement is a necessary ingredient in the uses of games
>
> (Aarseth 2001)

As well as forms of textual analysis originating in literary and film studies, there are also those approaches that look at the wider cultural context of gaming. Indeed, the culture that digital games has created is now taking charge of its own through the establishment of websites (IGN.com, gamespot.com), blogs (filefront.com) and online video content (channelflip.com) that cater for various tastes and needs, and the texts they produce are complementary to those of the games themselves. The growing ability of the consumers to manipulate the games themselves, either by hacking the codes or by using editing software that game developers provide along with the game, also allows for the user to create their own texts that they can then share with others over the World Wide Web. The gaming consumer thus becomes the producer of another text using the tools that the originator has provided. This practice of customization of programs and hardware is usually referred to as 'modding' (from modification).

Such an approach could justify and detect trends from both users and developers to use this interactivity, playing or speculating on the fact that a game has an editor or flexible content management. One interesting case is the so-called 'machinima' (Machine Cinema) of 'Red vs. Blue', a fan film project based on the capability of players to capture in-game clips when playing *Halo* (2001). The founders, a fledgling film-maker and his friends, use the footage gained from such in game moments to create comedic clips that they offer for viewing on their website (www.machinima.com). Gus Sorola and Burnie Burns are now celebrities within their admittedly small circle of admirers, but find themselves invited to film festivals and seminars. Indeed, Giddings and Kennedy see the player as a whole part of a player-machine complex, a 'cybernetic organism' (cited in Rutter and Bryce 2006: 142–3). The constant input/output, player decision/computer reaction 'ballet' makes it difficult to determine which of the two is actually in control, in which case it is easier to view the combination as a harmonic entity. The already mentioned 'MMORPGs' are now played by millions online, creating virtual communities (such as *Second Life* (2003) or *Entropia* (2003)) that are now possibly more than traditionally 'video games', but are 'life simulations'. All of these have become viable communities with social rules and their own economies. The later are particularly renowned for now allowing people to produce customized equipment for the players' in-game personae such as clothing, jewellery, virtual real estate and services (see Chapter 1).

Recommended reading

Aarseth, Espen (1997) *Cybertext: Perspectives on Ergodic Literature*. Baltimore and London: John Hopkins University Press.

Gamestudies: The international Journal of Computer Game Research (www.gamestudies.org).

Newman, James (2004) *Videogames*. London and New York: Routledge.

Rutter, Jason and Bryce, Jo (eds) (2006) *Understanding Digital Games*. London: Sage Publications.

Wolf, Mark J.P. and Perron, Bernard (eds) (2003) *The Video Game Theory Reader*. New York and London: Routledge.

Case Study: *Bioshock* (2007)

Gérard Kraus

Released in August 2007, *Bioshock* is a first-person shooter video game by 2K Boston/2K Australia (previously known as Irrational Games). Available for PCs and XBox360, it was highly anticipated ever since it was first presented in a close to final form at the Electronics Entertainment Expo (E3) in spring 2006. From that first appearance the title was able to collect a number of 'best of show' awards from the specialist press and websites dedicated to gaming. It went on to win the prestigious 'Best Game' award of the British Academy of Film and Television Arts in October 2007, while also being nominated for the 'artistic achievement' category. In December 2007 the US Spike TV Video Game award gave it the 'Game of the Year', 'Best XBox360 Game' and 'Best Original Score' prizes, while also nominating it for four more categories.

The developers of *Bioshock* acknowledge that the game is the spiritual child of *System Shock* (1994) (developed by Looking Glass Studios) and *System Shock 2* (1999) (developed by Looking Glass and Irrational Games). Irrational Games was founded by a number of ex-Looking Glass people, among them Ken Levin, who is generally regarded as the defining creator behind the later part of the *Shock* series. In *System Shock*, the action takes place on a space station whose controlling computer has gone rogue. In *System Shock 2*, it takes place on a spaceship whose occupants have been taken over by an alien force. The second game in the series also introduced a guiding voice, a narrative technique later used in *Bioshock*. For many critics, the game developed the narrative structure and depth of the video game in a way previously unimagined. As Kristina Reed puts it:

> *BioShock* isn't simply the sign of gaming realising its true cinematic potential, but one where a game straddles so many entertainment art forms so expertly that it's the best demonstration yet how flexible this medium can be. It's no longer just another shooter wrapped up in a pretty game engine, but a story that exists and unfolds inside the most convincing and elaborate and artistic game world ever conceived. It just so happens to require you to move the narrative along with your own carefully and personally defined actions. Active entertainment versus passive: I know which I prefer.

> (Reed 2007)

Set in an alternate 1960, *Bioshock* places the player in the role of a plane crash survivor named Jack. Cast adrift in the Atlantic Ocean, he discovers the underwater dystopian city of Rapture, populated by mutated beings and mechanical drones. A wealthy but world-weary industrialist had originally created the city, a place where governmental rule and theological and moral concerns are put aside in order for man to fulfil his own destiny. In particular, it portrays a world in which science has been pushed to the extreme and created possibilities that eventually lead to the demise of society. Trapped inside this complex narrative world, the player has no other option but to fight through waves of mutated city dwellers to uncover what has led to the city's downfall.

As this suggests, *Bioshock* is perhaps best understood as one recent example of the game industry's efforts to render the FPS more interactive. FPS can be traced back to the controversial *Wolfenstein 3D* (1992) in which the player was an allied prisoner of war escaping from a titular castle, mowing down hordes of Nazi soldiers (and their more esoteric experiments) with a pistol, machine or Gatling gun, which can be picked up (along with other items), as they progress through the various levels. *Doom* (1993) and subsequent FPS have gradually improved graphics; however, they still remained, at the heart, simple 'shoot 'em ups'. While some FPS, notably *Half-Life* (1998) and its sequel added interesting narrative strands to the genre, *Bioshock* developed this trend towards a more narrative-driven, first-person game with strong role-playing elements.

The primary aim of video role-playing games (RPGs) is the evolution of one's character. Where in FPS the only change was usually only superior armour and weapons which add to the increased interaction skills of the player, RPGs possess point systems that reward action with heightened skills of the player character. An example of this would be increased 'health points', skills that multiply the damage dealt with a weapon, and so on. RPGs also add an element of player character evolution to a game at the same time as adding an extra layer of decision-making: the player decides what his character is going to be good at. The RPG elements in *Bioshock* take the form of customizable weapons and body, as well as a camera, which allows you to take photos of the various enemies, in turn giving damage bonuses towards fighting them in the future. Finally, the game borrows from the survival horror genre in which a solitary character has to survive in adversarial conditions. *Bioshock's* Splicers, residents who have overdosed on genetically altering substances, are similar to *Resident Evil's* (1996) zombies and the conventions of a dark, post-apocalyptic setting are also met.

In the following, I look at *Bioshock*, and through it illustrate some of the principles in relation to the study of video games introduced in the main chapter. In my analysis, I refer to the way the game plays and is played on a PC rather than the XBox360 version; these changes are mainly reflected in the different control element, as there are few differences in the game content itself.

It is the nature of the FPS that a game is played from the first-person perspective with the currently selected weapon taking up part of the screen and small displays indicating the ammunition count, health point level, map of the level and any other information the player needs. Some games offer to customize the amount of information displayed thusly as a minimum of these is more beneficial to the immersive qualities of the game. In *Bioshock* the graphic elements can be split up into four distinct situations. There is, of course, the game play graphics in which the player is exploring the underwater city, picking up items and killing foes. In this, the weapon at hand is displayed prominently in the centre of the frame. A dial which indicates the number of rounds left in a gun, and in reserve, as well as what type of ammunition currently loaded in the weapon, is located in the bottom left-hand side of the screen. The top left displays the health point level as well as the level of Eve, the substance that fuels the genetically induced powers like throwing lightning, fire or ice, or use telekinesis.

For the more 'cinematic' moments during which the player has little or no input on what is happening on screen, these three elements disappear leaving a clean frame looking onto a scene as it develops. This is the case at the very start of the game but also, at major revelatory moments, spectacular narrative developments and key scenes. Most of these scenes are rendered in a way that does not distract from the general in-game graphics, with the exception of the end cinematic which are of much higher quality and can be seen as a reward for completing the game. The player has the ability to interact with or 'hack' in-game machines. In these cases the view changes to that of the items available for purchase or customization and, in the case of a hack, a puzzle. The player is removed from the immersive first person and presented with a more detailed view; notable here is the lack of a hand actually coming in to move the tiles, an element that pervades the other view.

In terms of interaction, there are the various interface menus that deal with the configuration and management of the game as well as an orientation map that position the player character in the current level. The interfacing is done through the keyboard and mouse. In the game the mouse movement corresponds to the player character's head and body movement; the various buttons on mouse and keyboard are assigned with various actions or menus that the player can perform. The numeric buttons allow the player to select one of his character's weapons to use while the function keys select which plasmid power to use. The space key makes the character jump while 'C' makes him crouch. The right mouse button serves as the trigger; pressing it will fire a weapon or activate a power. The algorithm, generating all this, has a number of tasks in itself. I have already mentioned the graphics and the interface, but one of the other important aspects that add to the immersive quality of the game is the sound and music. It is worth noting, for example, that the player encounters phonographs throughout the game that play songs from the 1940s and 1950s as background music. These include Noel Coward's *20th Century Blues*, Rosemary Clooney's *It's Bad for Me* and Johnnie Ray's *Just Walking In The Rain*. On one level, the songs clearly help to aid player enjoyment and immersion, but they also add another level of narrative and thematic meaning to the game as a whole – perhaps reflecting the work of Dennis Potter's TV serials like *Pennies from Heaven* (BBC 1978), *The Singing Detective* (BBC 1986) and *Lipstick on my Collar* (Channel 4 1993) (see Creeber 1998).

The dark atmosphere (introduced by the full moon and clouds' icon at the beginning) is continued within, with sparse lighting throughout, creating shadows and dark corners out of which Splicers can jump at the character. The framing, namely the subjective view, does not allow for the encompassing field of vision that a third person view would allow. This, in a sense, heightens a feeling of paranoia and uncertainty. The soundscape of the game, with its period songs playing and its dramatic score (underlining some events and most importantly the constant noise of dripping water and whales singing), serves both to locate the setting and also disorientate the player.

I find it particularly helpful, for an analysis of *Bioshock*, to look at the opening sequence and the cleverly disguised tutorial that is included therein. The game presents its world and mechanics in the first 10 minutes, a period in which the player gets introduced to the graphics, interface, interaction needs and algorithm of the game. A title card informs the player that it is 1960 and you (Jack) are in the Atlantic Ocean, or rather flying above as the faded-in point of view shot from within an aeroplane suggests. The screen then goes black as the roar of engines and the gasps of the passengers followed by impact, explosion noises and screams of the passengers, indicate that the plane has crashed. The *Bioshock* logo, dripping with water, and superimposed to a cityscape, indicates the title and with it the start of the game.

The screen then fades from black to display air bubbles being whirled around in water; this is followed by a handbag floating by, a propeller, still rotating, whizzing dangerously close to the point-of-view shot as well as other debris sinking to the bottom of the ocean. The view then tilts upwards and moves towards the surface through which one can recognize flames billowing. Once surfaced the algorithm shifts from purely cinematic to the player control. Significantly, the player finds his character surrounded by a ring of fire with only one way out, further highlighted by a trace of kerosene igniting towards the only exit. On the other hand, through the black smoke, the player can make out the shape of a lighthouse, bathed in the ominous light of the full moon and harkening back to the gothic and horror genre iconography. Once outside the immediate danger, the player must swim towards a set of steps leading up to a door and a first instance of entrapment, when the door closes upon the player's entry and triggers the lights inside to switch on and reveal a bust of the city's creator Andrew Ryan and the slogan: 'No Gods or Kings, only Man'. Once inside the player has no other option but to board a bathysphere (a spherical deep-sea diving submersible which is lowered into bodies of water with a cable) that serves to transfer the action from the outside to the underwater city.

This sequence thus introduces three major elements of the game; first, water, through the title cards but also the general surroundings, hinting at the isolation and desolate state of the city; that is, 'the playground' for the experience to come. Second, the image of the moon, shrouded in clouds and the general lighting conditions of this opening scene use the iconography and lighting that is arguably well known from horror and gothic fiction and cinema. Third, the player is on his/her own; there are no survivors as proven by the lack of strugglers in the water or on the way to the Bathysphere and the shutting of the doors behind him.

The 'trip down' serves as an introduction to the world of Rapture, the underwater utopia. One is presented with the ideology behind the city through an educational-style film playing on the hatch of the bathysphere. The audio track continues its rousing monologue when the cityscape is revealed, glowing in neon lights and appearing to be active. The end of the transfer hints at the things to come as a radio message warns of the 'Splicer' mutants and a light breaking just as the vehicle is about to enter the city. What should be the welcome hall of the city is bathed in darkness as a resident is killed by one of the mutants and proceeds to attack the bathysphere. A voice introduces itself as Atlas and, claiming to want to save the player character, asks one to follow the instructions. What the algorithm does then is guide the player through a number of in-game situations and explains the keys to press in order to make the character jump, fire, heal, reload, and so on as well as some tips on how to use the game's environments.

As this description suggests, the narrative of *Bioshock* partly uses the sort of dystopian themes found in science-fiction books like George Orwell's *Nineteen-Eighty Four* (1948) and Aldous Huxley's *Brave New World* (1932). The developers have also stated that the city's ideology is based on the writings of Ayn Rand who was an uncompromising advocate of rational individualism; her notion of 'Objectivism' developed in books such as *The Fountainhead* (1943) and *Atlas Shrugged* (1957). Objectivism holds that the proper moral purpose of one's life is the pursuit of one's own happiness or 'rational self-interest'. It argues, therefore, that the only social system consistent with this morality is full respect for individual rights, embodied in a pure and consensual capitalism. Weighty issues for a video game, but such philosophical and political themes are clearly suggested through Andrew Ryan's (suggestive of Ayn Rand?) presence in the game. As this speech suggests:

> I am Andrew Ryan and I am here to ask you a question:
> Is a man not entitled to the sweat of his own brow?
>
> No, says the man in Washington. It belongs to the poor.
> No, says the man in the Vatican. It belongs to God.
> No, says the man in Moscow. It belongs to everyone.
>
> I rejected those answers. Instead, I chose something
> different. I chose the impossible. I chose ...

But the game also blends an aspect of detective fiction in this highly intertextual world, with the player taking the role of the investigator slowly revealing what has happened. The narrative is told from a classical 'visitor's perspective'; the action plays around him with revelations along the way. The background to the fall of Rapture is told through voice recorders that the character can pick up and listen to in order to flesh out the story. This is not a goal of the game but nevertheless an inventive way to develop the story without relying on clumsy cut scenes, as listening to them does not stop the flow of the game. The game never reveals a third person view or reveals the player character's identity and leaves the player to make moral judgements which, in turn, result in one of three possible endings in which the aftermath of Rapture's fall are played out.

What I hope this brief analysis shows, then, is just how far video games have come since their first arrival on the cultural scene in the early 1970s. Its philosophical, literary and musical intimations reflect a complex, sophisticated and intertextual narrative world that is reflected in its intricate construction of character which include strong role-playing and immersive elements. While the media often dismiss such video games as simply violent and dangerous, this is an example of an intelligent and complex game that asks its audience to become an active and imaginative part of its artistic creation and development. As a critic on the *Chicago Sun-Times* review put it:

> I never once thought anyone would be able to create an engaging and entertaining video game around the fiction and philosophy of Ayn Rand, but that is essentially what 2K Games has done ... the rare, mature video game that succeeds in making you think while you play.

(cited by Wikipedia 2008)

Acknowledgements

I would like to extend my thanks to Andy Yu and Rod Munday for their expert opinions.

6 Digital music: production, distribution and consumption

Jamie Sexton

Music culture is undergoing rapid change on a number of levels: the production of sounds, their distribution and consumption, and the broader music industry, are all being transformed by digital technologies, in line with social and cultural patterns. Shifts in musical culture are occurring on a global scale, though the rate and nature of change is subject to geographical variation (see Chapter 8). The aim of this chapter is to focus on the impact that digital technologies have wrought upon the musical landscape, as well as to probe some of the theoretical issues that such changes have given rise to.

Music production

Production-wise, digital technologies intensify many of the shifts that have already occurred, in particular the move away from mimicking a live performance towards creating an 'artificial' sound world. When recording technologies entered the musical world in the late nineteenth century, the production of records tended to follow a philosophy of *documentation*; that is, a recorded artefact attempted to reproduce closely a live performance (Toynbee 2000: 73). A few gradual shifts followed; for example, the introduction of electrical recording instruments such as microphones and amplifiers led to the then scandalous technique of 'crooning'. The croon was an enhancement of the voice through artificial means, an 'affront to the documentary regime' (ibid.: 77) which over time has become domesticated and, contrary to its initial reception, embedded in a regime of 'truth' connected to intimate confession (Penman 2002).

It was in the 1950s and 1960s that a move away from documentation dramatically took shape. The emergence of electric guitars, magnetic tape, modular synthesizers and multitrack recording, led to the creation of virtual 'sound worlds' as opposed to documents of live performances. Within the avant-garde pockets of academic music departments the manipulation of sound was being explored even further through the advent of *musique concrète*, where recorded environmental sounds were manipulated and edited together to form sonic montages. Avant-garde techniques were increasingly smuggled into pop productions, leading to more complex recording techniques and the rise of the producer as a creative figure (as opposed to a functional engineer): George Martin, Joe Meek, Phil Spector and Brian Wilson all gained reputations as sonic alchemists, capable of using the recording studio in a creative and constructive manner. Ideas as to what constituted the primary 'song' were shifting: while some recordings still attempted to reflect the live performance, many musicians were now attempting to mimic recorded sound when they performed live.

The idea of the studio as a creative constructive hub led to remixing forming a central component of musical culture. While *musique concrète* can be broadly conceived as a form of remixing, it nevertheless arranged 'found sounds'. The main culture of remixing relates to the recreation of pre-existing *music*, though other found sounds are used often for colour and other purposes. It was in Jamaica in the late 1960s and early 1970s that remix culture really began to flourish to suit the purposes of dance hall culture. Producers and engineers would remove vocals and gradually begin to add effects such as reverb, delay and other noises, out of which the subgenre 'dub reggae' evolved. The rise of disco music in the USA during the 1970s also contributed heavily to remix culture as extended edits of hi-NRG tracks, tailored to the dance floor, led to the emergence of the 12-inch single. Such remixing was taken to new levels with the rise of hip-hop in the late 1970s and early 1980s, which was based upon the repurposing of other music samples, mainly through embedding 'breaks' or through assaulting found sounds via the technique of 'scratching'.

Digital technologies, which began to filter their way into mass production throughout the 1980s, accelerated existing trends and perhaps shifted them from marginal to dominant practices. The rise in a number of digital synthesizers and sequencers, as well as the ease of interconnecting different components through the musical instrument digital interface (MIDI), led to a growth in electronic music in the late 1980s and onwards, including house, techno, jungle, ambient and a number of other generic forms. (Although it should be pointed out, a lot of early techno music was produced with analogue equipment.) While more traditional musical 'groups' playing live instruments continued, the growth of individual, electronic music-makers led to a blurring of the distinction between the musician and the producer, and between the 'instrument' and 'studio'. It also led to the massive rise in the use of musical 'samples', thus giving rise to legal wrangles and debates over copyright, as well as arguments over what actually constituted musical 'creativity'. Key here was the rise of reasonably priced samplers in the late 1980s, which could integrate samples fluently within the overall track; they also provided user-friendly sound manipulation tools (such as time-stretching and pitch-shifting), sample looping functions and editing facilities (Berk 2000: 195).

Digital technologies have made it easier to match and mix existing sounds into a new composition. As such, the archive becomes increasingly important. Many musical artists now spend a lot of their time searching for music in order to find usable samples (the more obscure these samples the better, in that there is a desire among many producers to avoid being 'obvious'). Contrasted to traditional skills involved in playing a musical instrument, the creativity of many electronic music producers often lies in their ability to find, imagine and then skilfully *rearrange* existing cultural artefacts. This relates to Lev Manovich's observation that New Media generally is more concerned 'with accessing and reusing existing media objects as creating new ones' (Manovich 2002: 36). Thus, the notion of *variability* becomes a chief aesthetic trend within the digital world: 'Instead of identical copies, a New Media object typically gives rise to many different versions. And rather than being created completely by a human author, these versions are often in part automatically assembled by a computer' (ibid.: 36) (see Chapter 1).

Related to digital media and variability are the concepts of *automation* and *manipulation*. New digital hardware and software permits previously laborious tasks to become easier in line with increasing automation. So, for example, in contrast to physically editing magnetic tape, many digital programmes allow one to magnify a visual representation of sound waves, highlight and then edit a particular section, as well as 'undo' any results deemed insufficient. It is much easier to make back-up copies of digital works to make numerous edits. Furthermore, copying numerical code does not result in the quality degradation that characterizes chemical media. The manipulation of pre-existing sound becomes easier and thus increasingly forms the raw material out of which new music is constructed.

The increasing manipulability of music leads to an increasing severance from 'real-world' referents, or more precisely, from sounds that can be produced by humans playing instruments in 'real time'. In pre-digital forms of remixing sound was 'ripped' from one context and placed into another, yet the sound itself still bore the trace of human presence (i.e. beat samples in hip-hop records were created by human drummers playing in real time). Compare this to the beats that feature within many recent forms of music, such as jungle: the drumbeats are often too fast and sinuous for human capabilities. The programmable sequencing of sounds and the ability to process them in myriad ways takes music into a more cyborgian realm. 'With sampling,' argues Simon Reynolds, 'what you hear could never possibly have been a real-time event, since it's composed of vivisected musical fragments plucked from different contexts and eras, then layered and resequenced to form a time-warping pseudoevent' (Reynolds 2002: 360). Yet, while digital production often manipulates existing sound beyond recognition, it still uses more identifiable samples quite widely. In practice, while the reuse of recognizable music is problematic in terms of clearing copyright permissions, many do so (either by covering songs or through using samples) because of the cultural currency that existing music contains, linking as it does to memory and emotion. The musical soundscape in a digital age is thus a blend of the 'real' and the 'illusory', the recognizable and the strange, the old and the new.

Perhaps one of the most important developments in digital music is the role such technologies have played in opening up participation within musical production. I do not want to overstate such access: not *everybody* has the potential to engage in such production. Nevertheless, the opportunity for people to create music has undoubtedly increased; in particular, the possibility of people creating music *individually* has certainly grown. Thus, there has been a relative democratization and individualizing of musical production with the rise, in particular, of cheap, powerful computers and a concomitant rise in musical production software (including freeware and differently priced programs).

The late 1990s and early 2000s saw the increasing permeation of computers into the domestic sphere. In tandem, more music began to be produced on computers: hardware began to be complemented by software, and a variety of different music was increasingly produced on desktops and laptops. Different software programs allow one to record, sequence, mix and produce sounds (both sounds inputted from external instruments and produced entirely within the computer). These can range from expensive, professionalized software to more affordable, low-tech production tools. Such tools enhance access to producing decent quality recordings; previously, if people wanted to record they would have had to rent out studio space. Now, if they have a decent computer and some software, they can create at home at their own convenience; hence the rise of what has been termed the 'bedroom producer'. As computer software allows different sequences and instruments (real or virtual) to be layered upon one another and finely edited, it enhances the ease with which solitary individuals can produce complex audio tracks and entirely conflates the role of the creator and the producer. In some senses, this could be seen as leading to the *isolation* of the musician (as I will go on to discuss, this is not necessarily the case). Perhaps more importantly, it points to a *fragmentation* of musical production, in the sense that the 'parts' of a record that used to be combined from people playing instruments together in real time are now more likely to be created separately, then built up in a more fragmented fashion. Added to this, the rise of networking means that individuals can collaborate in a more piecemeal fashion: one person can create a 'part' then send it to someone else to work on (see Chapter 7).

More people are now able to create tracks that conform to a 'professional' standard, yet there are also opportunities for people with little musical skill or knowledge to become more involved in creative acts, however minimal these may be. Thus, at the more 'professional' end of the music production scale, people will need to train to learn reasonably complex equipment and invest in rather expensive software (which can nevertheless be pirated). For less experienced participants, a number of cheap or free tools allow one to manipulate music on a more 'basic' level. For example, free editing software allows people to upload tracks and to play around with basic sound manipulation procedures, such as editing bits out of the track, applying effects (e.g. echo, delay, tempo change) and applying fade-ins and outs. More advanced software allows one to create music from scratch (as with virtual synthesizers) or to create edited amalgams, popularly known as 'mashups'. These developments demonstrate how consumers of music in a digital age can increasingly engage in some form of production, thus exemplifying what Jenkins has termed 'participatory culture' (Jenkins 2006b).

While participatory culture levels the divide between production and consumption, we do still make distinctions between these areas, even if they can overlap at times (see Chapter 7). It is, therefore, to the issue of consumption – as well as the highly important area of distribution – that I now turn.

Distribution and consumption

The introduction of the CD (compact disc) on the mass market in 1982 heralded the arrival of digital music consumption. That the CD soon superseded the cassette as the most popular consumption format demonstrates its importance, though it is perhaps not hugely significant in terms of affording new ways in which consumers could experience music. The chief advantage of the CD was that it provided much better audio quality than the cassette but was also much more portable and durable than vinyl (it also helped that huge amounts of money and energy were pumped into promoting it, though this, of course, never guarantees the success of a format). CDs promised durability, as Philips promoted the format with the motto 'perfect sound forever'; consumers soon found that they were prone to digital 'jitters', while some have estimated that the shelf life of an average retail music CD is no more than seven to ten years (Friedberg 2002: 33). One of the most significant aspects of the CD was that it did enable music listeners to access tracks randomly, which for some was a great boon in terms of experiencing music in more 'user-friendly' ways. Nevertheless, there were some things about CDs that did not match up to cassettes: in particular, it would be a long time before people could record onto CDs, so the cassette remained a popular format for making music compilations. Additionally, because CDs were physically wider than cassettes, the 'CD Walkman' did not supersede the cassette Walkman in terms of popularity because it was a more cumbersome device to carry. It was not until the growth of the mp3 as a popular consumer format that digital portable devices began to replace the analogue Walkman (see below).

Subsequent digital formats did not take off in the way that electronics and music companies would have wished: DAT and mini-disc (MD), for example, made only limited inroads into the consumer industry. Worse was to follow for the corporations with the rise of the Internet and the ability to distribute and consume music in new ways. As is now well known, the music industry was taken unawares by the growth in distributing mp3 music files even though the roots of the format lay in corporate strategies to standardize digital data (Sterne 2006: 829).

The sharing of music files started around the mid-1990s: at this point, it was difficult to download music because of very slow connection speeds (which is why files were compressed) and it was not that easy to find particular music. The emergence of Napster in June 1999 changed things dramatically. Aware of the growth in file sharing, Shawn Fanning created a central server that linked users together and searched their respective folders to find specific tracks. Suddenly, file sharing was big news and the record industry had to take notice. They had a similar problem with the availability of cheap, recordable cassettes in the early 1980s, which had led to legislators granting music labels a portion of every sale of blank audio cassettes (Alderman 2002: 3). Yet, illegal copying of cassettes was limited to the extent that they often only swapped among a small network of friends. By contrast, it is possible to endlessly copy mp3s and distribute them to a virtual network of millions. In 1999, when Napster emerged, connection speeds were gradually beginning to rise and computer adoption was increasing. Unsurprisingly, the music industry clamped down: in December 1999, the Recording Industry Association of America (RIAA) filed a lawsuit against Napster, leading to its closure in February 2001 (it re-emerged as a legal service in 2003 after being purchased by Roxio).

A huge debate about copyright issues in the digital age and the conduct of the record industry followed that I do not have the space to delve into here (for an overview of debates, see Frith and Marshall 2004). What did follow was a tussle between the official industry and the activities of those deemed illegal by that industry. In light of Napster's demise, a number of newer peer-to-peer programs emerged that often used open-source software and therefore could not be identified with any particular persons in regard to legal action. The record industry, realizing the difficulty of shutting down such programs therefore adopted a new strategy of targeting individuals who shared large collections of their music through virtual networks, a controversial tactic, particularly regarding the extremely heavy fines and sentences that some have received.

Despite these punitive measures, illegal file sharing still occurs on a large scale. It coexists now, though, with the legal distribution of copyrighted electronic files. The record industry realized that it needed to offer a legal alternative to downloading music if it was going to remain a dominant force. For a new generation of music listeners, who often listen through portable devices and computers, the digital file is extremely versatile because it can be transferred between devices with ease and does not consume physical storage space. As of January 2007, digital files account for an estimated 10 per cent of the international music market – amassed through both online and mobile phone sales – and this will undoubtedly grow in the future (IFPI 2007). As digital downloads now increasingly impact upon music charts around the world, the individual single, as opposed to the long-playing 'album', reassumes importance as downloads are sold on an individual track basis. What is different from when the 7″ vinyl single in its heyday is that singles were then often used to sell albums; now, with every track on an album a potential single, the tables have arguably reversed. For his 2006 album *The Information,* artist Beck produced music videos for every track: in this sense, the album can be thought of as a platform for creating future revenue from all of its singular elements.

Nevertheless, there is still some dissatisfaction with paid legal downloading, often distributed via formats such as Advanced Audio Coding (AAC) or Windows Media Audio (WMA) rather than mp3, in order to embed Digital Rights Management (DRM) restrictions into files. Consumers have expressed dissatisfaction with DRM, which limits the amount of times a user can copy the file and, often, the type of hardware the files can be transferred to; there has also been dissatisfaction with the pricing of virtual files (Anon 2005). When people were downloading free, illegal tracks, they did not worry too much about the loss of sound quality entailed by digital compression, but this is not the case when it comes to actually paying for them. In addition, consumers have also complained that when they buy a CD, they are free to rip the contents and transfer the files in whatever manner they please, which actually means that digital online files are *less* flexible than their physical counterparts. The lack of flexibility inherent in DRM has led many within the industry to argue against it, and there are signs now that many record companies are willing to ditch it. EMI announced in April 2007 that it was going to offer enhanced digital files without DRM protection *alongside* its normal DRM-protected files via iTunes, though at the cost of 20p more per file (EMI 2007). Currently, this selling of tracks in both DRM-protected and unprotected versions at different prices looks set to become widely adopted.

There are other strands to Internet distribution and downloading beyond the activities of the major record companies and the illegal activities that so trouble them. The net offers new ways for music acts to distribute their music and to establish themselves within a virtual community. Both unsigned bands wanting to gain exposure, as well as musicians merely wanting to share their music among a network, can disseminate their music online. A key development here was the buzz created around the Arctic Monkeys in the UK through their songs being circulated on the net by fans (who had ripped songs from demo CDs given away at gigs and had created a site based around the band on MySpace). Even though the band claimed to have played no part in this process, it led to recognition and hype within the music press and on radio, and they eventually signed with record label Domino. Their debut single and album went straight to number one in the record charts; the album – *Whatever People Say I Am, That's What I'm Not* (2006) – became the fastest selling debut album in UK chart history. Nevertheless, despite the antipathy expressed by the band towards conventional industry, it is telling that they ultimately signed to a record label. While Domino is an independent label, it nevertheless has issued publishing rights in the USA and New Zealand to EMI. This demonstrates the importance of traditional industrial mechanisms if one wants to make a living through making music, even though new promotional and distribution processes are both challenging and complementing older forms. Certainly, musicians can bypass the music industry and have been able to do so now for a long time, particularly since the rise of 'DIY' culture in the late 1970s (see Chapter 1). New forms of distribution and connection enhance such possibilities, though the lure of signing for established record companies in order to broaden one's profile and make more money will remain tempting for many.

Established musicians can also make use of new technologies to enhance their presence: official websites, for example, enable acts to post news of what they have been up to, discographies, general information, discussion forums, as well as access to exclusive content (such as audio and audio-visual material). Often there will also be the chance to purchase music and other related merchandise. There are also a lot of other sites that often emerge in relation to music acts, or types of music more generally, which means that it is now far easier to gain access to information and material related to artists than previously. In addition, a host of music e-zines (electronic magazines distributed by email or posted on a website) are available on the web as well as critical blogs. The growth of the music e-zine once again harks back to the rise of 'DIY' culture in the late 1970s and the rise in self-produced fanzines. Today, though, it is far easier to create an online zine (no costs of publishing are involved) and to distribute it (because the very fact of putting it on the web means that it does not need to be physically distributed). The potential size of the audience is also much higher and, while it is not easy to gain a wide audience some online zines, such as *Pitchfork* and *Drowned in Sound*, have gained a substantial readership. The advantages of online zines are that, in addition to writing about music, audio and audiovisual material can also be included. One of the most popular features to spring up on e-zines recently has been the inclusion of podcasts by various staff writers.

Finally, it should be mentioned that digital technologies increase the importance of the music video. This visual side of music has undoubtedly been of great importance previously, in particular with the rise of MTV in the 1980s. Now, however, with the increase in specialist digital channels, there are even more music channels. Music videos feature as attractions of a variety of websites and are also one of the most popular forms of material to be downloaded on sites such as YouTube and Google Video (the short nature of such works perfectly suited for watching streamed material online). Furthermore, they are also beginning to prove popular as material that can be downloaded and watched on portable devices, such as mobile phones or portable media players (PMPs). The importance of the music video is indicated by the fact that, at the same time downloads became acceptable for chart ranking without an accompanying physical release; video downloads also counted towards the singles chart in the UK (IFPI 2007). It could be argued, then, that as the formats music is stored on become less material and increasingly stripped of visual dimensions (album covers, reproduction of lyrics and other information), such loss is compensated by music's increased connection to other visual formats such as music videos and web-based data flows.

Conclusion

While many trends identified with digital technologies and music can be traced back to older technologies, there is an acceleration of certain processes. These include: the recontextualization of pre-existing music; the increasing 'visual' nature of music (either the visualization of music in terms of wave displays or visual accompaniment *to* music); and the continued blurrings between production and consumption (though certainly not to the extent that such categories disintegrate). One particularly important aspect that I have yet to dwell upon in detail is the *proliferation* of music and the implications of this.

Since the advent of recording technology, the 'archive' of music recordings has continued to grow, though this has done so at a greater rate in more recent years as cheaper formats lead to even more archive releases. In tandem with this development, the growing access to production and recording technologies has also led to a growth in contemporary music being distributed in some form. Finally, because virtual music files take up far less physical space than previous formats, it is easier for consumers to collect more music than previously, a process hastened by those who have taken advantage of the amount of 'free' music obtainable through the Internet.

In this sense we are living in an era of musical 'abundance', in which both historical and contemporary recordings are increasingly accessible. This is one factor that is crucial in understanding the rise in musical recreation; not only because it is becoming easier to manipulate previous recordings, but also because there are so many recordings available that it almost becomes obligatory to somehow engage with such materials. Digital technologies, therefore, have led to a renewed cultural valuation of 'the past', not just in this sense but also in other respects. To conclude, there are two important ways in which 'the past' becomes revalued in relation to the present, which is seen as somehow lacking (unlike in the above example, where the past is merely something to be poached in order to fuel the present and future).

First, the age of being able to find so many recordings that were once difficult to find, as well as information on such recordings, has led some music critics to decry the age of 'abundance'. While many critics have embraced blogging and the opportunity to express unedited opinions online, there is a general feeling that this abundance leads to a stockpiling, name-checking, consumer mentality that draws away from the music itself. Thus, music critic Simon Reynolds has argued that:

> The web has extinguished the idea of a true underground. It's too easy for anybody to find out anything now [...] I sense that there's a lot more skimming and stockpiling, an obsessive-compulsion to hear everything and hoard as much music as you can, but much less actual obsession with specific arty-facts [sic].
>
> (Reynolds 2007)

It may be the case that when there is so much to listen to, then people may not be able to pay as much attention to specific records as they once did. This is possible, but it is mere conjecture. It seems to be more the case that established music critics of a certain age are reacting to this age of abundance, ruing the fact that their roles as cultural custodians are perhaps under threat. Embedded within such attitudes is a degree of nostalgia for a time when records and information about them were scarcer and, therefore, obtaining artefacts and related knowledge entailed much more investment and commitment.

Second, some people reject digital technologies – either partially or completely – in favour of analogue technologies, whether this is in the production or playback of music. Within production, for example, some musicians bemoan the lack of 'human-ity' in the sounds made by digital synthesizers, hence the rise in the value of analogue snyths such as Moogs. Consumption-wise, there are those who herald the 'warmer' sounds of vinyl and its related physical nature (where sleeve artwork comes into its own), or those who are rediscovering the joys of the cassette, particularly valued as a very personal form of making individual compilation tapes (Paul 2003). There are a number of reasons behind such moves. They may signal a form of consumer resistance to shifting formats and the expense that this entails – a refusal to adopt to the newest format as dictated by major industries. On the other hand, they can be elitist moves, finding value in objects that were once, but are no longer, mass consumer items and thus using them to stand out from the 'crowd'.

Whatever the motives behind such 'rearguard' moves, they certainly highlight how older technologies and cultural artefacts continue to play an important role within the digital age. Digital technologies have largely replaced analogue technolo-gies in the everyday production and consumption of music, but these older technolo-gies continue to play a role in niche cultural sectors. The ascendance of digital has not eliminated analogue; rather, it has shifted the ways in which some cultural actors value and interpret analogue equipment as it takes up a minority position within the contemporary audioscape.

Recommended reading

Bennett, Andy, Shank, Barry and Toynbee, Jason (eds) (2006) *The Popular Music Studies Reader*. London and New York: Routledge.

Sexton, Jamie (ed.) (2007) *Music, Sound and Multimedia: From the Live to the Virtual*. Edinburgh: Edinburgh University Press.

Shapiro, Peter (ed.) (2000) *Modulations: A History of Electronic Music*. New York: Caipirinha.

Toynbee, Jason (2000) *Making Popular Music: Musicians, Creativity and Institutions*. London: Edward Arnold.

Case Study: The iPod

Jamie Sexton

The iPod has been a phenomenal success for Apple, leading the field in the rapid consumer take-up of DAPs (digital audio players). This has subsequently fed into the growth of PMPs (portable media players), which are capable of a broader range of multimedia functions and have been on the market since 2005 (these include a number of iPod models, such as the iTouch), and more recently the multimedia mobile phone, most famously embodied in Apple's iPhone (launched in 2007). In 2006, the iPod was estimated to account for 76 per cent of global DAP and PMP sales, and in April 2007 it was announced that Apple had sold over 100 million items, making it the fastest selling music player in the business (Sherwin 2007: 30). Why has it been such a success? In this case study, I try to account for some of the reasons why the DAP, in particular, has proved so popular and the issues that its use has generated. I also look into why the iPod has conquered the DAP market so successfully, to the extent that the iPod itself is now synonymous with the DAP (and PMP), even though it is only a particular brand of such a player (similar to how the Walkman, which was a brand of personal stereo, generally came to refer to personal stereos in general).

The success of the iPod is reflected not only in its name referring to DAPs and PMPs generally, but also through the prevalence of the term 'podcasting'. Podcasting is a name given to any type of audio content that can be downloaded from the Internet manually or, more often, automatically via software applications such as 'ipodder'. Its name reflects how it is suited to being downloaded onto mobile audio devices (it is often in MP3 format) though it need not be played in this way. According to Richard Berry, the term can be traced back to an article by the British journalist Ben Hammersley in early 2004 (Berry 2006: 143).

The increasing mobility of global populations is one of the major contexts within which to place the rise of portable media. With the development of the railway system in the nineteenth century, people were able to move across terrain with more ease, and in line with this, the portable book emerged for reading on journeys, while the book and newspaper stand became a regular feature at the station (Urry 2006: 363). Throughout the twentieth century, as more forms of transportation have emerged and as travelling has increased, so newer mobile media technologies have materialized, which include the car radio, the transistor radio, the portable computer, the hand-held video game and the cell phone or mobile phone. These mobile media forms are an important historical tradition within which to place the personal stereo, or the Walkman, which was the most important mobile precedent of the iPod.

Sony's Walkman, a cassette player small enough to carry around on the move, and connected to headphones, was introduced in 1979 and was an unexpected success. The growth of people adopting the Walkman (or a different brand of personal stereo) was so great that it constituted a social phenomenon and gave rise to extensive critical opinion. The fact that people could now move around and constantly be connected to music of their choosing was seen as significant. Previously, portable radios and cassette players enabled this function, but they were socially intrusive to the extent that they disrupted public space through enforcing one's sounds on others. Personal stereos enabled the listener to remain cocooned in their own sound world. This led critics to lament the ways in which people were becoming cut off from their social surroundings and locked in their own private audio bubbles (as noted by Hosokawa 1984: 165). This tended to overlook the fact that in the Victorian era the book was itself used as a kind of shield on the train to 'cope with new speeds as well as the embarrassment of sitting in an enclosed compartment with strangers' (Urry 2006: 363).

Less censorious analysts focused on the new relations that the Walkman brought into play between, for example, the private and the public, or the ways in which Walkman users enjoyed a new sense of empowerment by aestheticizing journeys through urban (or country) environments. Private and public demarcations, while never entirely stable, were nevertheless complicated further by the Walkman user being able to carry their private audio worlds into public space (Bull 2001: 188). The sense of control over everyday life has been expressed by both analysts and Walkman users: users, for example, have often expressed how the Walkman opens up a fantasy world in which they sometimes feel like they are part of a filmic experience (Bull 2006). Hosokawa has argued that the Walkman creates a kind of 'secret theatre', an imaginative, private space for the user that is nevertheless signalled to others who are unaware of its content (Hosokawa 1984: 177). The Walkman was also seen as important for the manner by which it took music from its previously common settings and recreated the environment upon which it became nomadically superimposed, thus altering the 'given coherence of the city-text' (Hosokawa 1984: 171). In this sense, anonymous social spaces could be audibly inscribed with personal meanings and rendered intimate (see Chapter 7).

Since the advent of the Walkman, there have been a number of different variations on the mobile cassette player, including the Discman and the MD Walkman, though these did not have the impact of the original tape-based mechanism. Portable DAPs first appeared on the market in 1998, though at this time music storage space was limited and stored on an external flash drive rather than an internal hard drive. While some early models were quite popular, DAPs were controversial because it was believed (by the record industry) that they encouraged illegal downloading. By the end of the 1990s, DAPs were capable of storing music on internal hard drives and this was the beginning of their ability to store large amounts of music files (around 5GB at this point).

In 2001, the Apple iPod was launched, which eventually became the market dominator, as opposed to the more established Sony. The reasons as to the massive success of Apple in this area are numerous, but there are some factors that stand out:

design, usability, advertising and the launch, in 2003, of the Apple iTunes store. The actual technical production of the player was designed by the company PortalPlayer, who were hired to work on the creation of the iPod, with Apple contributing demands regarding the look, feel and operability of the device. Apple had already built a reputation in design and usability with its Macintosh computers (Kelly 2007: 195–6). When the iPod was launched, it was notable for its slimline design and its central scroll wheel (soon replaced with a click wheel), which made it easy for users to find and arrange music.

Apple also undertook a sustained advertising push to promote the product, which became particularly marked around 2003. Using simple, yet striking, adverts – often featuring a silhouette dancing against a coloured background with iPod in hand – television, magazine and billboard adverts became ubiquitous. Apple skilfully targeted a core youth audience through use of music accompanying the television advertisements: the three original advertisements featured hip-hop, garage and techno music, respectively, which were the three best selling genres at the time (Wheeler 2003). Its public relations (PR) division also went into overdrive, securing around 6,000 iPod and iTunes stories within major publications worldwide by the end of 2003. The company also forged lucrative partnerships with other companies such as Volkswagen and Pepsi (Cuneo 2003: S2). Apple was able to fit the product into its general brand image, in which the purchasing of an Apple product was seen as a lifestyle choice, associated with 'hipness', leisure and elegance. By contrast, Sony only really began to build up a sustained advertising campaign for its DAPs in 2004, at which point it was generally considered too late (Anon 2004: 14). Meanwhile, Apple had already captured a majority of this expanding market.

The launch of the iTunes store was another factor in Apple's huge success with the iPod. As previously mentioned, the record industry was expressing some concern about DAPs due to issues of piracy. With the iTunes store, Apple established links with many major record companies to provide a legal, downloadable service. The timing of the launch of iTunes music store was also important: it was released in the USA in April 2003 and in France, Germany and the UK in June 2004 (by which time it was PC-compatible), to be closely followed by its launch in numerous other countries. This era coincided not only with prevalent iPod advertising, but also with the real growth of an online legal music market. While many were still downloading illegal files, others wanted to enter the virtual music world in a less risky manner. The iTunes store, as Kelly has pointed out, guarantees a standard technical quality (which illegal downloading cannot), is 'safe' to use and can also definitely be transferred to, and played on, an iPod (Kelly 2007: 196). This latter consistent connection was important as not all music files could be played on all DAPs. In this sense, the iTunes store may have helped to sell the iPod and vice versa, hence the fact that the store has dominated digital music sales in a similar manner to the player dominating DAP sales.

In light of the huge rise in the consumption of iPods and other DAPs, analyses of the changing ways music is being experienced are again materializing. From one perspective, the iPod does not seem to be a particularly radical progression from the Walkman: the mobility of individuals through public space, who can nevertheless remain connected to a private audio realm, remains constant. Yet, even if the ubiquity of the iPod does not constitute a drastic break from the phenomenological states associated with the Walkman, there are important differences between the two devices.

First, the growth of large hard drives to store music on has led to the increased portability of music. With the Walkman, one had a portable device but often had to choose a very limited amount of music to carry around because each 60–90 minutes of music had to be stored on a single cassette. This sometimes led to people spending quite a bit of time actually mulling over what music they should take with them on each particular outward excursion (Bull 2001: 184). In contrast, the iPod allows people to store a huge amount of music on a tiny device without any supplemental material. The size of hard drives differs according to each model, but most devices have the space to store vast amounts of music. Many iPod users have enthused about the way in which it is possible to take their entire record collections with them on the go (Bull 2005: 344). Thus, physical restrictions become increasingly overcome due to the virtual nature of digital music, and this allows a greater degree of mobile choice. This, in a sense, gives people greater control of their private sounds in public space. Previously, Walkman users had spoken of how they would create specific tapes to take with them on journeys to create a nomadic 'mood' (Bull 2001: 185). Yet, this would need to be planned in advance; if the chosen tape(s) did not, as anticipated, match the mood, this sense of 'control' may have dissipated. With the iPod, the huge amount of music at one's disposal allows users to match mood and music off the cuff, so to speak.

This 'off-the-cuff' quality of the iPod is a result not only of its storage capacity, but also because its digital nature affords users to programme, randomize and skip tracks. In this sense, the device is like a portable jukebox. People can listen to entire albums on the move, they can listen to assembled 'playlists' (akin to a compilation tape), or they can let the player select tracks at random. This latter function has given pleasure to some users, who tend to enjoy the mixture of surprise (you don't know what's coming next) and control (it's going to be a track that you've put on there and if you don't want to listen to it at that moment then you can skip it). The random function can also give rise to unanticipated moods in the user. Dan Laughey has described how a student who he interviewed experienced a 'strange' mixture of feelings as he listened to a set of random tracks from his collection, some of which were 10 years old. He 'experienced odd feelings of happiness, regret, anger and embarrassment as he recalled songs that were attached to memories of particular events and episodes in teenage years' (Laughey 2007: 181). In this sense, the iPod takes the personalization of the Walkman into new territory. First, it can aid the customization of music to fit the current mood of the individual, who can flick through tracks at will and 'fit' the music to the current mood. Second, the user can give up a degree of control and let the random function inject a level of surprise, which may produce particular moods sparked by memory, as the sequence of songs connect with emotions buried deep within the individual.

One final important difference between the iPod and the Walkman is that the latter was almost uniformly used as an 'in-between-device'; that is, it was used on journeys between destination points (Bull 2005: 345). The iPod may be used as a mobile device but it is also used in a number of other settings: at home, in the car (it can be fitted into car stereos), and at work. It can be plugged into other machines with ease while its capacity, as well as its randomizing and programmable functions, make it ideal to play anywhere. At home, for example, it offers more flexibility than a CD in terms of programming one's entire collection into a coherent sequence of songs that one is in the mood for. In this sense, its status as a kind of personalized mobile jukebox is suited to customized listening within a variety of contexts. If the Walkman was a gadget that blurred the divisions between the private and the public, it was nevertheless only used in public settings in order to render them more personal. The iPod, however, is a device that can be used in both personal and public settings in order to enhance the individual's audio experience.

While Apple has certainly been dominant in the DAP and PMP markets, it is by no means guaranteed that this will always be the case. Sony and Creative, in particular, are attempting to compete in the market. Apple's success, meanwhile, is not always met with consumer satisfaction and the gap between hype and reality has led to many complaints about faulty iPods. Retail analysts Olswang have reported that 'iPod owners are twice as likely to have had to ask for a repair to their player, than owners of other brands' (Inman 2006: 6). Nevertheless, such complaints have yet to dent Apple's market dominance; the likelihood of Windows – whose Zune player was launched in the USA in November 2006 – doing so in the near future is remote. (Currently, the product had yet to be released outside the USA, which will surely dent its chances of success.)

The Zune has a relatively large screen, which makes it ideal for watching moving images on the go. Entering the PMP market at such a late stage, Microsoft is obviously gambling on the growth of portable moving image viewing. Currently, there does not seem to be the same demand for video on the move as there does music, though the future direction of PMPs is moving towards multi-functionality (and, hence, many iPods now contain video, as well as audio functions). Mobile phones have long offered multi-functionality and the fact that many people use such devices to listen to music on has forced Apple to respond. In reply, they have launched the 'iPhone', which is a telephone, PMP, Internet device and camera, among other things. The iPhone, a characteristically sleek Apple gadget, also includes a state-of-the-art multi-touch sensing screen, which is scratch-resistant and tailored for ease of use with one's fingertips. (Apple subsequently launched the 'iPod touch', which added the multi-touch sensitive screen and wi-fi networking capabilities to the iPod.) Launched in the USA in June 2007 and in the UK, Germany and France in November 2007, currently, the device was in its early stages of market penetration. Inevitably, the hype underpinning its launch was so forceful that it was sometimes difficult to distinguish between advertising and reporting in relation to the product. Nevertheless, early reports and sales were generally positive, if not unanimously so. Whether the iPhone marks the stage where the DAP and PMP become significant, yet short-lived media phenomena, or whether it fails to penetrate the market in the same manner as its music-focused progenitor, remains to be seen. At which point the fog of hype currently obscuring attempts to assess the product rationally will have shifted onto a number of more modern lifestyle gadgets.

7 Participatory culture: mobility, interactivity and identity

Matt Hills

Digital culture has undoubted already impacted in a variety of ways on contemporary life, but one of the increasingly significant developments it has ushered in relates to mediated communication 'on the move'. Of course, as with many so-called New Media developments, this is not something wholly new; 'old media' such as analogue radio has been handily portable for decades, and the Walkman personal stereo became a massively popular analogue device, in the 1980s, for privately listening to recorded cassette tapes in public space (see Chapter 6). Despite these sorts of precursor, it can nevertheless be argued that digital, mobile media does indeed offer a series of distinctively portable possibilities.

First and foremost is the fact that 'computer-mediated communication' (CMC), can now be utilized in ever-more mobile forms. Emails can be accessed and read while users of BlackBerries or similar devices are out and about, and wireless or 'wi-fi' broadband coverage is becoming increasingly commonplace, at least in urban areas of high population density in the Western world. Computers, telephones, photographic media, even television and video: the long-held concept of 'media convergence' is finally beginning to see fruition within consumer culture, and it is in the arena of mobile media where the interfaces and intersections of different media technologies are perhaps most visible. However, as Henry Jenkins has pointed out, convergence is not merely the bundling together, in one device or delivery mechanism, of different strands of media type of content:

> Convergence does not depend on any specific delivery mechanism. Rather, convergence represents a paradigm shift – a move from medium-specific content to content that flows across multiple media channels, toward the increased interdependence of communications systems, toward multiple ways of accessing media content, and toward ever more complex relations between top-down corporate media and bottom-up participatory culture.
>
> (Jenkins 2006a: 243)

Convergence, in this sense, is more about 'multi-platforming', where media texts and audiences perhaps start to move almost seamlessly across different platforms such as television, online on-demand radio, podcasts, user-generated content, digital video, and so on. One of the especially intriguing things with 'nomadic' or 'mobile' communications is that the very concept itself has therefore become somewhat amorphous. Given that some information and communication technology (ICT) users and consumers may be accessing the same services (the web, even television and radio) via mobile, wireless devices, while others may be accessing these through (in practice) fixed-point desktop terminals in the home or workplace, or even old-fashioned television sets dealing with digital television signals, then how can we start to delimit the range and scope of 'mobile' media? Is blogging, for example, something done sitting at a desk, or something done *in situ*, perhaps out on the street, standing in a doorway with a lightweight notebook and a borrowed wireless network? (see Gillmor 2006).

Nomadic communication

Dealing with something like the mobile phone may seem the clearest option, but I would argue that it is the fuzzy edges of 'mobile' media, where networks and services previously thought of as 'static' are now becoming increasingly accessible on the move, where we can learn more about the possibilities of 'nomadic' communications in digital culture. Furthermore, 'mobile' media are not always something distinct from 'fixed-point' digital media; increasingly, mobile digital devices – mobile phones, camera phones, iPods and the like – have been techno-culturally defined as symbiotic with consumer 'hub' personal computers (PCs) or laptops through which digital content libraries are archived/backed-up, and through which images and captured video are uploaded to the web to be shared via social networking sites. Again, there are very fuzzy edges around the 'mobile' or the 'nomadic' here, as many of these technologies call for, or incite, the 'bringing home' of ported, portable digital data to a central – possibly fixed – PC, conceptualized as the 'storage' space or archive for files. As such, mobile digital media needs to be seen as defined in interaction and interrelationship with less self-evidently portable ICTs.

How, then, have digital communications devices begun to shift our experiences and uses of the media towards the nomadic? Here, I introduce three significant changes:

1   the move away from conceptualizing 'mobile' media as something belonging to 'public' rather than 'private' space ('nomadic' communications may now find their mobility within domestic space rather than outside it, or in opposition to 'home' territories);
2   the volume of media 'content' that mobile devices such as MP3 or MP4 players can now routinely handle on demand, and outcomes related to this factor;
3   the possibilities for self-expression and articulations of self-identity offered by 'nomadic' digital media.

(Marshall 2004)

In short, these three areas of interest could be summed up as interrogating the 'where', the 'what' and the 'who' of digital mobile media. Along with, and threaded through, thinking about these issues, I also want to flag up some of the critiques that have been made of emergent mobile digital cultures. These concerns relate partly to the 'always-on' nature of specific devices and networks (Middleton 2007) – that is that lines between 'work' and 'private life' may be eroded – and partly to the use of digital communications technology in controversial youth-cultural practices such as the posting online of 'happy slapping' videos (Nightingale 2007). As with many previous 'new' media, mobile digital devices (e.g. camera phones) have been partly interpreted as challenging old systems of power and regulation, hence allowing youth subcultures to engage in activities thought of as threatening to the social order. Though it may not be in any way possible to construct a 'balance sheet' of cultural developments, pros and con, in this area, it does remain important not to fall into premature cultural celebration or condemnation. Digital culture is never simply 'one thing' which can be monolithically assessed as a 'good' or 'bad' series of practices, and it is also fast-moving and flexible. For example, there is a fair chance that by the time this discussion sees print, it may already have been partly superseded by further media technological developments. Perhaps digital culture extends 'planned obsolescence' and the notion of constant 'upgrading' into habitual patterns of consumption and self-conceptualization, even in the world of academic commentary.

The where, what and who of digital mobile communications

Rather more traditionally, 'mobile' media have been thought of in a specific way as devices which offer mobility *outside the home*, rather than forming part of a domestic media set-up. Indeed, in this sense, 'mobile' media can be said to be about taking a sense of the home(ly) out into the cultural world. This meaning is emphasized in Raymond Williams's infamous account:

> I can't find an ordinary term for it, which is why I have to call it one of the ugliest phrases I know: 'mobile privatisation'. It is private. It involves a good deal of evident consumption. Much of it centred on the home itself. The dwelling place. At the same time it is not a retreating privatisation, of a deprived kind, because what it especially confers is an unexampled mobility ... It is a shell you can take with you.

> (Williams 1977: 171 cited in Bull 2000: 179)

The 'shell ... you take with you' is 'centred on the home' but it is not inevitably in the home; it takes the familiar, or a seemingly protective layer of it, out into unfamiliar public space. This is one of the main arguments in Michael Bull's excellent study of personal stereo usage, that Walkmans – and latterly iPods, we might hazard – enable users to 'mediate the "other" ' in terms of their own narcissistically oriented intention (see Chapter 6). The description of this experience might be described as 'culturally solipsistic travelling' (Bull 2000: 181). Like Williams's 'mobile privatization', this is a depiction of a culture of blocking-out, with the screening-out or sounding-out of urban space and its others amounting very nearly to 'a state of cultural autism' (Bull 2000: 181) for its headphone- or earphone-wearing consumers. By taking familiar audiovisual content with them, users can arguably retreat, within public spaces, into their own (semi-)private realms of familiar media consumption. Multi-modal, multimedia consumption is, in this style of account, freed from its more usual domestic terrain: 'Internet-enriched media consumption is no longer fixed in a domestic environment, ... media suffuse and permeate daily life and many of us are increasingly "multi-taskers"' (Talbot 2007: 172).

However, this extension of 'the private' into public space has not always been viewed negatively, with David Jennings instead suggesting that although (2007); (see also Jenkins 2002 and 2006a: 244–5; Lévy 1997):

> The increasing ubiquity of portable devices that absorb people's attention in public spaces may create the impression of a population retreating into cocoons ... with the spread of inexpensive wireless networks, these devices are sprouting more social features that encourage sharing and communicating between people, bringing them together rather than keeping them apart.
>
> (Jennings 2007: 179–80)

Regardless of positive or negative commentary, what these scholarly accounts share is the basic assumption that nomadic communications are centred around types of 'mobile privatization', whether this is a 'screening-out' of the unfamiliar, or an extension of contact with one's pre-existent social networks. The 'private' is thereby carried out, or along with, the 'public' self. What interests me in this context is the possibility that so-called 'nomadic' digital communications may actually now have moved beyond 'mobile privatization' and into its reverse; 'private mobilization', if you like, whereby 'public' spaces are brought – with wireless network mobility – into the home. In other words, rather than 'home' constituting a fixed point or 'base' that is bounded and set apart from the cultural world, domestic spaces enabled with wi-fi broadband are now increasingly not just pervaded by multiple media flows and multiple social networks; they are also targeted as consumer spaces for a range of wireless technologies. 'Mobile' technology is hence arguably just as present within the home as it is outside it. And here, 'mobility' or 'nomadism' may be about being able to move from room to room with a wi-fi networked laptop or music player, as well as different occupants of the domestic space having their mobile phones to hand.

The assumption that 'mobile communication = mobility in public space' is thus only part of the story here. Mobility can also mean mobility of ICT devices and network access points around the home, thus deconstructing the old-school opposition between 'fixed'/cabled domestic media technologies – the television at the hearth of the household – and 'mobile' personal devices which cross over into public space. 'Private' media consumption and communications technology is itself increasingly unanchored from fixed spaces within the home, capable of being 'ported' or carried from living room to study to bedroom. These may seem like relatively trivial and micro-level versions of mobility, undeserving of the label of 'nomadic' communication, but I would argue that such wanderings and trajectories nevertheless form part of a shifting media ecology and cultural anthropology in which arenas and contexts of cultural life that have conventionally been separable – home/school, home/work, family/friends – can all now begin to communicatively interpenetrate and intersect in complex but possibly newly routinized ways. As has been observed, there's 'a need … to ask "what's new *for society* about the New Media?" rather than simply "what are the New Media?" ' (Flew 2002: 10).

For example, one of the early cultural anxieties about mobile telephony was that it would render users open to mechanisms of surveillance and contactability at all times, blurring cultural categories of public/private in new ways:

> the mobile works ambivalently, rendering the subject available within networks of emotional support and contact, but also opening up the continued possibility of critical scrutiny and surveillance … The 'object weight of communication' implied by the mobile has to be read through the individual's psychological projections of its significance. The mobile can play the part of a technological *injunction* … as much as a technological *conjunction*.
>
> (Sussex Technology Group 2001: 220)

And though mobile communications have now moved towards increasingly multi-modal and multimedia data streams (Cranny-Francis 2005: 56), some of these anxieties have remained culturally consistent. Catherine A. Middleton has carried out interesting ethnographic work on Canadians' use of BlackBerries, PDA-style devices with miniature keyboards which enable users to access and respond to email while they are on the go:

> The BlackBerry does give its users a mechanism to exert control over the management of daily communication tasks, but by virtue of its always-on, always-connected nature, it also reinforces cultures that expect people to be accessible outside normal business hours. Rather than just a tool of liberation for its users, the BlackBerry can also be understood as an artefact that reflects and perpetuates organizational cultures in which individual employees have little control and influence.
>
> (Middleton 2007: 165)

Middleton's conclusion is that 'BlackBerries are loved by their users yet frequently loathed by their users' closest friends and relations', precisely because use of these mobile devices tends to be tied into organizational cultures that 'reinforce overwork and promote unrealistic expectations for employee engagement in their jobs' (Middleton 2007: 175). Any notion of work/life balance is eroded here, as the potential reach of employers'/work issues extends into leisure time and the domestic sphere, possibly even being reinforced as an expectation or requirement of the work culture concerned. Far from being a version of 'mobile privatization' where the home(ly) is carried 'like a shell' of meaning and identity into the outside world, this scenario is one of intrusion into the domestic, or what I would call the 'private mobilization' of work cultures which threatens to deconstruct work/leisure and public/private binaries from the outside in. As such, cultural concerns about 'contactability' which surrounded the mobile phone during its widespread consumer adoption may now have been partly relocated around always-on email account access, and the cultural labour expectations surrounding this. Far from 'nomadic' communications necessarily being liberating for consumers, they may be restricting for some workers, who become unable to move beyond the range or reach of work communications. Again, we can see a version of the celebratory/condemnatory matrix here, with mobile digital media being linked to specific critical discourses that it is important to continue to bear in mind.

Though I have begun with the 'where' of digital mobile media, and its cultural ramifications, it is not really possible to separate this out from the 'what' and the 'who' of digital culture, and hence these can only really remain analytical, structuring devices. Given that proviso, I now move on to briefly focus more centrally on the issue of media content. Henry Jenkins has argued that one device has become a near-totemic object in discussions of digital culture, but in a way that is related to changes in the delivery and experiencing of digitized content:

> The video iPod seems emblematic of the new convergence culture – not because everyone believes the small screen of the iPod is the ideal vehicle for watching broadcast content but because the ability to download reruns on demand represents a major shift in the relationship between consumers and media content.

> (Jenkins 2006a: 253)

Now dubbed the 'iPod classic' by Apple, in order to differentiate it from the touchscreen and wi-fi enabled 'iPod Touch', this emblem of convergence culture has largely achieved such status – issues of design aesthetic aside – by virtue of popularizing the personal downloading and organizing of music/video 'libraries' of digital files. Though we might assume the analogue personal stereo to be highly reminiscent in usage to the iPod – both are music-listening devices complete with headphones – there are significant differences. Of the Walkman, Michael Bull's study noted that:

> many users have special tapes containing music only listened to on their personal stereo. This music might have some personal association for them functioning as an 'auditory mnemonic' or alternatively might merely put them in the desired mood for the journey or day ahead ... The metaphor of keeping 'on track' is instructive as it indicates a joining together of mood and duration ... [which] reduces the contingency of the relationship between desired mood and time.

> (Bull 2000: 19)

However, because of storage limitations with old analogue Walkmans, users either had to carry a few relatively bulky tapes with them, or plan out in advance what music they were likely to want to listen to while they were on the go. Managing mood, by linking types of music to types of journey (to/from work), meant that Walkman users typically were required to assess, in advance, what particular music they would want to make use of. Not having the 'right' tape to play resulted in the personal stereo being deemed useless or 'dysfunctional' (Bull 2000: 20). By contrast, the storage capacity of iPods – now often comparable to laptop hard drives – means that users can carry their *entire* music collections/libraries with them. Ipods enable the portability of vastly more information than seemingly comparable analogue devices, and, of course, with the arrival of the video iPod, such devices became multimedia/multi-modal.

Storing whole media collections of content that can be accessed portably and on demand; this is one of the key shifts and developments of digital culture. Users of the 'iPod classic' can watch television content on the iPod's smallish screen, whether this content is recorded from digital television or a series of files downloaded over the Internet. And they can organize or customize this content in a variety of ways by 'tagging' it with specific categories:

> There may also be more spontaneity in the way that we build and use our collections of music and other media in the digital age ... We won't need to think of music simply in terms of artist and album title, or of film and television solely in terms of lead actors and genre. Instead, we'll be able to choose among a much wider range of organizing factors, from mood to date of release.
>
> (Jennings 2007: 81–3)

In this context, media content is no longer schedule-led, nor even necessarily organized by conventional genres, given that individual users can customize the music/media categories within their 'libraries'. Digital culture is, significantly, a culture of 'on-demand' access to content; whether paid for or shared peer-to-peer, users expect to be able to access media content when they want to and where they want to, being bound neither to broadcast times (and places), nor in some cases to official release dates/in-store availabilities (in instances where music tracks are leaked, pre-release, to the Internet).

By rendering massive quantities of media content portable in almost credit-card size devices, objects such as the iPod have radically altered what it means to be a media consumer in the twenty-first century. As P. David Marshall has commented:

> the digital media form is ... what I would describe as indiscrete as opposed to the more discrete and defined commodities – films, television programs, albums – that the media industry has produced in the past. ... the technology ... hails us quite differently than a television program or film.
>
> (Marshall 2006: 637)

That is, 'old media' content is transmitted to consumers as finished, fixed 'products' requiring the consumer to participate in the audience identity of watching at specific times/spaces. Digital media culture does not fix media products in quite the same way; consumers can download specific tracks, for example, rather than having to acquire predetermined 'albums' of music (Flew 2002: 110). They can also choose the time and place of media consumption, perhaps only downloading and beginning to watch a television series when they know in advance of committing time to it that its narrative reaches a form of conclusion, or that a specific number of episodes/series have already been produced. Television and film hail the consumer as an object to be recruited; digital culture tends to hail consumers of its media content as co-marketers (Murray 2004: 21) or even 'brand evangelists'. According to Derek Johnson:

> Steven Johnson ... describes fans' cross-platform engagement with *Lost* [a TV show available through iTunes – MH] as evangelism, where the multiplat-formed experiences and discoveries of a minoritarian hardcore audience work to interest greater numbers of viewers. ... While in the later 1990s online content was seen as a 'magnet' for attracting fans ... the multiplat-forming practices of the twenty-first century were conceived as means to make fans into magnets for building viewership.

> (Johnson 2007: 68)

Despite these changes, and the seeming encouragement of consumer interaction along with the rise in the nomadic audiences' 'power' over when and where to consume media texts, Mary Talbot has cautioned against doing away with models of media power, noting that 'receiving "officially approved messages" in podcasts is no different from receiving them in other formats' (Talbot 2007: 173). And Derek Johnson's (2007) analysis of digital television/multi-platform audiences similarly recognizes the need not to overstate increases in audience 'power', thereby retaining a critical focus on how media producers continue to attempt to manage what are deemed industrially acceptable forms of audience activity.

Digital media content which can now be readily accessed and consumed via mobile, portable devices are not, of course, restricted to commercial music and film/television. A further way in which digital media culture has evolved is towards not just content that can be customized/collected by consumers, but also towards the increased creation of user-generated content. This user-generated content (UGC) can be camera phone images (see Gye 2007) or captured digital video which once taken on a portable, personal device can then be uploaded to the web and shared at sites such as YouTube:

> By mid-2005 ... the moral concern associated with camera phones shifted ... to the moral outrage occasioned by the British phenomenon of 'happy slapping' ... this panic inadvertently confirmed the entertainment value that could be extracted from the online sharing of camera phone videos and images. ... The giant corporations of cyberspace – News Limited, Yahoo!, Microsoft, Google – all reacted to the perceived potential commercial value of social networking and its capacity to attract user-generated content as entertainment.

> (Nightingale 2007: 290)

In her analysis of this situation, Virginia Nightingale suggests that the 'mobility of the camera phone increases the likelihood that it will be used for controversial purposes' (2007: 291). 'Happy slapping' has been just one example of such controversy; this is the term given to attacks on members of the public by camera phone-toting youngsters who then video these incidents and post the recordings online. Innocent bystanders can thus become the targets of humiliating online footage, and though this may be thought of as a minor infringement or prank, it can also be thought of as a new type of mediation-led criminal activity; attacks on people in public space, motivated largely by the desire to digitally film and upload such exploits to online user communities. As Nightingale points out:

> the online user community is routinely expected to share the burden of site surveillance. ... advertisers are attracted to the ... interest that the presence of controversial material generates, but cannot risk their products being linked to content that might damage brand images.
>
> (Nightingale 2007: 291)

The increasing integration of mobile image-making technology into everyday life has thus not been without its flash points and moral panics, and again not without critical commentaries. But looking beyond these headlines and spectacular transgressions, the rise in online sharing of UGC derived from mobile digital camera (phone)s suggests that digital culture will continue to see a far wider range of media content providers and generators than ever before.

Having said that, though, major media corporations, established brands and key players are all highly likely to retain their positions of professional power. UGC tends to lack markers of media professionalism, often being relatively low-resolution, non-broadcast-quality digital 'reality footage'. However, this 'guerilla' or 'underground' media-making does carry values and connotations of rebellious authenticity, as opposed to the professional, high-gloss values of the media mainstream. And UGC taken from camera phone images has found a place within the era of twenty-four-hour rolling live news, with broadcasters such as the BBC's *News 24* willing to use relatively low-resolution digital coverage from members of the public who have witnessed natural disasters, freak weather conditions, and so on (see Chapter 3).

If mobile digital communications technology has facilitated an expansion in sources of media content (one of the 'whats' of nomadic/mobile communication), as well as allowing audiences to access content in new ways and increasingly on their own terms (the 'where'), then it has also posed new possibilities for the 'who' of media culture, or the articulation of self-identity via:

> an increasing desire to personalize media. This personalization is enacted further through the use of iPods and MP3 players that allow individuals to download and then program their playlists and thereby eliminate the mediating of broadcast radio. The rapid expansion of mobile phones, PDAs and Blackberries, with a variety of features including cameras, downloadable ringtones, different skins to accessorize their look ... further underlines how New Media personalizes one's media use and environment.
>
> (Marshall 2006: 638)

This personalization, or cultural process of individualization, suggests that digital culture from mobile telephony onwards into iPod use, and beyond, has been powerfully linked to forms of self-identity, self-expression and self-display (see below). P. David Marshall argues that media representations – images of others and social/ cultural groups – have begun to be displaced in the cultural imaginary by 'New Media forms of presentation' (Marshall 2006: 644). People are beginning to routinely produce and consume images of themselves, whether these are created as profile images for social networking sites, as avatars, or within practices of personal digital photography. And though it may be assumed that different generations of New Media users are more or less comfortable with these developments, it can no longer be assumed that mobile digital media are limited only to the young. In such a context, self-identity is not only presented and displayed through the embodied self, and attention needs to be paid to 'the ways in which individuals present, or construct, their identities [online via] … the aesthetics and construction methods of … "brico-lage" ' (Lister et al. 2003: 246).

Certainly, such processes of self-presentation are evidently not only an outcome of mobile digital media, and a massive body of scholarly work has analysed these shifts in relation to cyberculture more widely. But it can certainly be argued that the rise in consumer take-up of mobile digital media has accelerated and contributed to these cultural patterns. One further emblem of this process, other than the video iPod mentioned by Jenkins (2006a), is the way in which mobile telephones have become multimedia devices working 'not simply as communicative conduits but also as "handy" or pocket containers of data, media content, photo archives and secure microworlds' (Richardson 2007: 205). As micro-worlds of the self, current mobiles promise much more than merely ways of texting, emailing or speaking to social contacts or loved ones. They may proffer possibilities of nomadic communication, but they also work to mirror and secure the self-identities of their owners thanks to stored media content, phonebooks and saved texts. Akin to the proverbial yuppies' filofax of the 1980s – a bound paper file in which allegedly all crucial information about the owner's life and social world could be kept – mobile phones have become culturally and ideologically loaded objects, made to ontologically secure and carry presentations of self-identity. There is an irony or possible paradox here. The proliferating range of devices aimed at liberating consumers from the fixed places and times of older analogue media have, perhaps, ended up reinforcing and fixing presentations of self-identity through their customizable, multimedia and data-storage capacities. But versions of Raymond Williams's 'mobile privatization', the extending of 'private' self-identities and consumer tastes/images into public spaces, have also met their match through what I have termed 'private mobilizations' of work culture, and the erosion of cultural boundaries between public and private from the outside in, as well from the inside out.

Recommended reading

Flew, Terry (2002) *New Media: An Introduction*. Oxford: Oxford University Press.

Jenkins, Henry (2002) Interactive Audiences? in D. Harries (ed.) *The New Media Book*, pp. 157–70. London: British Film Institute.

Jenkins, Henry, (2006) *Convergence Culture: Where Old and New Media Collide*. New York and London: New York University Press.

Jennings, David (2007) *Net, Blogs and Rock 'N' Roll*. London and Boston: Nicholas Brealey Publishing.

Case Study: Social networking and self-identity

Matt Hills

In the preceding chapter I noted that 'nomadic' digital media tend to be defined in symbiotic relationship to fixed-point PCs thought of as storage or uploading centres. Of course, this situation may well change as portable devices are able to carry more and more data as well as being wi-fi-enabled themselves (like the iPod Touch, although this is currently not blessed with much in the way of data storage). The current situation means that services and sites thought of as culturally significant within mobile digital culture – YouTube or Flickr, for example – can involve the uploading of digital files which are captured on the move, but which may then be posted online through (relatively) fixed-point PCs. And social networking sites such as Facebook might also, similarly, involve the sharing of digital images taken on camera phones or dedicated digital cameras, which may then be uploaded and accessed through a variety of less portable/nomadic PCs.

However, it is interrelated to home and work PCs, the rise in digital mobile media has arguably had a major impact on concepts of self-identity for generations of devoted users – not just college students – and it is this issue that I want to zero in on in more detail here. P. David Marshall has noted that:

> among American University students the pervasive use of Facebook.com and Myspace.com is remarkable. These sites are organized to connect friends, but also provide techniques for checking out others. ... These kinds of sites describe the wider proliferation of the presentation of the self.

> (Marshall 2006: 639)

University students may be able to access such sites through fixed-point university networks, but given that Facebook is no longer restricted to those with education-based email addresses, its potential constituency is massive, with users' primary access points now becoming potentially mobile, as well as being based within the home (some workplaces have begun to block access, however, given fears over lost worker productivity). The site began life as a US phenomenon largely limited to college students, a cultural space which Victor Burgin has argued is and was especially liminal, being particularly linked to experiments with identity, and hence to forms of narcissism:

> American colleges still actively cultivate a familial atmosphere. The dormitory room is a transitional space. It lies between the primitive space of

infantile omnipotence under maternal protection and the adult space of civil society ... For [object-relations psychoanalyst] Winnicott, 'this area of playing is not inner psychic reality. It is outside the individual, but it is not the external world'. What better description could we have of the space of the Internet?

(Burgin 2004: 51–2)

For Burgin, the US college system is one which liminally acts between 'child' and 'adult' identities, being precisely transitional, and thus combining elements of play, child-like assumed omnipotence and adult responsibility. His perhaps rather overblown conclusion is that the Internet, in sum total, corresponds to this state of playfulness and liminality between reality and fantasy. A more measured conclusion – though even then, one which may be prone to overgeneralization – would be to view the early rise of Facebook as linked to these cultural meanings and processes of transition; adopted by a generation of users placed at similar stages in the life course, collectively on the cusp of cultural categories of child/adult, Facebook would seem to offer the possibility for identity play and experimentation as a potentially narcissistic vehicle for one's visibility to others:

We must be careful ... not to lose sight of genuinely new modes of identity play in networked media. Indeed, in some ways cyberculture does not so much ignore 'lived experience' as argue that we are more and more 'living' in networks, a union of the immediate and the mediated.

(Lister et al. 2003: 254)

And while Facebook has been thought of most centrally, of course, in relation to social networking, what this sometimes misses out is the extent to which Facebook and its ilk, with their 'union of the immediate and the mediated', place a new-found digital-cultural emphasis on the presentation of self. Such an emphasis typically hinges on, and reinforces, the use of mobile digital media to capture and image moments of self-expression, identity and play.

For example, one has a Facebook Profile picture along with a customizable Profile space where all sorts of applications including 'virtual bookshelves' and 'music collections' can be set up. Consumer taste is thus heavily foregrounded; friends can rank and review movies, and gauge their compatibility with others' interests. Self-identity is explicitly made a matter of one's assorted enthusiasms and fandoms. But the self is not just presented through fan-consumer identities; given the centrality of the Profile picture, users tend to update these frequently, and they become a short hand for changing, up-to-the-minute performances of self. As Lisa Gye has argued of personal camera phone use, by 'reinforcing the intensely personal, camera phones may also participate in this narrow economy of self' (2007: 286). And the Facebook Profile picture seems to form a part of this 'narrow economy of self'; different subgenres of picture have emerged, ranging from the 'glamour' shot in which the self is seemingly auto-objectified for others and thought of as a type of 'model', to the potentially resistant 'quirky' or non-representational picture where object correlatives or abstract images stand in for the self.

Profile pictures have also started to be thought of as corresponding to a type of photographic opportunity while users are on the go or participating in offline social events; for instance, on a summer break at the UK's south coast in 2007, I encountered young holidaymakers who were no longer posing simply for holiday snaps; instead, they were self-reflexively and quite self-consciously 'taking Facebook Profile pictures' on Brighton Pier. The fact that Facebook Profile pictures are thought of as constituting a specific genre or mode of photo is evident from the fact that at least some users have championed 'Anti Profile' pictures of themselves, that is, images which are deliberately and knowingly less than 'perfected', posed and wholly flattering shots.

Mobile digital technologies like personal photography and image-capture may be culturally evolving not just towards the creation of UGC such as 'reality' footage but also towards altered and increasingly 'photographic' conceptions of self-image. As Lisa Gye observes, digital cameras and camera phones 'are set to extend our way of looking at the world photographically and in doing so bring changes to how we understand ourselves' (2007: 287).

The use of camera phones to generate images that commemorate and testify to one's presence at specific cultural events has also become a significant use of these technologies, and gig-going, for example, has become a massively mediated cultural ritual, as Chris Chesher has observed:

> Once the U2 show itself started ... people in the audience started using their mobile phones in a different way [i.e. not to contact others in the audience – MH]. They held them up, pointed them towards the stage, and began recording the show as still images or video. ... The sound is invariably distorted, with the screams of nearby fans overriding the music. Videophones therefore produce a cinema of convenience, not a deep relationship with the moving image.
>
> (Chesher 2007: 222)

But this 'cinema of convenience' or digital still-photography of the same status, seems to be conceptualized, culturally, in the same way as Facebook profile pictures; it is recorded via mobile devices precisely in order to be shared online as a marker of one's cultural taste, and one's consumer status ('I was there'). As Chesher goes on to observe:

> [I]n the weeks following the show, some of these phone and digital camera images circulated further from the stadium ... The images were available most easily on the Internet, where photo-sharing sites ... and video-sharing sites ... made these files and media streams available around the world.
>
> (Chesher 2007: 222–3)

P. David Marshall argues that this concept of the self (and its activities) as a series of images anticipating the scrutiny of online others leads to a new kind of 'public privacy' in which the self is constantly and narcissistically performed, auto-objectified, for an imagined audience:

With photos and other personal details, Facebook and Myspace generate public privacy into a new form of narcissism. This narcissism is actualized through New Media and it is specifically modalized around a mediatized version of the self: the representations of celebrity have now been liberated to become the basis for the potential public presentation of the self.

(Marshall 2006: 639–40)

The proliferation of mobile digital media and communications technology appears to have partially democratized image-making and media creation, but at the same time it has arguably extended the cultural regimes of specific types of image along with potentially narcissistic concepts of selfhood. Rather than interpreting the U2 fans he considered ethnographically as narcissistically imaging themselves, Chesher analyses this use of mobile image-making as a corrective to, or at least a variant perspective on, the 'professional' image-making strategies surrounding live rock concerts:

Many personal blogs featured images and reports on the shows ... Someone who was interested in the U2 show would get a very different impression watching these clips by comparison with the professionally edited live videos. They would see a fragmented composite of amateur images from different positions, evidence of a multiplicity of experiences.

(Chesher 2007: 222–3)

However, critical as well as celebratory readings are possible with regard to this New Mediatization. It could be argued that by gathering and posting such concert footage clips, fans are presenting themselves as bearers of high levels of fan cultural capital (broadly speaking, fan status that would be recognized as such by fellow fans). Rather than simply witnessing and digitally mediating events such as this pop concert, such uses of digital cameras and camera phones can be interpreted as forming a further part of personal image-making. Posting this type of content reflects on the user's online identity and bears future imagined audiences' approval in mind.

The rise in digital cultures of narcissism and 'public privacy', in Marshall's terms, has also meant that mechanisms for protecting the relative 'privacy' of data are called for:

Users are generally happy for certain types of personal data to be published as long as their privacy is protected – and it is seen to be protected. When the Facebook social network redesigned its service so that it was easier to track when other people had posted new journals or photos, users rebelled, claiming that it made it too easy to indulge in stalker behaviour.

(Jennings 2007: 192)

Although nomadic communications and mobile image-captures may be 'brought back' to Facebook profiles, users seem to favour the notion that not each and every of their online additions should be trackable, in general and in principle, by a mass, unknown audience. Privacy levels can be modified by Facebook users, and restricted to 'friends', but the importance of the Profile photo is that this will show up as visible to unknown others. As such, the cultural circulation of the Profile pic cannot be hemmed in or dictated by the self, and it hence functions as the lingua franca, or the perfectly exchangeable self-as-commodity, of Facebook.

The articulation of nomadic/mobile communications media with cultural constructions and expressions of self-identity has also been testified to in Ingrid Richardson's work on 'pocket technospaces'. Richardson argues that mobile telephones have become powerful symbolic bearers of the self, especially by acting as storage spaces for what is felt to be intensely personal data:

> We both desire and know the impossibility of achieving a neat, compact, and foldable being-in-the-world. Yet this 'as-if' sense of containment is a common experience of mobile phone users; interviewees in my study frequently referred to their phones as microcosms of their lives, far exceeding the containment capacities of wallets and handbags.

> (Richardson 2007: 213)

iPods may also act in this way, of course, furnishing the user with an aesthetic and informational sense of a 'neat ... compact' being-in-the-world which folds together considerable amounts of data, if not whole music collections and assorted photos and videos (see Chapter 6). Perhaps the leading cultural impact and presence of mobile digital media has, which I have suggested here, been their ability to become 'microcosms' of, and mirrors for, presentations of self-identity. Whether it is the Facebook Profile picture, or captured images/footage of leisure events such as high-profile rock concerts, or iPod music libraries, varieties of mobile digital media have not simply acted as additions to prior cultural practices and discourses. Rather, in a range of ways digital mobility appears to be presaging and supporting broader shifts in cultural activity, partly away from the consumption of media representations and partly towards the conceptualization of the self as a presentational image directed at imagined others, as well as a symbolic entity 'contained' and carried in personal digital devices.

8 The digital divide: scarcity, inequality and conflict

Last Moyo

The development and spread of digital media across the world has culminated in the centrality of these media in the social, political and economic activities of people and organizations in many countries, especially in the developed world (see Dutton 2003; Hamelink 2003; Slevin 2000; Hacker and van Dijk 2000). For example, in most developed countries, computers and mobile phones are increasingly becoming indispensable to how people communicate, vote, buy, trade, learn, date, work or even play (see Dalessio 2007; Haldane 2007; Webster 1997, 2004). Information technology enthusiasts argue that this means that such countries are living in the age of the information society, which they define as a post-industrial society (see Chapter 1), where information service industries and the new information and communication technologies (ICTs) are at the helm of the socio-economic and political processes of societies (see Bell [1973] 2004).

In principle, the openness and accessibility of the Internet is perhaps reflected by the ever rising popularity of the medium. For example, according to the Internet World Statistics website, which gets its figures from organizations such as the International Telecommunications Union (ITU) and Nielsen/Net ratings, in September 2007, there were approximately 1.2 billion Internet users in the world (about 18.9 per cent of the world population) and the growth rate between 2000 and 2007 was about 245 per cent (see Internet World Statistics 2007). However, critics like Robert Hassan argue that although there is a significant minority of people in the world that may be using New Media, the growth of the so-called information society is undermined by the fact that the benefits of the digital media and the Internet are 'not flowing evenly and smoothly ... within countries or across the world' (Hassan 2004: 165). For example, while countries such as North America account for about 20 per cent of the world's Internet users, continents like Africa represent only 3 per cent of the 1.2 billion users (see Internet World Statistics 2007). This disproportionate distribution of Internet access across the world and within countries has generally been referred to as the 'digital divide' (see Norris 2001; Hamelink 2003; Haywood 1998; Holderness 1998). According to Pippa Norris, the phrase has gained currency particularly in reference to the Internet users and has become 'shorthand for any and every disparity within the online community' (Norris 2001: 4).

What is the digital divide?

Academics have generally defined the digital divide as being primarily about the gap that exists between people who have access to the digital media and the Internet and those who do not have any access (see Norris 2001; Meredyth et al. 2003; Servon 2002; Holderness 1998; Haywood 1998). The disparities in the ownership and access to these media can potentially affect the access to information from the Internet by the disadvantaged communities and also create or reinforce the socio-economic inequalities based on the digital marginalization of the poorer classes and regions of the world. For example, in 1999 Thailand had more cellular phones than the whole of Africa while the USA had more computers than the rest of the world combined (see UNDP 1999: 75). Similarly, around the same period, the industrial countries (which have less than 15 per cent of the people in the world) had 88 per cent of Internet users. North America alone (with less than 5 per cent of the people) had more than 50 per cent of all users (HDP 2003: 75). As such, the imbalance or disparities of the diffusion of the digital media and the Internet between the information-rich and the information-poor all over the world has generally been used as the main defining criterion of the digital divide where universal access to New Media is seen as part of the solution to the development and democratization challenges that face many communities across the world (see Chapter 9).

However, some scholars believe that the question of the digital divide is multidimensional and more complex than just the question of access to the digital media and the Internet by various people, countries and regions (see Hassan 2004; Norris 2001; Servon 2002). They contend that defining the divide merely on the basis of access to computers and the Internet is actually simplistic and undermines not only the seriousness of the problem, but also the potential solutions to the problem in terms of public policies. As Lisa Servon argues, the digital divide 'has been defined as a problem of access in the narrow sense of possession or permission to use a computer and the Internet' (Servon 2002: 4). She argues that ownership and access do not necessarily amount to use in all cases because some people who have access may not be skilled users of the Internet or in cases where they have the skills, they may not find relevant content online to become consistent users. While physical access to the computers and the Internet is certainly one of the key variables for defining the digital divide, there is a need to broaden the concept by looking at how other factors such as literacy, technological literacy, content, language, network and the costs that are associated with Internet access, help in the understanding of the digital divide.

Technological literacy is mainly about the skills and the ability of the individuals and communities to use the digital technologies and the Internet effectively to address their socio-economic and political needs. For example, the lack of hardware and software operational skills can act as a barrier not only to using the Internet, but also in content production, hence creating the digital divide even among those with access. However, technological literacy is seen by some critics as being just one of the many types of literacies that are needed for the effective use of the digital media and the Internet (see Carvin 2000; Damarin 2000). Andy Carvin, for example, argues that basic literacy (the ability to read and write), informational literacy (the ability to comprehend the quality content), adaptive literacy (the ability to develop new digital media and Internet usage skills) are all important parts in understanding the complex nature of the digital divide. In other words, without basic literacy people cannot read or produce online content while failure to understand the quality of information on the Internet may also keep many potential users away from the medium. Adaptive literacy implies that Internet users must consistently develop usage skills that will help them to cope with new technological demands in software and hardware.

Content barriers of the divide are about the lack of participation by certain groups of people in the production of online content and the failure by those content producers to address the specific informational needs of certain types or groups of users. Servon argues that the marginalization of content that addresses the needs of the poorer people comprises another dimension of the digital divide because 'when disadvantaged groups log on, they often find that there is no content there ... [because] ... information that is directly related to their lives and communities and cultures does not exist' (Servon 2002: 9). She also observes that this is primarily because 'the content ... hardware, software, and the Internet reflects the culture [and] tastes of those who create the products and the early users – largely middle and upper class white men' (ibid.: 10, see also UNDP 1999). In support of a needs-oriented understanding of the divide, Meredyth, Ewing and Thomas also argue that the debate about the digital divide is no longer necessarily about universalizing access to computers, but about how and why people use new technologies and the Internet (Meredyth et al. 2003). They argue that appropriate content can attract marginalized groups and communities to the Internet.

Another point that is closely related to the sensitivity to the usage needs of content is that of language. Language can act as a barrier to people with access and literacy skills and hence exacerbate the digital inequalities between those who understand the most dominant Internet languages such as English and those who do not. For example, another United Nations and Social Council (2003) Report titled, the *Role of ICT in Bridging the Digital Divide in Selected Areas* argues that while access to computers and the Internet has become extremely high in the Asian and Pacific region, the hindrance to the effective and consistent use of the Internet is the marginalization of the region's local languages. It posits that, while there are over 4,000 languages in the region, 68 per cent of the websites are in English which most people do not understand. This suggests that there is no one single digital divide, but that there are many types of divide based on various factors (see Norris 2001; Meredyth et al. 2003). Pippa Norris's typology of the various types of the digital divide such as the geographic divide, social divide and democratic divide may perhaps provide a framework in which the intricate connections of access, literacy, content, language, gender, race and age in the digital age can be examined in detail (see Norris 2001: 3–25).

The geographic divide

The geographic divide is mainly about access or lack of access to the digital media and the Internet because of geographic location. As Norris argues, the availability of digital opportunities and the subsequent inclusion or exclusion from the information society can be influenced by where an individual lives in terms of their proximity and access to the digital information networks (Norris 2001: 23). The geographic divide is multidimensional and can refer to national, regional and global disparities in levels of access to the digital media and the Internet. Whereas the national and regional divides focus on Internet access levels in different localities or regions within a country, the global divide is about disparities in access between people living in the highly developed economies of the north and those living in the less developed economies of the south.

Trevor Haywood argues that the global divide is developing within the context of old inequalities as access to computer networks is seemingly 'laid over the same old patterns of geographic and economic inequality ...' (Haywood 1998: 22), thus replicating real-life inequalities in a digital form. In other words, the global divide seems to follow the contours of the historical economic imbalances between the countries of the north and those of the south due to many reasons such as the colonial legacy of underdevelopment, the failure of post independence free market reforms and the current unfair trade policies that benefit the developed countries at the expense of the developing poor nations. Poverty is one of the major problems that is exacerbating the global digital exclusion between regions. For example, '1 in every 5 people in the developing world lives on less than US$1 per day and 1 in 7 suffers from chronic hunger' (Accenture et al. 2001: 7). Again, according to John Baylis, Steve Smith and Patricia Owens:

> [O]ne fifth of the world's population are living in extreme poverty ... , one third of the world's children are undernourished ... , half the world's population lacks regular access to essential drugs ... , more than 30,000 children die a day from easily preventable diseases.

> (Baylis et al. 2001: 202)

Such acute levels of poverty and deprivation have tended to force most of the countries of the Third World to prioritize development in the areas of public health, housing, provision of clean water and education, instead of developing the telecommunications infrastructure to ensure the inclusion of their citizens in the so-called information age. The focus on such basic social needs invariably means that the telecommunications networks which are so indispensable for Internet connectivity are still relatively poor in most of the countries in the south compared to those in the north, mainly because access to information is one among an endless list of social needs. The disparities in telecommunications also inevitably affect the level of digital opportunities that can be available to the people living in a particular region of the world because the Internet relies on telephone networks. The following examples demonstrate some of the disparities that aggravate the global divide which are caused by infrastructural problems:

- More than 80% of the people in the world have never heard a dial tone, let alone 'surfed' the web or used a mobile phone (UNDP 1999: 78).
- Africa, which has about 739 million people, has only 14 million telephone lines, which is far less than lines in Manhattan or Tokyo (Panos 2004: 4).

- Sub-Saharan Africa has about 10 percent of the world's population (626 million), but has only 0.2 percent of the world's one billion telephone lines (ibid.: 4).
- The cost of renting a connection averages almost 20 percent of per capita GDP in Africa compared to nine percent for the world, and only one percent for the high income countries (ibid.: 4).

Clearly, the poorer telecommunications infrastructure in Africa and other developing nations has serious ramifications on the digital divide. For example, while the Internet is generally perceived as creating opportunities for cheap, reliable and instantaneous communication in the north, the poorer telecommunications infra-structure in some countries in the south means that Internet access may be limited to very few people while the majority of the people find it unaffordable because of the prohibitive connection and service charges that are worsened by lack of economic opportunities. In essence, the 'digital divide is but an indicator of the deeper economic malaise of poverty and economic exclusion (Hassan 2004: 68) and it 'cannot be reversed without tackling the plurality of factors that leads to inequality ... [because] ... access to ICTs should be embedded in a more general perspective on inclusion, development and poverty reduction' (Servaes and Carpentier 2006: 2).

Given the serious global economic imbalances, the digital media are most likely to further entrench the global digital divide and continue the creation of a global information class structure of the information-rich global north and information-poor global south (see Norris 2001; Hassan 2004). In the words of Norris, the former class being ' ... one for those with income, education ... connections giving plentiful information at low cost and high speed' while the latter being 'for those without connections, blocked by the barrier of time, cost, uncertainty and dependent upon outdated information' (Norris 2001: 5–6). In addition to infrastructural barriers, socio-cultural factors such as language, class, gender and education further compound the north–south divide because they influence the numbers of people with potential to consistently use or not use computers and the Internet. For example, regarding the gender factor, European countries are generally perceived to be relatively affluent and liberal, and this means that women in those countries are more likely to have a computer and to be connected to the Internet compared to their Asian and African counterparts. Consequently, the global divide must also be seen and understood through the prism of the local or internal factors that affect the social structure of the information society in terms of participation of people. Language has also increased the global gap between information 'haves' and 'have-nots' because, while only less than 1 in 10 people speaks English, 80 per cent of the websites and the computer and Internet user interfaces are in English (see UNDP 1999: 78).

However, it is imperative to note that although the north–south divide is very pronounced, there are still differences in the levels of access and effective usage of the digital media and the Internet between countries of each region. For example, of the estimated 322 million Internet users in Europe, the UK represents about 12 per cent, Russia (9 per cent), Poland (4 per cent) and Romania (1.5 per cent) (see Internet World Statistics) 2007. These variations may be influenced by socio-cultural differences including national economic performance and national telecommunications policies which may have an impact on the availability and affordability of computers and Internet services to the end-users. The digital exclusion experiences in Africa are also not uniform and homogenous. For instance, there is an interesting example of Benin where more than 60 per cent of the population were illiterate in the late 1990s; hence, there were only a mere 2,000 Internet users in the country at the time (see UNDP 1999: 78). Again, by 2007, most of the Internet users in Africa were generally from South Africa (6 million), Nigeria (8 million), Morrocco (6 million) and Egypt (6 million).

Social divide

The social divide is about differences in access between various social groups due to socio-demographic barriers such as class, income, education, gender, age and race. For example, class is one of the major determinants of digital inclusion or exclusion. Mike Holderness argues that 'it remains the case that the sharpest, most clearly enumerable divides in cyber space are those based on where one lives and how much money one has' (Holderness 1998: 37). In most cases, affluent people tend to live in places with good telecommunications infrastructure with broadband and wireless networks, whereas poorer people who live in ghettos are less likely to have good sanitation, let alone a good telecommunications network (see Hoffman et al. 2000; Ebo 1998). The general trend in both the developed and developing countries is that the richer classes are the first to own and use these cutting-edge media technologies while the poorer people only get them as a result of the 'trickle-down' effect when prices of computers and Internet connection become affordable. Again, the Internet itself is capital-intensive and subsequently most poor people are kept in its fringes because computers, modems, software and Internet Service Providers' monthly subscriptions may not be affordable to them.

For example, according to British Telecommunications (BT), 'of the 9.5 million adults living on low incomes in the UK, 7 million (74%) are digitally excluded' (British Telecom Report 2004). In Africa, where a large majority of the people are poor, Mike Jensen argues that by 2002, 1 in 35 people had a mobile phone (24 million), 1 in 130 had a personal computer (5.9 million), and 1 in 160 had used the Internet (5 million) (Jensen 2002: 24). As a result, Norris observes that, as far as the income divide is concerned, popular access to computers and the Internet requires the elimination of the financial barriers which aggravate the physical access divide which, in turn, has a multiplication effect on other types of divide such as gender, race and literacy (see Norris 2001). However, it must be noted that there is a significant number of people who have higher incomes but are digitally disengaged due to other impediments such as age, technological literacy, technological phobia and the lack of motivation. Similarly, lower income does not always result in digital exclusion because in many cities in Asia, Africa and India poor communities may not have access to the Internet in their homes, but can develop consistent use of it in public libraries, cyber cafés, rural Internet centres and other public access points. In research I conducted between 2003 and 2007 in Zimbabwe, I discovered that there was a developing trend of consistent email use in cyber cafés by the poor urban factory workers and unemployed women to communicate with their exiled relatives now living in the UK, Australia, America and New Zealand (see Moyo 2007).

Education is also one of the elements of the class divide. Most of the digitally excluded people are more likely to be less educated and be less well paid in their jobs, although this does not necessarily mean that they do not use the Internet. For example, the United Nations World Food Programme (UNWFP) has an innovative seasonal online fund-raising campaign in Africa that connects the poor, less educated small-scale farmers in rural areas to sell part of their cash crops online (UNWFP 2007). Similarly, one can also find that educated old people may frequently use the Internet more than the young uneducated and unemployed youths in the urban areas of the developed and developing world. However, as Suzanne Damarin argues, the general trend is that education or lack of it further amplifies the gap between those who can use the Internet and those who cannot because the probability of using the Internet always increases with one's level of education due to the mainstreaming of new ICTs in education (see Damarin 2000: 17).

Other variables such as gender, race and ethnicity further complicate the social divide because, as Servon argues, social discrimination has led to the exclusion of meaningful participation of women and black people even in countries such as the USA (see Servon 2002). She argues that in the USA, 'schools in low-income areas that overwhelmingly house children of colour are much less likely to provide quality access, training, and content than are schools in wealthier districts [where white people live]' (ibid. 2002: 10). In terms of gender, women appear to be marginalized due to the domination of patriarchal interests in most societies since the use of digital media and the Internet is subject to social shaping (see Preston 2001; Slevin 2000; Scott 2005). For example, 'women accounted for 38% of users in the United States, 25% in Brazil, 17% in Japan and South Africa, 16% in Russia, 7% in China and a mere 4% in the Arab states' (UNDP 1999: 62). The report also notes that, even in the USA, the typical Internet user is a young white male because usage patterns are invariably embedded in socio-cultural values that predispose men to technology than women.

Democratic divide

The democratic divide refers to the fact that there are people who can use the digital media and the Internet as tools and resources for participation in political activism and those who cannot. It is about 'those who do, and do not use the panoply of digital resources to engage, mobilize and participate in public life' (Norris 2001: 4). In essence, the democratic divide is closely interwoven with the notion of citizenship where citizens (as opposed to subjects of a monarchy) are seen as constantly reviewing their social and political contract with the state against abuse. This divide is therefore about people who can and cannot use the Internet's plethora of resources and facilities such as information and news in websites, blogs, podcasts and other interactive forums such as discussion forums, email and voiceovers for civic engagement.

Participation in cyber activism ranges from the individual to the institutional where people organize themselves into civic groups to defend certain interests. As an institution, civil society has been variously referred to as 'a sphere of public life beyond control of the state' (Colas 2002: 25), the 'bulwark against the state' (Keane 2002: 17), or 'the infrastructure that is needed for the spread of democracy and development' (Anheir et al. 2001: 3). The Internet has been central in civic engagement processes at national and global levels (see Chapter 8). Interesting examples of civil organizations that fight to hold their governments accountable to citizens using the Internet include, the *US Human Rights Network* (USA), *Muslim Council of Britain* (UK), *Australian Council of Women and Policing* (Australia) and *Kubatana Civic Network* (Zimbabwe). At a global level, civil society has also used the Internet to network and mobilize its members against certain inter-state decisions that determine global policy which affect people's lives at national levels (see Naughton 2001; Aronson 2001). For example, organizations such as *Amnesty International*, *Green Peace* and the *International Forum on Globalisation* extensively use the Internet as part of their cyberactivism and civic engagement on issues like human rights, environment and unfair globalization practices. The *Battle for Seattle* protests against the WTO in 1999 and the anti-Iraqi war cyber solidarity movements in the post-September 11 (9/11) are some of the interesting examples of civic resistance where the Internet played a larger part in mobilizing people to resist state and inter-state decisions.

The democratic divide is also affected by other divides such as such as literacy/illiteracy, urban/rural, men/women and the young versus old. Regarding literacy; on the one hand of the divide there are cyber activists who may have physical access to computers and the informational literacy to decode political messages, while on the other hand there may be those who either have access but have no skills or those without both. The democratic divide is therefore complex because it does not merely end with access or lack of it, but also emphasizes media literacy which, according to James Potter, is not merely about active engagement with media messages at cognitive and affective levels, but also involves computer literacy and visual literacy especially as media and media texts continue to converge on the Internet in ways that demand reader and user sophistication (Potter 2001: 4–14). The news media and civic organizations are still in the process of learning how to exploit the full potential of the Internet as a multimodal medium. Digital advocacy can therefore be viewed as a process that remains in transitions as individuals and 'organisations are still learning how to use the potential of the Web to do more than just act as a static form of electronic pamphlet or poster' (Norris 2001: 190). In addition, Roger Fiddler posits that, due to lack of sophistication by users 'personal computers ... are still used by most people as little more than electronic typewriters' and that 'even with new user-friendly software and the addition of a mouse, personal computers remain decidedly unfriendly' (Fiddler 1994: 32).

Similarly, the sophistication of users may vary according to class, race, age, and the rural and urban divide and this has ramifications on the democratic divide.

Conclusion

The new ICTs and the Internet appear to play a very significant role in people's lives by providing huge amounts of information that helps citizens to make informed choices not only in politics and business, but also in the simple challenges that they face in their daily lives such as shopping or choosing the best school or university for their children. The various digital divides discussed in this chapter epitomize a serious problem of information poverty that affects billions of people in the age of the so-called information society where, as many international human rights instruments state, information is supposed to be a human right (see Article 19, UN Declaration (1948); Article 19, International Covenant on Civil and Political Rights (1966); Article 9, African Charter (1981)). This is partly because the information society discourse is market-driven and also embedded within the neo-liberal globalization process which prioritizes the interests of the global corporate forces over those of billions of poor people without access to the Internet (see Preston 2001). While information and communication are legally perceived as human rights, the big communication industries are not attracted to investing in poor countries and communities because they do not make any profits because these marginalized groups tend to prioritize other social needs instead of information.

However, according to the former UN Secretary General, Kofi Annan, the struggle for food, shelter and clothing is by no means separate from that for information. In 1999 he stated that, 'People lack many things: jobs, shelter, and food, health care and drinkable water. Today, being cut off from basic telecoms services is a hardship almost as acute as these other deprivations and may indeed reduce the chances of finding remedies to them' (Annan 1999: 6). The problem of the digital divide must not be left to the market forces alone if the inclusion or participation of marginalized people in the information society and globalization processes is to be realized. Solutions to the problems of access, infrastructure, content, technological literacy and various forms of discrimination must take a multi-stakeholder approach in terms of the crafting of policy responses and the implementation of agreed strategies. Otherwise, it can be argued that in weak and ailing economies, the full potential of the Internet may never be realized as it tends ' ... to connect the connected more than the peripheral' (Norris 2001: 95).

Recommended reading

Castells, Manuel (1999) *The Information Age: Economy, Society and Culture*. London: Blackwell Publishers.

Hassan, Robert (2004) *Media, Politics and the Network Society*. Milton Keynes: Open University Press.

Norris, Pippa (2001) *Digital Divide: Civic Engagement, Information Poverty, and the Internet Worldwide*. Cambridge, USA: Cambridge University Press.

Servon, Lisa (2002) *Redefining the Digital Divide: Technology, Community and Public Policy*. Malden, MA: Blackwell Publishers.

Wyatt, Sally et al. (eds) (2000) *Technology and In/Equality: Questioning the Information Society*. London: Routledge.

Case Study: Virtual war

Sebastian Kaempf

In the 1990s, discussions of the so-called 'CNN factor' (the political effects resulting from emergence of uninterrupted, real-time global television coverage) following Western interventions in Iraq and Somalia examined some of the important issues raised by media representation and security. Yet, by the twenty-frist century, the emergence of New Media technology has fundamentally started to transform not only the means through which contemporary war is being waged but also war's visual representation. Contemporary war has a new front line, one where war is no longer fought physically but virtually and where the actors involved have replaced bombs and bullets with weapons in the form of bites and bandwidths.

This case study investigates these changes and assesses the ethical implications for the 'War on Terror'. A particular emphasis is placed on the growing use of digital images and videos as strategic weapons in the context of the post-9/11 conflicts between the US military and its adversaries in Afghanistan and Iraq. Such an examination is discussed in the context of prevailing military conditions of asymmetry as the latter not only impact on the ways in which the US military and its adversaries in Afghanistan and Iraq have waged a virtual war of images (disseminated through blogs, YouTube, mobile phones and websites), but also how these digital images have been interpreted by their target audiences.

Waging war in the New Media age

To grasp the current changes in the visual representation of war waged in the New Media age – which in themselves have largely arisen in reaction to the 'perception management' campaigns run by the Pentagon – we first need to understand the two central characteristics ascribed to US warfare in the post-Cold War world. First, the acquisition of new military technology and the restructuring of US forces through technological innovations brought about by the so-called 'Revolution of Military Affairs' (RMA) allow the US military to wage net-centric wars that have created conditions of asymmetry wherever the USA intervened (Smith 2002: 355–74; Bacevich 1996: 37–48). Since the collapse of the Soviet Union, the US armed forces have possessed military capabilities far in excess of those of any would-be adversary or even a combination of the latter (Bacevich 2005: 16). Second, the global military predominance that resulted from these technological innovations has allowed the USA to conduct wars in ways that have become increasingly riskless to US military personnel *and* to civilians in target states. At the heart of this 'postmodern' (see Chapter 1) US warfare lies the capacity to apply force without suffering the risk of reciprocal injury (Kahn 2002: 7). Waging riskless wars, James Der Derian writes, 'Is the technical capacity and ethical imperative to threaten, and, if necessary, actualise violence from a distance – *with no or minimum casualties*' (Der Derian 2002: xiv–xv).

Yet, besides reducing the risks of combat to US military service personnel, the increased involvement of military lawyers in the target and weapons' selection process has contributed significantly to US operations falling in line with the principle of non-combatant immunity (Kennedy 2006; Farrell 2005: 137; Ignatieff 2000: 197). This has permitted the USA to also limit civilian deaths during contemporary conflicts for it possesses a historically 'unprecedented capability to create discriminate destruction' (Farrell 2005: 179).

Most importantly, however, these technological innovations went hand in hand with the attempt to gain control over the media representation of the wars in which the US armed forces became involved. This trend towards 'embedded journalism' (an embedded journalist is a news reporter who is attached to a military unit involved in an armed conflict) originated as a consequence of the disastrous Vietnam War, where US decision-makers experienced the power of the media to shape the (negative) perception and the outcome of a war (Herring 1986; Isaacs 1997). The subsequent quest to regain the ability to control the representation and thereby shape the perception of US wars among the US public (and a wider Western audience) temporarily culminated in the 1991 Gulf War and the Kosovo bombing campaign in 1999. The controversial phenomenon of 'embedded journalism' therefore needs to be understood as a response to the recognition in the Pentagon and the White House that contemporary wars are principally media wars, that is, spectacles that not only take place on a battlefield under the observing eyes of journalists but also that these wars are generally won by the warring faction which succeeds in using (and thereby manipulating) the media entertainment networks as part of its military strategy (Münkler 2006: 72–6). This does not mean that the media has necessarily lost its political independence but that the information it can publish and the images it can use are generally controlled by the Pentagon's 'perception management' campaigns. Perception management is a term originated by the US military. The US Department of Defense (DOD) gives this definition:

> perception management – Actions to convey and/or deny selected information and indicators to foreign audiences to influence their emotions, motives, and objective reasoning as well as to intelligence systems and leaders at all levels to influence official estimates, ultimately resulting in foreign behaviors and official actions favorable to the originator's objectives. In various ways, perception management combines truth projection, operations security, cover and deception, and psychological operations.

> (Department of Defense 2001: 411)

Over time, US efforts at 'perception management' have become more sophisticated and central to the conduct of war. Especially since 9/11, the Pentagon has been more aggressive in attempting to manage the media, control the flow of information, and shape the coverage of US operations abroad. The Bush administration has set up multiple information management centres, so-called 'war rooms' with the aim of co-ordinating media messages and dominating the news cycles during 'Operation Enduring Freedom' and 'Iraqi Freedom'.

This control of the print media and television channels has been central not only to creating but also sustaining the popular notions of 'costless wars', an imagination underwritten by the repeated replay of 'bomb's eye views' transmitted from precision-guided missiles (PGM) as they descend to their predetermined targets. Carefully selected images conveyed by US operations suggest a 'grammar of killing' that avoids the spilling of blood. They present US operations as precise, discriminate and clean. At the same time, the now taken-for-granted capabilities of 'smart bombs' and associated military marvels have been effectively marshalled in support of a rhetoric of meaningful discriminacy between combatants and non-combatants that has at times even averred to infallibility (Beier 2007). In other words, this ability to frame the perception of US operations as humane and surgical has been essential to creating and sustaining the legitimacy of US warfare in the eyes of the public (Der Derian 2002: 9–17; Owens 2003: 595–616).

Thus, the reality of the postmodern battlefield as seen by the US public is principally mediated through media technology (Virilio 2002). Postmodern war has largely become electronic with the actual war being waged not over real territories but virtual maps and geographies generated by computer simulations and data supplied by satellites (Gray 1997). For Der Derian, the Gulf War in 1991 constituted the beginning of 'virtual cleansing', a process of the sanitization of violence that has aimed at overpowering the mortification of the human body (Der Derian 2002: 120). By enlisting US soldiers and the US public in virtual and virtuous ways, this newly evolving media-infotainment warfare has not only altered the physical experience of conflict through the means of technology but has also sought to evade the fact that the US way of waging war is still about killing others (Der Derian 2002: xvi–xvii; Virilio 2002).

US warfare has achieved lethal perfection with a degree of impunity that is historically unprecedented. In other words, it has created conditions of asymmetry that allow the USA to increasingly wage virtual wars that expose (US) citizens to an instantaneous reality of war that is propagated to be sanitized of sacrifice and the spilling of (innocent) blood. Waged increasingly by computer technicians and high-altitude specialists, it is becoming increasingly abstract, distanced, and virtual. This phenomenon of 'virtual cleansing' was noted by Michael Ignatieff during the Kosovo air campaign:

> War thus becomes virtual, not simply because it appears to take place on a screen but because it enlists societies only in virtual ways ... These conditions transform war into something like a spectator sport. As with sport, nothing ultimate is at stake: neither national survival, nor the fate of the economy. War affords the pleasure of a spectacle, with the added thrill that it is real for someone, but not, happily, for the spectator.
>
> (Ignatieff 2000: 191)

This means that new networked computer systems, simulations and precision-guided weapons systems have created a real-time virtual reality of war that no longer requires personal sacrifice while mobilizing US citizens to experience war as some form of not-quite-real 'spectator sport' (McInnes 2002; Mann 1988).

War today is increasingly being waged in the fourth sector, conducted not only by the dispatch of Tomahawks in the air or Kalashnikovs and suicide attacks on the ground, but also by means of bytes, bandwidths, digital images and computer simulations. With the emergence of New Media technology, however, the sanitized images of US warfare created by smart weapons technology, 'embedded journalism', and the Pentagon's 'perception management' have been fundamentally challenged. And while broadcasting used to be an expensive affair, all that is needed today is a computer, a small camera, a little bit of software and an Internet connection to get a message across a large audience. New Media technology in that sense provides a cheap and user-friendly means to produce competing virtual realities and create rival narratives in order to influence the perception of a certain conflict. As a result, the most critical battles in the 'War on Terror' have not been fought in the mountains of Afghanistan or the streets of Baghdad, but in the newsrooms in places like New York, Atlanta, Cairo or Doha and – most importantly – in various Internet forums, through YouTube, in chatrooms and blogs (Bumford 2005). Most of these (new) media outlets are removed from the tight control of the Pentagon's public relations (PR) specialists and thereby offer platforms through which the uninterrogated virtual reality offered by US operations can be put into question. These outlets have enabled US adversaries to reconceptualize public media as a battle space and to employ public relations as a weapon (Ignatieff 2004a).

It has taken US decision-makers a long time to grasp the significance of what the evolution of New Media technology meant for the nature of war. In February 2006, Donald Rumsfeld, the US Secretary of Defense, conceded that:

> Today, we are engaged in the first war in history – unconventional and irregular as it may be – in an era of emails, blogs, cell phones, Blackberries, instant messaging, digital cameras, a global Internet with no inhibitions, hand-held video cameras, talk radio, 24-hour news broadcasts, satellite television. There's never been a war fought in this environment before.
>
> (Rumsfeld 2006)

In other words, the USA, for the first time in its history, is waging war in an age in which the means through which the visual representation of conflict is produced and disseminated are undergoing revolutionary changes.

But while the US military has principally been slow to realize the significance of New Media technology as a powerful propaganda tool – according to Rumsfeld, 'the US government still functions like a five and dime store in an eBay world' (Rumsfeld 2006) – al-Qaeda has been much quicker and more skilful in adapting to fighting wars in today's New Media age. From of the beginning, al-Qaeda has seen the New Media message as integral to its campaign. For instance, Ayman al-Zawahiri, Osama Bin Laden's chief lieutenant, recognized that, '[M]ore than half of this battle [against the

United States] is taking place in the battlefield of the media. We are in a media battle in a race for the hearts and minds of Muslims' (Lewis 2001).

This key statement shows that al-Qaeda is pursuing a deliberate strategy, not with bullets but with words and images. And based on the evidence of al-Qaeda's fight against the 'infidels' in Afghanistan and Iraq, Bin Laden's network has discovered New Media technology as a powerful strategic means to disseminate propaganda and influence public opinion. For example, between the events of 9/11 and the end of 2006, al-Qaeda has released over 50 video messages, most of which were 'aired' through the Internet (Hegghammer 2006a). This employment of New Media technology by al-Qaeda marks the emergence of the terrorist as a film director. The group, which runs a professional PR committee, goes at great length to film all its operations which, through the Internet, can go directly to its target audience without going through a filter such as CNN or the BBC. So, in many ways, the purpose of using extreme violence is to create a media event. In marketing terms, these visual messages serve as recruitment posters for the insurgencies in Afghanistan and Iraq as well as powerful symbols of defiance against the world's biggest military force.

In a sense, it is the strategy of the disadvantaged military actor who creatively employs a new information outlet that not only bypasses US 'perception management' but also evades US military power in order to win against the 'infidels' politically (Anon 2004; Bergen 2002: 1–23). In other words, it is classical guerrilla strategy adjusted to the age of New Media technology: to seek out the enemy's weak and unprotected flank while avoiding the latter's military strength. Prevailing conditions of military asymmetry have compelled Bin Laden's terrorist network to adjust by exploiting the restraint in contemporary US warfare; that is, the need for the US military (to appear) to accomplish both high levels of casualty-aversion and civilian protection in order to be legitimate in the eyes of the US people. Al-Qaeda's asymmetric strategies therefore aimed at delegitimizing US operations by challenging the visual representation of US warfare as clean, humane and surgical. With the evolution of New Media technologies, the US ability to condition the representation of the battlefield is gone. The media control and exclusivity that General Norman Schwarzkopf possessed during the early 1990s and from which NATO still benefited during the Kosovo campaign is broken (Münkler 2006: 72–6). New Media technology has become a means of visual resistance.

This raises the much wider question as to whether virtual war has ever been as humane, clean and bloodless as suggested. Previously, the Pentagon could portray virtual war as bloodless because it owned the airwaves and made all the editorial decisions as to what got shown on the news. In this context, the question of whether virtual war was clean was one that we could never really answer: all we could say was that it appeared so, based on the coverage we had seen on the news. But things have changed, and the advent of 'pirate' technologies has given rise to the growing view that in reality virtual war is not actually clean. In that sense, the emergence of New Media technology has an effect similar to the opening of a new archive which – bit by bit – delegitimizes previously generated assumptions.

In the context of the 'War on Terror', US adversaries pursue the delegitimization of the US war machine by actively dehumanizing warfare. In Afghanistan and Iraq al-Qaeda cells have systematically used human shields, located their operational headquarters in Mosques, targeted international aid workers, and deliberately blurred the distinctions between combatants and non-combatants (Cordesman 2002: 23, 35; Human Rights Watch 2002: 40–4). While some of these strategies are not entirely new, New Media technologies have provided insurgents/terrorists with a qualitatively new way of waging war. They not only provide al-Qaeda with an asymmetrical means to break out of the military inferiority on today's battlefields and to directly strike at a Western 'spectator-sport' audience, but also a means to delegitimize the Pentagon's carefully crafted image of bloodless wars.

This is done in two ways. First, by revealing (and, in the process, often exaggerating) the actual violence wrought by US war-fighting tactics and thereby exposing US images as propagandistic representations of warfare. Here, al-Qaeda has countered the live footage of 'smart missiles' hitting their military targets in central Kabul with Internet video footage showing the civilian cost of war on the ground. It has used the Internet and instrumentalized traditional media outlets such as al-Jazeera to claim that over 7,000 Afghan civilians were killed during the US bombing campaign (while the most reliable figures range between 1,000 and 1,300 civilian casualties) (Conetta 2002a; Herold 2002; Todenhofer 2002; Bearak 2002).

Al-Zarqawi's terrorist networks in Iraq have been quick to understand that New Media devices have the power to frame a single US atrocity and turn it into an image that can sap the legitimacy of a military operation among Western and Arab publics. The underlying assumption is that the willingness of the US public to commit atrocities in its defence is limited by moral repugnance. In other words, by deliberately employing the Internet, blogs and digital video footage, al-Qaeda has been able to shape a counter-reality to the one produced by and, until recently, exclusively conditioned by the US war machine. While the latter has tried to make the victims of war disappear (Conetta 2002b), the former has placed death fully back at the centre of its New Media strategy.

Second, al-Qaeda, the Taliban and Iraqi insurgents/terrorist actively dehumanized warfare by producing digital images and Internet videos that celebrate the shedding of blood at the time when the US representation of war suggests a grammar of killing that is bloodless and surgical. The best examples can be found in the public beheading videos that dominated al-Qaeda's PR campaign between 2001 and 2004. These videos announce that al-Qaeda sets its standards in barbarity and that no one, not even women, are regarded as innocent. One of the most prominent victims was Margaret Hassam, the country director of CARE International. Her innocence (having lived as a social worker in Iraq for over three decades and being married to an Iraqi) was precisely the point of her kidnapping and ritualized decapitation. The purpose of the beheading video was not to kill the hostage (an act which could have been accomplished much more cleanly with a bullet in the back of the head). Instead, the purpose has been to create an event to be videoed, designed as a virtual bomb to target the US hope that it was possible for foreigners to do good deeds in Iraq. Images such as these are designed to erode the political will of the US public to continue its military commitment in Iraq. Al-Qaeda understands that broadcasting ritual slaughter can have devastating effects: following the footage of similar killings of soldiers and relief workers from Spain and the Philippines, both countries – responding to the public outcry at home – immediately withdrew their entire military forces from Iraq.

At a time when the legitimacy of US warfare is sustained through a visual representation that literally denies the fact that war is still about killing others, public beheading videos have been used by al-Qaeda as a strategic weapon designed to shock, frustrate and frighten a spectator sport warfare audience. These are not casual acts of sadism but a calculated attempt to provoke in order to draw the USA and its allies into acts of revenge. They are deliberately crafted to offer a juxtaposition of dehumanizing images to the humane images conveyed by US netcentric warfare. Thus, digital images and Internet videos have been used as strategic weapons aimed at exploiting Western inabilities to stomach the shedding of (innocent) blood. Terrorist leaders such as Bin Laden and Al-Zarqawi's know that the only way of forcing a US withdrawal lies in swaying the political will of an electorate that places its soldiers at risk (Hegghammer 2006a). This is where digital images become a virtual weapon of war, a way to test and shatter the US will. Al-Qaeda is counting on the futility of the US's moral disgust as the first step towards cracking the will to continue to fight.

Yet, it is important to remember that the use of New Media technology has not been an exclusive practice among US adversaries but has also occurred increasingly from *within* the American war machine itself. Mobile phones, blogs, MySpace and YouTube have also empowered the individual US soldier to become a potential journalist. Thus, besides the terrorist as YouTube impresario, there has also been the US torturer as digital video artist. The Abu Ghraib pictures and mobile phone video footage taken by US military personnel were certainly never just intended for private use. Some of them were meant as a spur to other torturers (and actually uploaded onto personal websites) while others were supposed to be shown to other prisoners to warn them what awaited them if they did not co-operate. Here, the digital image has become an instrument of coercive interrogation. But irrespective of whether this footage uncovered a systematic illegal abuse of prisoners or 'simply' proved to be the exception, it has further complicated the Pentagon's 'perception management' (Hersh 2004). New Media technology allows US soldiers to capture and publish their personal experiences in ways that are beyond the Pentagon's control. In a sense, this development marks the merger of the warrior with the war reporter. Every US serviceman and woman can become a potential war reporter whose digital footage – as in the case of the abuse of hooded detainees at Abu Ghraib which was broadcast by the television magazine *60 Minutes II* in late April 2004 – has the potential to further delegitimize US operations in the eyes of the public. The political scandal resulting from the torture pictures damaged the legitimacy and public image of the USA in the execution of the ongoing military operations in Iraq.

Conclusion

This case study has hopefully illustrated how New Media technology has started to transform the experience of war for it allows the production of competing virtual realities. A new means of disseminating information, New Media technology has enabled US adversaries to break the Pentagon's exclusive ability to frame the perception of US warfare by creating virtual counter-realities that aim at delegitimizing US operations in its global 'War on Terror'. As a result, twenty-first-century warfare has not primarily been waged over the military predominance in Kandahar or the Sunni triangle, but over the conflict's representation and public perception. Contemporary war has morphed into a battle of digital images, or what Paul Virilio famously termed a 'cybernetic war of persuasion and dissuasion' (Virilio 2002: ix). Here, the prime strategic objectives are no longer the elimination of the enemy's military forces but the (re)shaping of public opinion. It is in the realm of (new) media battlefields where questions of victory and defeat are decided.

9 Digital democracy: enhancing the public sphere

Last Moyo

Michael Saward argues that '... defining democracy is a political act' (Saward 1994: 7). By this, he implies that there is no one universal definition or model of democracy. As such, it is important to point out right from the start that all definitions and all models of democracy are contestable. This chapter merely seeks to establish working definitions of democracy to explore debates around digital media, particularly the role of the Internet and mobile phones in their creation of a democratic 'public sphere'. Digital democracy is used here to refer to 'a collection of attempts to practice democracy without the limits of time, space and other physical conditions, using [new] ICT ... as an addition, not replacement, for traditional analogue practices' (Hacker and van Dijk 2000: 2).

The public sphere

As a theoretical concept, the public sphere has its basis in the emergence of the capitalist society in western Europe during the transition from feudalism to a free market economy. The advent of capitalism led to the rise of a bourgeoisie class who were antagonistic to the landlords who wanted to cling to political power although the feudal edifice was crumbling because of the shift in the means of production and decline in religious beliefs. From the humble beginnings of the enlightenment period in the seventeenth century to its pinnacle in the eighteenth century, a gradual but enduring shift from a religious consciousness to more secular ways of conceptualizing human existence developed with the quest for knowledge as the rallying point. Reason began to be seen as the basis for human emancipation and the quest for knowledge became one of the main preoccupations of society (see Chapter 2).

According to Jurgen Habermas, nowhere was this quest for emancipation more evident than in the literary works of philosophers, but also in the rise of a reading public who sat in coffee houses and salons to discuss topical issues of the day. Habermas (1989) also shows how these British coffee houses and French salons soon became a platform where this newly emerging class shared information about commerce, politics and their new lifestyles. Later, newspapers became a central aspect of this activity in terms of the political concerns and other important issues. The early newspapers were often read in groups in coffee houses and salons in Britain, Germany and France.

The coffee houses and salons marked the genesis of the 'public sphere' while the advent of the print and electronic media meant further augmentation of its scope and breadth. Since Habermas's delineation of the bourgeoisie public sphere, this concept has become central in social, cultural and critical theory, especially in directing political thought on the role of democratic institutions like the media, parliament and civil society (see Garnham 1992, 2002). In modern societies, media institutions, civil society and universities have come to be normatively regarded as public spheres where the concept is used mainly for performance evaluation especially with regard to their political functions and democratic obligations to do with public debate. In essence, therefore, what is attractive about the public sphere theory according to Robert Holub is ' ... its potential foundation for a critique of society that is based on democratic principles' (Holub 1991: 3). As Monroe Price puts it, it is generally used as a 'technique for evaluating speech practices and media structures to measure progress towards a democratic society' (Price 1995: 24).

It can be argued that Habermas (1989) conceptualized the public sphere as ideally a platform where everyone (regardless of class, income, creed, gender, race and ethnicity) has a right to sit and share ideas with others on any socio-economic and political issues that are of public interest and concern, through fearless critical and 'rational' debate. In line with Habermas's view, Holub adds that 'The public sphere is a realm in which individuals gather to participate in open discussions. Potentially, everyone has access to it. No one enters in discourse ... with an advantage over another' (Holub 1991: 3). His concept of the public sphere underscores four important points about the ideal public sphere and these are participation, non-discrimination, autonomy and rational critical discourse.

1   *Participation and non discrimination:* this means that the public sphere must be an open forum for all. If anything, a public sphere must thrive from the plurality and diversity of opinion thus creating a market place of ideas.
2   *Autonomy:* a public sphere has to be autonomous because an autonomous environment is conducive for critical and rational debate, where people can employ full use of their mental faculties without fear and favour.
3   *Rational or analytical debate:* this is the crux and essence of the public sphere. According to Habermas, people in the coffee houses and salons had allegiance to the 'authority of better argument against hierarchy' (Habermas 1989: 36). Fear and favour were seen as an affront to rationality and analysis which are the sinew of a functional public sphere.

Despite these egalitarian claims, Habermas's version of the public sphere has been criticized as a subtle way to universalize bourgeois class interests over other class interests of working-class people. Bourgeois public spheres were elitist liberal spheres based on liberal thinking that was erroneously projected as articulating universal interests and concerns. The bourgeois public sphere is seen as far from being an embodiment of rationality, but rather a sphere that excluded other forms of thinking or world views, and political concerns like those associated with the proletariat, peasants and women. Nancy Fraser also argues that in class societies, thinking of an all-inclusive non-discriminatory homogenous public sphere, is mere romanticization of the public sphere concept. She refutes the notion of a single public sphere arguing for plural spheres which she calls 'alternative public spheres', 'competing public spheres', 'counter public spheres' and 'subaltern public spheres' (see Fraser 1992). Fraser makes a compelling and persuasive argument that a single public sphere serves only to entrench class relations of domination and subordination, which are not in the interests of democracy.

The models that these alternative public spheres take have not found interesting intellectual nuance and delineation, but John Keane believes they comprise micro public spheres, meso public spheres and macro public spheres (see Keane 2004). Micro public spheres tend to be small involving an institution, a community or an association that may be advocating for certain interests. They represent nascent public spheres. Examples of micro public spheres include political pressure groups or civic organizations that operate at a small-scale level. Micro public spheres have the potential to transform to be large scale or even be national, depending on the availability of resources for expansion, the political context and initiative for growth and expansion. The advent of the Internet has also further enhanced the capacity for expansion even at a global level.

Meso public spheres are large scale or national and have the capacity to become international. They tend to be political public spheres and generate a lot of interest and participation from the ordinary citizens who may seek the betterment of their standard of living and general welfare. The macro public spheres are global in scale and they may deal with issues that affect individual nation-states, but give them global publicity. Examples include Amnesty International, Green Peace, Human Rights Watch and many others.

From the coffee houses to cyber forums

It can be argued that the major attributes of an ideal public sphere are interactivity or deliberative democracy, openness and accessibility to all, unfettered freedom of expression and freedom of information exercised and enjoyed within the context of just laws, supremacy of, and loyalty to a 'rational' and 'critical' discourse as opposed to threats and violence. Given these attributes, to what extent can it be argued theoretically that the Internet, at least in principle, is able to simulate an ideal public sphere?

The Internet is generally hailed as an open platform and hyper-interactive medium. Although participation on the Internet is curtailed by factors like access, costs, censorship, lack of technological literacy and technophobia, it can be argued that generally the Internet is a relatively open and accessible public sphere where anyone who has access to a wired computer can freely express their views as long as they remain within the law and do not infringe on other people's rights. However, it must be pointed out that in countries like China, the Internet is heavily controlled and under surveillance and is therefore not as open and as accessible as in Western countries (see Moyo 2007). However, the openness of much of the Internet as a public sphere can be seen in the diversity and plurality of the voices on the net that are represented by the websites of political parties (right and left wing), Christian and

Muslim sites (radical and moderates), civil society and government sites, that coexist with each other online. The plurality and diversity of these sites (some with hyperlinks) make the Internet potentially the biggest single public sphere. Through the usage of email, e-chats and webcasting to create democratic discussions between members, the Internet can also be regarded as a fairly autonomous and independent public sphere.

Internet interactivity implies that Computer Mediated Communication (CMC) must approximate the dialogic, deliberative, communicative and democratic ideals of the Habermasian public sphere. Online interactivity can be defined as the means that are available on the Internet that generate electronic conversations or discussions (audio, video or text) that can approximate real-life verbal exchanges that were the basis for the Habermasian public sphere. Martin Lister et al. (2003) also says that interactivity can also be seen as referring to a range of ways by which users can interact with and participate in shaping, modifying, redefining and expanding online texts. Technically, this may include editing, attaching, forwarding texts and even creating hyperlinking counter-texts to the existing myriad of texts online (see Lister et al. 2003).

Practically, interactivity online is manifested through a number of applications such as email, computer-to-mobile text messaging, electronic chats and discussions, forwarding and voiceovers (Voice Over Internet Protocol (VOIP)). Most of these functions and applications make the Internet a unique medium in the sense that unlike radio or television that is somewhat locked within a transmission, top-down and linear model of communication, the Internet seemingly enhances lateral, interactive and discursive communication where there is not excessive gatekeeping. Paschal Preston argues that the email, chat forums and other interactive functions make the claim that the Internet is akin to the Habermas public sphere not necessarily an exaggeration. He asserts that:

> Undoubtedly, these Internet based developments [i.e. interactive applica-
> tions] represent new opportunities to create novel forms of Habermasian
> (political and cultural) public spheres centred around open access, egalitarian
> and transparent debate. Especially where such Internet applications manage
> to challenge and resist domination by commercial and other section inter-
> ests.

(Preston 2001: 209)

First, it is important to note that Paschal sees these Internet applications as only providing an opportunity for an open and interactive public sphere. It is an opportunity that may be realized and taken advantage of by other people, ignored by some, is ambivalent to others, lost by the weak or poor or hijacked by the strong and dominant. Second, Paschal raises a vital point about how the strong and dominant commercial and political interests in society always take advantage of New Media to promote their sectional interests. To that point can be added another about techno-logical literacy (see Chapter 8). The interactive potential of all these applications can only be achieved if the Internet users are able to manipulate the Internet's interactive potential to the fullest.

Unlike the old analogue media, the Internet brings in a convergence of text, audio and the visual in political dialogue in the public sphere. As such, the Internet is celebrated as an interactive sphere, not only in the technical sense, but also in terms of the comparative sense of the interactive ability of all communication technologies in history. Comparing the openness and interactive potential of the old mass media to the new digital media such as the Internet, Jeff Chester argues that:

> What old media are not ... is participatory. We may read newspapers and magazines, listen to radio and recordings, or watch film and television, but the odds of any of us actually contributing to the mass media ... are small. The mass media industries tend to be closed systems, dominated by a relative handful of interlocking giants, with room at the margins for alternative expression perhaps, but with the vast majority of ... independent voices ... excluded.

> (Chester 2005: 15)

Almost everywhere, the state and the market forces seem to use the mass media to promote the status quo and allow participation and criticism only to a degree where the elite's interests remain safe. Apart from that, the old mass media as a form of technology arguably frustrate, rather than promote interactive, multi-directional communication because feedback in most cases is not instantaneous like the Internet, except for programmes such as talk shows. This is probably why Hans Enzensberger demonstrates cynicism with those media compared to the Internet. According to Enzensberger 'In its present, equipment like television or film does not serve communication, but prevents it. It also allows no reciprocal action between transmitter and receiver; technically speaking it reduces feedback to the lowest point' (2000: 52).

The public sphere potential of the Internet is also augmented by the fact that, unlike the mass media of newspapers, the Internet is not linear. As far as the Internet is concerned, we cannot speak of the senders and receivers of information in the traditional transmission sense of old communication technologies. In Internet communication, senders can be receivers and receivers can be senders of information. The Internet, therefore, changes the conventional relationship between the senders and receivers by making it dynamic, fluid and dialogic – elements which are linchpins of egalitarian political public spheres where discussions must materialize into solutions to certain political questions (Chapter 7).

Broadband and wireless network connections have also 'revolutionized' interactivity in the Internet public sphere. To use the technological determinism superlatives and hyperboles, compared to dial-up methods, fibre-optics broadband and wireless technologies are said to be transmitting huge flows of data with 'lightning speed' (Chester 2003).

Convergence is the integration or fusion of media of diverse textual backgrounds such as newspapers, radio and television, to form one robust versatile medium. It can also be seen as the 'co-operation', 'alliance' or 'merger' between print, broadcasting and online media (Berger 2001: 27). Guy Berger's view is important because it implies that convergence can actually be understood at two levels. The first level could be said to be that of merger or fusion of text, sound and video into one text in a single medium. Television and the Internet provide good examples of this fusion. The second level of convergence is that of co-operation between various media (telecommunications, broadcasting, print) that in reality remain separate entities but have merged online thus creating new challenges in terms of content and institutional regulation for policy makers.

Consequently, the Internet perhaps represents the most advanced medium probably for all types of communication in the sense that it combines the strengths of the other media such as video, text and voice. Theoretically, convergence benefits the public sphere because it has transformed it into a multimedia sphere where users may potentially benefit from text, sound and video simultaneously to express a point of view or construct meanings. In essence, the Internet user enjoys what can be dubbed as multimodality in the sense that with a VOIP and a web camera, Internet users can enjoy interactive verbal conversations that are enhanced by a sense of visual presence. They can also use applications like *MSN or Yahoo Messenger* to chat in cases where they need to clarify issues in written formats. The web camera also gives a platform for no-verbal communication through facial expressions and gestures.

Further benefits of Internet users are harnessed from the fact that the Internet is amenable with other media in the sense of co-operation. For example, through email, the Internet can communicate with mobile phones, television, and also provide feedback to other online media like online and offline newspapers. Hence, it can be argued that the Internet has such an immense communicative potential for those who are able to use it because 'its applications provide radically new opportunities for the handling, storing, distribution and processing of all forms of information (visual, audio, data, etc.) within a common digital mode' (Preston 2001: 27). Furthermore, Preston also adds that (ibid.: 208), 'the Internet is widely [seen] as a particularly flexibly communication system that is relatively open or responsive to user based ... innovation and one that represents significant new opportunities for "horizontal" non-commercial and more egalitarian forms of communication'.

According to James Slevin, the advent of the World Wide Web (WWW), a multifunctional application, has further enhanced online interactivity because it is able to allow 'users to send electronic mail, chat, transmit files and automatically load helper applications when these are needed' (2000: 38).

The concept of interactivity is closely linked to that of digitality. Digital media texts as opposed to analogous texts imply high mutability and reproduction of data, hence users of the Internet can also change, edit and add to the electronic messages they receive. Digitization also implies the Internet's ability to accept high data inputs, disseminate large corpuses of data, reliability, flexibility, economic efficiency, plus faster access to data (see Hamelink 2000: 11). This is because, as opposed to analogue media where the input data must always stand in analogous relationship to one another in a physical form, digital media converts all input data into numbers (coded to represent some cultural form) which can easily be stored and retrieved faster and cheaper. Hypertextuality is the Internet's ability to link a text to a network of other texts that are outside, above and beyond itself (Lister et al. 2003; Landow 2001). This has not only brought greater choice for information sources for the Internet user, but also comes with greater challenges for higher aptitudes for information processing.

Digitization and hypertextuality on the Internet do not only mean that any technically skilled Internet user is able to participate in online local as well as global public spheres through using a range of applications available for CMC, but also means that the Internet user is well 'armed' with ubiquitous information to support logical debates in both online and offline public spheres. Digitization, for instance, has made the Internet one of the best media in terms of the compression of time and space. Martin Lister uses an example of email and argues that compared to the ordinary letter that is sent through the postage system, the email is by far faster, interactive, and has the ability to transmit a lot of data (Lister et al. 2003: 18).

Hypertext and hyperlinks lead Internet users as public sphere participants to more information and related information sources, which, as argued earlier, if used properly can promote more critical and analytical interaction in online and 'offline' public spheres since the public sphere must be ideally constituted of a reading public. Information and information access are two most critical resources for any public sphere and hypertextuality and digitization make the Internet possibly the largest repository of information. Furthermore, although some of the information is protected and given an economic value, most of the information online from the media, civic organizations, government, political parties and some international organizations is freely accessible to all Internet users thus implying active participation in the public sphere of the Internet by those who are connected. Frank Webster also underscores the significance of free access to information in the public sphere, 'Information is at the core of the public sphere, the presumption being that within it, actors make clear positions in explicit arguments, and that their views are also made available to the wider public' (1997: 102). Information is therefore indispensable to all democratic public spheres. However, the critical question is, to what extent does the free and publicly accessible parts of the net have useful information? Are the billed or password-protected sites more informative than the free sites? If so, what does this mean in terms of the privatization or broadening of participation in the online spheres?

As stated earlier, the general trend in online public spheres that act as early warning systems to corruption, poor governance and human rights violations, is that they are always freely accessible, although at times members may need to subscribe to participate in a range of debates they offer in their discussion forums.

But what are some of the problems of the Internet as a public sphere? Generally, the problems range from social exclusion due to poverty, prohibitive costs of cutting-edge technologies, shrinking public and individual access due to corporate profiteering, counter surveillance technologies, poor connectivity, poor technologies, lack of relevant content, technophobia, commercial intrusions like pop-up adverts and virus attacks. It must also be noted that other writers disagree with the whole idea that the Internet can be a public sphere. Trevor Haywood argues that the Internet is basically a centrifugal and fragmenting medium with poor chances of creating a meaningful public sphere and that 'We should not be surprised if it makes us more remote from each other ... .That which can connect us with others in far-off places can also reduce and inhibit the richest and most satisfying of human intercourse when we use it over short distances to replace meeting each other in real space (Haywood 1998: 27; see also Poster 1995; McChensey 1997). He further argues that the Internet is 'the enemy of truly collective reason and debate, and we must not fall for it' (ibid.: 27) and contends that, 'testing and reviewing information and knowledge within lively and articulate communities is still the most important safeguard to our democratic freedoms' (ibid.: 27). However, to counteract such views, emphasis must be given to the issue of convergence showing how the Internet does not replace previous existing public spheres, but is part of them and has also extended citizens' interactive capabilities.

Mobile phones and participatory democracy

Mobile phones are proving central in participatory democracy as a voting gadget, even in the LDCs (least developed countries) of Africa. According to Kristóf Nyíri (2004), people use mobile phone technology to express themselves on salient issues that have to do with global justice or even local issues that affect national development. They talk, share text messages and emails to make informed choices about important issues of national concern such as elections, referendums, national and workers' strikes. Mobinet Index, an AT Keaney and University of Cambridge study, argued that in 2004, about 49 per cent of mobile users in the world had mobile Internet and approximately 75 per cent used mobile data services such as email, news and short message service (SMS). Again, civil society as an arena for debate has been strengthened by the advent of mobile communication. In countries that are fraught with legal restrictions on mass media, mobile phones are increasingly used for networking and mobilization by civic groups (see Feltoe 2002; Moyo 2007). Journalism, a profession which is seen largely as an epitome of the public sphere, makes extensive uses of mobile technology to further broaden and augment its discursive potential through a myriad of ways that are available through mobile technology data services and email.

To discuss the democratic and interactive potential of mobile phones, it is important to outline mobile phone functions and their potential uses. Mobile phone functions comprise, inter alia, making and receiving voice or video calls, SMS (also referred to colloquially as 'texting') mobile Internet, radio, television, faxing (if connected to a computer), auto roaming, call diverting and digital camera.

Text messaging is normally done mobile to mobile, but in some countries even in Africa, one can also 'text' fixed line phones, computers or television. Full mobile Internet allows the mobile phone user to surf for information, send and receive emails and access other online-based media that provide news. The convergence of the mobile phone with other media like the Internet and radio creates greater hope for its public sphere potential, but needless to say, these functions are not of any use by themselves. Their capacity to create democratic conversations among citizens and between the rulers and the ruled, not only depends on the people's ability to use them, but also on the political, regulatory, technological and socio-cultural regimes of any given nation.

Making and receiving calls is one of the most basic functions of a mobile phone and yet if looked at closely from a communicative democracy perspective, it is no ordinary activity. Given that freedom of expression is the linchpin of the public sphere, the mobile phone can be seen as having a potential for dialogic democracy. In terms of their voice communication potential, mobile phones can make one-to-one calls and group calls where participants can discuss any ideas ranging from business to politics. In most cases, mobile phone conversations lay the foundation for the pursuit of issues in depth mostly through interpersonal or group communication. Daniel Chandler says that the more frequently people make contact by telephone, the more they seem to want face-to-face meetings afterwards (Chandler 1994b). Timo Kopomaa concurs with Chandler and argues that:

> The mobile phone does not decrease the number of face-to-face contacts – on the contrary it increases them and promotes them. People typically use the mobile phone for calling up a person they would like to meet or who they are on their way to meet. The mobile phone also gathers friends more frequently and in bigger groups together.
>
> (Kapomaa 2001: 2)

The mobile phone seems to be a multidimensional and complex gadget. It is on the one hand, a public sphere in its own right through mobile radio, mobile Internet, mobile television, while on the other hand it acts as a basis for arranging face-to-face group discursive forums. Interactive group calls on mobile phones approximate the public sphere interactive exchange although one can also argue that mobile phone verbal exchanges are not that interactive or flexible like face-to-face discussions. Technology failures like poor reception, breaks or network cuts, and other types of 'noises' may undermine the quality of mobile phone-executed discussions.

The mobile phone has also opened up a communication channel for citizens that were previously marginalized by other forms of telecommunications (especially in Africa where mobile phone growth is phenomenal), while also extending the interactive capacity of those that have always been in the mainstream of mass media and other forms of communications. For example, in most LDCs, ordinary people who do not have a fixed line but are now in possession of a mobile phone are able to participate on live radio and television talk shows, hence the direct link with broader public spheres through the mobile phone. From this perspective, the mobile phone is a means of not only accessing, but also participating in main public spheres of the mass media like radio and television. Auto roaming further augments an individual's chances of remaining within the public sphere in time and space as both an audience and a participant in mass media discussions. For instance, a tourist with a mobile phone that has radio reception remains attached to the principal public spheres of local and global radio stations. The tourist can listen to radio news from a mobile phone; participate through a mobile phone, and further link with private spheres of family or friends to verify on some issues. In a sense, therefore, mobile phones seem to transform traditional forms of communication and media consumption by extending one's interactive potential and by implication, the public sphere itself (Hulme and Peters 2001). Kapomaa sees the mobile phone as a public sphere that is in so many ways akin to the idealistic Habermasian sphere. He argues that:

> ... the mobile phone can be viewed as a 'place' adjacent to, yet outside of
> home and workplace, a 'third place' ... [akin to] ... coffee houses, shops, and
> other meeting places. The mobile phone is, in its own way, a meeting place,
> a popular place for spending time, simultaneously a non-place, a centre
> without physical or geographical boundaries.
>
> (Kapomaa 2000: 3)

'Texting' is another function of the mobile phone that seems to have a potential for interactive public spheres particularly for the youth; areas where the mass media are gagged or muzzled by the state; and indeed places where service charges for mobile phones calls are prohibitive. In parts of Africa, for example, 'texting' has not only been used in referendums, but continues to be used to support other 'guerrilla media' in the mobilization, organization and co-ordination of mass protests. The mobile phone's influence on the civil society can also be seen from the way the gadget is taking a central role in advocacy at a continental level. In 2004, some women's advocacy organizations solicited 'text' and online votes from Africans at home and in the Diasporas in support of the Protocol on the Rights of Women in Africa. Only three countries had signed the Protocol which had been adopted by the African Union the previous year. The public sphere potential of the mobile phone is gradually developing because of the greater confidence by its users about its technical capabilities. According to Hulme and Peters, the interesting thing is that the mobile phone is not only more than just some technology for making voice calls, but it is also beginning to be seen as such by communities across the world. They state that 'Perceptions about the mobile phone are already changing; the mobile is taking on a new meaning and has superseded its utility as a medium solely for voice telephone. It is increasingly perceived as a multi-purpose device' (Hulme and Peters 2001).

The centrality of the mobile phone may be due to its unprecedented expansive and pervasive nature which imply a greater public sphere where all members who are participants are potentially accessible anywhere and anytime in the world (be they in the street, bus, train, bathroom, or even toilet) as long as there is connectivity. The freedom provided by the mobile phone, indeed, means that people are always available, even when moving as it maximizes their contact potential (see Kapomaa 2000). The expansive and pervasiveness of the mobile phone public sphere is further augmented by such functions as roaming and call divert. Roaming allows a mobile phone user to use their mobile phone internationally and still link with family, friends, colleagues and the media as if she/he is in his or her country. Call diverting links fixed line with mobile line so that a mobile user can receive those calls directed at home or work when she/he is on holiday. The divert and roaming functions, in a way, render the answering machine obsolete.

Although 'texting' is largely seen as a practice of the youth, this is beginning to change as civic organizations are using it for political communication as previously stated. For the youth themselves, their 'texting public sphere' is further consolidated by a mobile-based cultural identity. One can argue that whereas the bourgeoisie public sphere was sustained through the celebration of newly found lifestyles and culture by the then middle class, the youth's 'texting public sphere' is also sustained by customized signs like the type of ring tones played, the screen servers used, and stickers which also connote a lot of underlying meanings within the youth community.

But why has 'texting' generally been seen as a youth activity? The answer to this question also shows the intimate relationship of the mobile phone with other ICTs. For example, Marge Eldridge and Rebecca Grinter assert that:

> One reason that teenagers use text messaging is to arrange times to chat and to adjust arrangements already made. For example, they sometimes text a message to a friend to see if it is a suitable time to phone them on a landline phone or to chat to them on the Internet.

(Eldridge and Grinter 2001: 1)

This observation about the dynamic nature of the mobile phone public sphere is very interesting. However, this may apply largely to western European countries and North America where young people also own mobile phones and service providers give concessionary rates for text messaging and voice calls as they compete for the market. Given the 'digital divide' (see Chapter 8) that affects poor countries such as those in the African and South American regions, the mobile phones and the fixed line phones are largely associated with adults and institutions, and therefore, tends to be conduits for serious verbal and 'textual' exchanges, although occasionally people also circulate jokes among themselves. For example, in Zimbabwe and other African countries, the 'text me' or 'beep me' practice is widely used by and associated with the young adult population due to prohibitive service costs.

Theoretically, mobile phones have a great potential to promote the 'timeous' and effective journalism for the news media. Journalists with mobile phones are not only expected to use SMS and data services, but also mobile cameras and the mobile Internet for their research. In journalism, the mobile phone has also extended the public sphere by 'converting' every person carrying a mobile camera to a journalist. Many news media stories nowadays, especially in western Europe and Northern America, depend on pictures of dramatic newsworthy events taken by ordinary people carrying in-built mobile cameras (see Chapter 4). This is because people do not always carry their cameras around but they are likely to have their mobile phones with them.

The mobile phone has broadened the breadth of the public sphere of news media in the sense that the public are now armed with a critical tool that gives pictorial evidence to their accounts of dramatic stories to the journalists. Mobile phone pictures corroborate eye witness accounts of stories as news sources. In a report called 'Information Rich Information Poor: Bridging the Digital Divide', the BBC's Kate Miller gives interesting examples where the mobile phone cameras have proved to enhance the news media public sphere. According to Miller, the following events took place in 2004:

- A flight from Switzerland to the Dominican Republic had to be turned around after someone with a mobile phone camera took a picture of a piece of metal falling from the plane as it took off from Zurich. According to the *BBC*, this was also reported by the Swiss daily, *Le Matin*.
- Two robbers who robbed a bank in Denmark were snapped by an individual with a mobile phone camera before they carried out the crime while waiting for the doors of the building to be opened (also reported in by the Danish regional paper *Aarhus Stiftstidende*).

In 2007, Saddam Hussein's execution was secretly recorded in a mobile phone video showing that his execution was not as dignified as the official state video had shown. The mobile video circulated extensively in the news media around the world. Clearly, mobile phone technology is making an impact on the news media public sphere. While the positive contributions of the mobile phone to the public sphere are clearly discernible (at least for societies that have these technologies), there is also cynicism about the ethical vacuum facing public members who are 'mobile phone journalists'. Do they know what to photograph, when to photograph, why to photograph or even how to photograph in a manner that does not undermine the quality of service of the journalism fraternity? Are the mobile phone cameras not going to plunge journalism into sensationalism brought by the 'mobile paparazzi'? If so where does this leave the news media public sphere in terms of a reasoned discourse characterized by analysis, fairness, impartiality, completeness and informed opinion?

Conclusion

But what can be said about the Internet and mobile phones which provide the infrastructure for these news media and civil society political public spheres? Clearly, the Internet's potential to create a public sphere is undermined by factors like affordability, accessibility and availability (see Chapter 8). However, while the cost of computers remains generally prohibitive globally, access to information via the Internet is seemingly improving because of the public access points like the Internet cafés and public libraries. Through institutional and public access in cyber cafés and public libraries, it can therefore be argued that the Internet (and mobile phones to a lesser extent) seems to be expanding information access throughout the world. Yet, it should also be noted that the Internet has not created political public spheres that exist in isolation from the traditional mass media due to convergence. As Roger Fiddler argues, 'the New Media do not typically replace existing media, but instead modify and [complement] them' (1994: 25). Perhaps we need to bear this in mind before we become too utopian about the emancipatory powers of the digital age.

Recommended reading

Calhoun, Craig (ed.) (1992) *Habermas and the Public Sphere*. London: The MIT Press.

Dahlgren, Peter and Sparks, Colin (1999) *Communication and Citizenship: Journalism and the Public Sphere*. London: Routledge.

Fraser, Nancy (1992) Rethinking the public sphere: a contribution to the critique of actually existing democracy, in C. Calhoun (ed.) *Habermas and the Public Sphere*. London: The MIT Press.

Habermas, Jurgen ([1989] 1992 Orig pub in 1989) *The Structural Transformation of the Public Sphere: An Inquiry Into a Category of Bourgeois Society*. Cambridge: Polity Press.

Hacker, Kenneth et al. (eds) (2000) *Digital Democracy*. London: Sage Publications.

Case Study: Electronic votes in Haiti

Tim Pershing

Digital voting systems and voter registration databases have become common in most developed democracies. They are not without controversy, as touch screen machines are hacked in minutes by examining experts and the lack of paper backup leaves any hope of legitimate review impossible. Major electronic voting systems manufacturers offer electronic electoral support worldwide, eager to tap the resources available in the 'democracy market'. In the USA, there are 50 individual state registration databases open for political manipulation. Each state has control of its elections machinery and the systems used vary widely: Oregon is vote by mail while New York State still makes just getting your name on the ballot extraordinarily difficult (unless you are the choice of either the Democrat or Republican party). The web has become a major tool in political party campaigning as its reach is used to motivate party members, raise funds, track events and generate protest. Bloggers fact check (or forge facts) and political gaffes become instant YouTube fodder. Cell phones and PDAs are ubiquitous as politicians communicate with their staff 24/7. Is all of this simply twenty-first century democratic politics, the use of new technology to pursue an advantage over your opponents, same as it ever was? Are electronic voting machines just another addition in the history of voting systems designed to protect the sanctity of the vote, or perhaps to manipulate it?

All this digital technology may be fine in Europe, North America and other developed countries where the electrical grid is taken for granted, the digital divide (see above) is defined by the number of computers in the home and the precursor to touch screen voting technology, the automated bank teller machine, is ubiquitous. But what about developing democratic states, places like Benin, Afghanistan, Mongolia or Haiti? Is twenty-first-century technology appropriate in nations where significant portions of the country still live closer to the nineteenth century? Which is the better choice; an elaborate digital database and scanable voting cards to ensure one person one vote, or a simple dip of one's thumb in indelible purple ink, ensuring the same 'one time only' result? Can digital democracy advance democratic norms and practices or is the democratic digital divide a chasm too broad to bridge in developing democracies (even with satellite systems, solar panels and wi-fi?).

The recent series of elections in Haiti can tell us a lot about hi-tech in a relatively underprivileged country. Haiti, just off the southern coast of Florida, is a land apart from its neighbours. It is by far the poorest country in the Western hemisphere and one of the poorest in the world. Electricity is scarce or non-existent in the vast majority of the country, and if lights are on its most often through a private generator. Port-au-Prince, the capital and socio-political hub of the country, survives on sporadic electricity of several hours a day, power that sometimes fails to appear for days, even weeks (although the electric bills keep coming). There are no traffic lights, and huge swathes of the city are blacked out every night. Try to imagine Belgium, with a similar sized population, functioning on the same electrical supply.

The landline phone system is archaic and is rapidly being replaced by competing cellular systems, although it will still be years before coverage is complete in Haiti's mountainous countryside. Illiteracy runs around 60 per cent, unemployment about the same. The main national highway is nothing but dirt in many places, and regularly floods to impassable in the rainy season. The majority of the population does not have running water, or even access to potable water. Lawless gangs run the slums of the cities and international drug traffickers move product through untended ports and airfields, destined for lucrative European markets. In 2000, Haiti's elected President, Jean Betrand Aristide, began a standoff with international and domestic opponents, ending with the country in chaos by 2004 and the President in exile in South Africa. The list of problems, from health care to education to corruption goes on. So it was with some surprise that in 2005, it was reported that the appointed interim government, put in place to manage elections after the departure of President Aristide, was considering touch screen voting machines for the upcoming national elections.

Touch screen voting? In Haiti? How would they be powered, who would pay for them, who would run them, who would trust them? In the end, touch screen technology did not come to Haiti in this election cycle, but several attempts at digital solutions to the logistical nightmare of running elections in Haiti did. There were many detractors to the introduction of such technology in such an infrastructurally challenged country. How do you supply electrical power for the computers or train and field the technicians needed? Would creating a centralized double-blind computerized tallying system? Would updated postings on the Provisional Electoral Council's website reduce vote fraud and produce unchallenged electoral legitimacy or result in charges of international conspiracy to manipulate the vote? Would illiterate peasants trust technology they have never seen before? How would people living in remote, roadless mountain villages gain access? Would the elected Haitian government have the capability to maintain, upgrade and continue to pay for a complicated, technological, sophisticated, electoral system? These questions have merit, and all found some level of answer in the approaches eventually used. Something else was found though, something common throughout history; when the latest technology is introduced into new environments, unintended consequences ensue. Think gunpowder into Europe, the airplane to warfare, and democratic governance to authoritarian states, where it can produce a Mandella or a Mugabe.

Despite efforts by the political elite (no doubt hoping to profit financially through the exchange) touch screen voting technology was eventually discarded in favour of old-fashioned paper ballots and hand counting, but other elements of the process implemented by the Provisional Electoral Council with the support of the UN mission, United Nations Stabilization Mission in Haiti (MINUSTAH) and the

Organisation of American States (OAS) were decidedly digital. The first stage was to register a majority of eligible voters, a tough task in a country where even the number of citizens is a rough guess. This was highlighted by the fact that the estimate of eligible voters used by the OAS (who took on the registration process) was 3.2 million, some 200,000 short of the number of voters registered (remembering that the desire was to register only a significant majority, somewhere above 70 per cent, of the eligible voters). Even though Haiti had experienced well over a dozen national elections (with an extremely wide range of considered legitimacy and participation), no registration database, paper or otherwise, remained. It was concluded that this time, a national identity card system could be utilized, as was successfully done in many new Latin American democracies. These cards, similar to a standard driver's licence, would contain the citizen's name, address (as far as possible), signature (if literate), thumbprint and two photos. It would also convey the voting centre where the elector would vote. The cards would have a shelf life of around a decade, and for the first time provide the majority of the Haitian citizenry with a standardized official identification card, and with it a sense of national belonging.

To do this, the OAS purchased hundreds of computers, digital cameras and thumbprint scanners. They initially established 424 registration centres across the country, but found that they were falling way below the needed registration level. This prompted the move to create 100 more registration centres, including the loading of computer, thumbprint scanner, digital camera and solar panels onto donkey backs for treks to remote mountain villages. The data was processed by Cogent Systems Inc. and the ID cards produced by Digimarc in Mexico. The process was not without faults, far from it. Many people have no address in a land with nameless roads, mountain footpaths, and no postal system to speak of. Names and addresses were often entered incorrectly into databases. Deciding which voting centre to assign each registrant was confusing, resulting in tens of thousands of voters required to walk a dozen kilometres or more through mountainous terrain or through dangerous urban neighbourhoods in order to vote. The whole system, from card manufacturing in Mexico to the purchase of computers and scanners had to be funded and purchased through the bureaucracy of the United Nations and the OAS and approved by the rancorous Haitian Provisional Electoral Council (CEP), the independent commission charged by constitution with the overseeing of elections. In the end, delays in the distribution of the national identity cards resulted in multiple delays in the election date, although some 3.5 million eligible voters (75 per cent?) were registered, more than enough to produce a legitimate turnout by international standards.

While the balloting and vote tally was all done by hand, there was another component where technology played an enormous, and controversial, role. This was the centralized Vote Tabulation Centre (VTC), run by the UN Electoral Assistance Section with software provided and managed by OAS technicians. The role of the Tabulation Centre, based in the SONAPI industrial park in Port au Prince, was to produce a computerized double-blind tabulation system in which all legitimately registered votes (from each of the 9,000 individual polling stations) would be counted and posted on the CEP website in real time. The result allowed any voter, candidate, party member or election observer to check the final count – polling station by polling station – against copies of the tally sheets posted outside the actual polling places. It also allowed observers to look for voting irregularities, of which there were many, one of which, an abnormally high incidence of blank ballots in many areas, would come to be the turning point in the election.

Pulling off the VTC in a place like Haiti was an audacious manoeuvre, and it did not come off without hitches. Most were a result of other problems forcing the VTC to adapt its counting procedures, such as the slow delivery of the Proces Verbal (PV) which led to public speculation of manipulation or fraud by political elites in cahoots with the always mistrusted international community (the OAS controlled the software and managed the technological aspects, which included US-based servers and the loading of data onto the CEP website). It also did not help that the initial 10 per cent of votes tallied came from the capital Port au Prince, which went 65 per cent the Lespwa candidate, the former President Rene Preval. This result, posted on the CEP website, coming from what would be Preval's strongest region, raised hopes of a first-round Preval victory. The next posting, incorporating votes from areas where Preval ran less well (although for the majority of the polling, well ahead of any of the other 33 presidential candidates) had Preval's total down in the lower 50 per cent bracket, with 50 per cent plus 1, the cut off for winning in the first round. As subsequent totals from the countryside were added in, the Preval percentage slipped under 50 per cent, and his supporters among the working poor and poverty stricken masses hit the streets in protest against the perceived theft of his first-round victory. In a move that got the world's attention, thousands of protesters swarmed the elite Hotel Montana, where the CEP had set up its press centre. Hundreds of hot protesters swam in the pool and lounged poolside as the UN landed troops on the roof to protect (needlessly) the hotels guests, among them Bishop Desmond Tutu, who took advantage of the opportunity and addressed the crowd. The move made it clear; Preval supporters were not trusting the system.

This is where the digital database both proved its worth and its faults. First, the UN technicians and CEP officials failed to understand how people would perceive the manner in which percentages of votes can change as various regions are counted (remember, Haiti's lack of infrastructure meant it took a week for all PVs to arrive at the VTC) and failed, in part due to the lack of media and communication capabilities, to explain how the system worked. Haiti has a short and tortured democratic history. In a country where electoral fraud was the norm, not the exception, the first odour is that of a rat. On the other hand, the system had clearly shown that the populist Preval, the choice of the urban poor and disgruntled former members of Aristide's Lavalas political party, was trouncing his conservative opponents who had inaugurated the street protests and international contacts that had sent President Aristide packing. While there was political turmoil over Preval reaching the 50 per cent plus one to win in the first round – the system clearly showed, by any margin of error, that the majority had clearly expressed their will.

As the vote tallies were being examined, the inclusion of not just the votes *for* each candidate, but the invalid ballots (due to multiple or improper marking) and the blank ballots (those left unmarked), were registered as well. In Haitian electoral law, the percentage of all votes cast is what is counted, and blank votes count as a vote cast (as in a 'none of the above' protest vote). An extremely high percentage of blank votes of up to 18 per cent were registered in many regions; an acceptable level is around 3–4 per cent. The result was enough to deny Preval a first-round victory, if the blank votes were added in. Virtually all observers, Haitian and international, agreed that no Haitian would intentionally walk for hours, then stand in line for hours, only to deposit a blank vote (voter turnout was a healthy 63 per cent). As the data became available, it was obvious to electoral observers that something was not quite right. A statistically reliable quick count performed by the US-based National Democratic Institute gave Preval 52 per cent in contrast to the CEP's 48.5 per cent, and Preval supporters swarmed the streets. It did not help matters that ballot materials that should have been stored at a UN military base were accidentally thrown away, resulting in images of people holding ballots and ballot boxes aloft as they paraded through the streets, now claiming physical evidence of an attempt to defraud the popular vote.

In the end, no matter what technology is used, elections come down to political realities. Preval, sitting close to the mythical 50 per cent plus one, was ahead of his nearest competitor, long-time conservative politician Lesly Manigat, by nearly 38 per cent of the vote – this in a field of 34 candidates. The international community had committed some US$70 million to the running of elections, and had barely been able to pull off a relatively peaceful first round. No one, it seemed, except for Manigat and third-place finisher Charles Henri Baker, really wanted a second round. A late night political fix was found by reapportioning the suspect blank votes across all candidates, a solution which gave Preval 51 per cent of the tally and a first-round victory (see the Elections Canada Website: www.elections.ca for detailed reports and statements on the 2006 Haitian elections as monitored by the International Mission for Monitoring Haitian Elections (IMMHE) and the Canadian Mission for Accompanying Haitian Elections (CMAHE)).

There was still a second round for parliamentary voting to pull off in April, and another round for local elections scheduled for June, but finally held in early December. The VTC was upgraded for the second round, based on lessons learned from mistakes made in the first round. Data, posted on the CEP website, allowed for observers to check all polling stations and identify patterns of electoral abuse or mistakes. Some of the high blank and invalid votes, it turns out, might have been due to poor instruction or mistaken interpretation of the electoral process by the poll workers (exacerbated by the sizeable last-minute politically motivated switching of electoral workers in some voting centres, putting untrained party partisans in charge of a not so simple system) in addition to low levels of literacy and some overly complicated elements of the process. Graphs produced from the data of the voting patterns provided interesting first time information on the voting structures of Haitian society, including the refutation of the political support of many formerly highly regarded public figures. It also provided interesting points for social science inquiry, such as the seeming pattern of high blank and invalid votes in the most rural regions, with lower rates in the bigger cities. Why was this? Better voter education in the cities and access to media? Perhaps a correlation between the greater illiteracy rates in the rural districts? Was it a failure of oversight of the process, leading to greater fraud and intentional vote manipulation (one of the problems in the elections was a lack of privacy for voters as they cast their ballots, leading to the potential for voter intimidation)? Additionally, because virtually all candidates campaigned relatively freely (aside from some figures tied to Aristide, who were illegally imprisoned to deny their participation), so their constituency (or lack thereof) was laid out for all to see. This data on the various constituencies, especially the surprisingly high level of support for the three protestant associated candidates for President, revealed for the first time a realistic picture of Haiti's political spectrum.

One thing is clear, digital technology has entered the Haitian electoral process, despite the country's deep infrastructural problems and underdeveloped political and economic systems. In many ways, Haiti jumped technologies, moving straight from the nineteenth century to the twenty-first century. In a country where the burrow is better known than the byte, there was great concern how people would handle such rapid technological advancement. Initial sceptics, this author included, came to admire the ability and desire to adapt into the contemporary technological world. With the cost of an Internet uplink system at US$1200.00 and wi-fi access at hotels and cyber cafés in most towns and small cities, Haiti's youth, especially, have begun to embrace the possibility of development through technological advancement. While the digital divide may be greater in Haiti than in most other countries in the world, that does not negate its potential for positive use, especially in transitioning to a viable democratic system. Jumping technologies can work, even if it is to the byte from the burrow.

10 After New Media: everywhere always on

Royston Martin

All media work us over completely. They are so pervasive in their personal, political, economic, aesthetic, psychological, moral, ethical, and social consequences that they leave no part of us untouched, unaffected, unaltered. The medium is the massage. Any understanding of social and cultural change is impossible without knowledge of the way media work as environments. All media are extensions of some human faculty – psychic or physical.

(McLuhan et al. 1967: 26)

At the height of the space race in the 1960s when affordable televisions and portable radios added another powerful dynamic to the development of the mass media, communication theorists like Marshall McLuhan helped retune thinking about the place of technology in society. They argued that what we do with media and what it does to us is an essential part of understanding the human condition.

Media and technology are part of the fabric, if not yet in the DNA of our evolution. People have recorded and transmitted versions of events for thousands of years. Cave paintings, cuneiform scripts and ideograms tell us that from our early beginning we developed a range of technologies to relay information, to represent our experiences, our thoughts and our feelings. What distinguishes us from other animals is our desire and ability to harness communication for self-expression and the exchange of ideas, for introspection and organization. Media is a product of technology, but its essence is human language, an auditory form of communication that preceded the need for technologies to record it.

Homo sapiens or 'intelligent' humans can be traced back around 250,000 years, our very early ancestors; homo habilis appeared on the scene two million years before that. To cover this huge period of evolution, we commonly use the term 'prehistoric' to mark the time before history began to be recorded in the written word; that breakthrough came relatively recently. Between five and six thousand years ago in Mesopotamia, now modern-day Iraq, Sumerians initiated the use of the written word with a stylus to record numbers impressed into soft clay. Within a thousand years the process was so refined, thanks to the development of a sharp wedge-shaped, cuneiform, stylus, that the marks began to represent syllables of the Sumerian language.

As Michael Cook notes in the preface to his book *A Brief History of the Human Race*:

Humans have taken to making history only in the last few hundred generations. For two or three thousand generations before that our ancestors were probably no less intelligent and insightful than we are now (or no more stupid and obtuse). But they were otherwise engaged.

(Cook 2003: xix)

Around a million years before the development of writing and recorded history, our ancestors made another huge technological and evolutionary leap forward. We cannot say where, when or who exactly discovered how to control fire, but what we do know is that it enabled our forbearers to cook a richer diet, which significantly improved their health, their strength and their overall position in the food chain. It is a very early example of technological determinism that states that technology has an inherent effect on society. Writing at the end of the nineteenth century, sociologist Thorstein Veblen argued that technology determines human development and that society organizes itself in such a way as to support and further develop a technology once it is introduced successfully (see Veblen 1995).

Alongside natural language and the written word, the development of technology has been key to our evolution. The wheel and the printing press, the telegraph and the Internet have had profound effects, not always positive ones, on what it means to be human. For every peaceful application of a technology there is often a violent one. And while media has accelerated individual emancipation and developed our sense of self and leisure, it has also been used for propaganda purposes, to incite conflict and to exert control.

The exploration of the tensions between utopian and dystopian visions of societies dependent on media and technology has inspired many. If a key characteristic of being human is the articulation of introspective thought, then a key characteristic of media is that it is often employed to explore and reflect on the affects that it has on us and how we use it.

Fritz Lang's 1927 film release *Metropolis*, for example, is set in 2026 where society is split in two, between planners, who live above the earth in luxury, and workers who live underground labouring slavishly to prop up the lives of the privileged. Lang produced the work midway between the Russian Revolution and World War II when the stresses between social classes were especially amplified in Europe.

The film, *2001: A Space Odyssey* (Kubrick 1968), loosely based on Arthur C. Clark's science fiction short story, the *Sentinel* (1948), concerns an alien race which uses a monolith-like machine to explore new worlds and, where possible, to trigger intelligent life. In the film version, the opening scenes shows one such device appearing in ancient Africa, million of years ago, where it inspires a starving group of our ancestors to conceive of tools in the shape of animal bones. They use them as clubs to kill other animals, a predator and the leader of a rival tribe. This ends a cycle of life-threatening famine and they move ahead. Drawing on the idea that technology could one day become sentient and turn against its creator, the narrative leaps through time and we quickly reach a point at which Bowman, one of the central characters, has to outwit his spaceship computer to stay alive.

During the space race and in the depths of the cold war in the 1960s when Clark was writing the screenplay for *2001*, the possibility that the development of weapons had taken the world to the point where technology could destroy the human race seemed very real. World War II had accelerated the development of the atomic bomb, and the positioning of ballistic missiles in Cuba led to a dangerous stand off between the United States and the Soviet Union, which raised the spectre of nuclear war.

Doomsday scenarios are not confined to history or to academic dystopian technological determinism. Religions, Judaism, Islam and Christianity, for example, all have apocalyptic end times with their own variations on the last day. The science fiction community has extemporized on similar themes to create elaborate fantasies where humans, robots, gods and monsters play out life and death struggles for the control of everything. But, that an unseen consciousness, in the form of God for the religious or a perfect computer for the sci-fi fan, is in existence, there is no evidence yet. Instead, there is the growing influence of social constructivists like Wiebe Bijker who argue that human action shapes technology and that its use and development cannot be understood without figuring out how that technology fits into its social context. As he notes in 'Why and how technology matters', 'Social shaping models stress that technology does not follow its own momentum, nor a rational goal-directed problem-solving path, but is instead shaped by social factors' (2006: 687).

He and others argue it is Darwinian evolution that drives development, and it is our relationship to and command of technologies, natural language and the written word that determines what we are. A big part of that is the human imagination; it drives the sense of inquiry about what is possible and what lies ahead.

Images floating in mid-air, virtual immersion in distant galaxies, cloned friends and infinite leisure time (thanks to a robotic workforce), are just a few of the intoxicating promises offered in mainstream and online magazines speculating on the future. Ray Kurzweil's book, *The Singularity Is Near* (2005), imagines that one-day human beings will live in perpetual clouds of 'nanobots', molecule-sized robots constantly altering 'microenvironments' to our exact requirements. Kurzweil thinks in the longer-term 'nanotechnology' will let us change our shape, offer immortality, and enable us to transfer our minds across the universe. Todd Seavey's *Neither Gods Nor Goo* (2008) interrogates some similar projections. Seavey points out that in contrast to Kurzweil, the thriller writer Michael Crichton paints a much more disturbing picture of that future in his 2002 best seller, *Prey*. It is a world where nanobots run amok forming 'nanoswarms', clouds that visually mimic human beings to infiltrate society and then destroy it. For the time being both visions seem to be safely in the realm of science fiction. But that is not to say that because something is hard to imagine the possibility of it becoming a reality is any less likely. The fifteenth-century inventor of the European printing press, Johannes Gutenberg, almost certainly would have questioned the idea that the Bible could instantly and invisibly be sent across the world and printed elsewhere (Columbus had yet to set sail for the Americas at this time).

In *The Language of New Media* Lev Manovich writes, 'Graphics, moving images, sounds, shapes, spaces, and texts that have become computable; that is, they comprise simply another set of computer data' (2002: 20). This economical definition of New Media brings into focus just how central computing technology is. However, this can hardly be described as a new phenomenon. Media convergence and 'interoperability' (referring to the ability of diverse systems and organizations to work together or 'interoperate') and widespread public use of the Internet have been possible for well over a decade. Remote electronically mediated social networks, online buying and selling; second lives played out in private online spaces are no longer new. The end of the age of New Media is approaching; the question is where will the digital revolution lead next?

The end of New Media?

Technological singularity is based around the concept that there is an imagined point somewhere in the future when computers become smarter than humans. In 2000, 'The Singularity Institute for Artificial Intelligence' (SIAI) was set up as a non-profit organization to develop safe artificial intelligence software. The Institute lists as its key mission to raise awareness of both the dangers and potential benefits it believes AI presents. The SIAI notes:

> There are several technologies that are often mentioned as heading in this direction. The most commonly mentioned is probably Artificial Intelligence, but there are others: direct brain-computer interfaces, biological augmentation of the brain, genetic engineering, ultra-high-resolution scans of the brain followed by computer emulation.

> (SIAI 2008)

Jocelyn Paine shows in her work, 'Computers, the Singularity, and the Future of Humanity' (2003) that the basic idea has been in circulation since the mid-1960s if not before. Paine unearthed a marvellously optimistic section from I.J.Good musings in the 1965 edition of Advances in Computers. In it he wrote:

> Let an ultra intelligent machine be defined as a machine that can far surpass all the intellectual activities of any man however clever. Since the design of machines is one of these intellectual activities, an ultra intelligent machine could design even better machines; there would then unquestionably be an 'intelligence explosion,' and the intelligence of man would be left far behind. Thus the first ultra intelligent machine is the *last* invention that man need ever make, provided that the machine is docile enough to tell us how to keep it under control. It is more probable than not that, within the twentieth century, an ultra intelligent machine will be built and that it will be the last invention that man need make.

> (I. J. Good cited in Paine 2003)

Good's prediction was wrong. At the outset of the twenty-first century what is most probably going to become a key defining characteristic of media and technology is its increasing ubiquity. In 'The Computer for the 21st Century' written for *The Scientific American* in 1991 Mark Weiser noted:

> The most profound technologies are those that disappear. They weave themselves into the fabric of everyday life until they are indistinguishable from it. Consider writing, perhaps the first information technology: The ability to capture a symbolic representation of spoken language for long-term storage freed information from the limits of individual memory. Today this technology is ubiquitous in industrialized countries. Not only do books, magazines and newspapers convey written information, but so do street signs, billboards, shop signs and even graffiti. Candy wrappers are covered in writing. The constant background presence of these products of 'literacy technology' does not require active attention, but the information to be conveyed is ready for use at a glance. It is difficult to imagine modern life otherwise.
>
> (Weiser 1991)

The explosion in the use of hand-held mobile devices like mobile phones, MP4 players and satellite navigation systems demonstrates how prescient Weiser's early 1990's post-desktop model of human-computer interaction was. He projected a world in which information processing is completely integrated into everyday objects and activities so that people, not necessarily aware that they are doing so, engage with many computational devices and systems simultaneously in the course of daily life. Today, our so-called surveillance society bristles with invisible wirelessly linked media, which simultaneously track people, to record with what, and with whom, they interact. Radio-frequency identification (RFID) tags, gesture and voice recognition CCTV cameras, bar codes and data mines are all part of the huge growth in the ubiquity of media and technology.

The tags, or 'spy chips', as they are known by their detractors, can be used for a huge number of purposes. Insert one into a vehicle tax disc and it can enable a driver to automatically pay a road toll; a similar tag injected beneath the skin of an animal can help its owner keep track of their valuable pet. Additionally, RFID tags can be loaded with biometric information and inserted into humans, something that could help save the life of a front-line soldier, for example. But tagging raises huge ethical questions if one imagines an unscrupulous government enforcing the practice.

The advance of media and technology towards becoming invisible, everywhere and always on does not have to be viewed unfavourably. The spread of free, easily accessible instant information – be it on, for example, health care or democratic election processes – are small examples of the potential the digital media has to help raise living standards. In 2007 the 'Linpack Benchmark' (a numerically intensive test to measure the floating-point performance of computers) clocked the IBM BlueGene/ L computer's benchmark performance at 478.2 TFlop/s ('teraflops' or trillions of calculations per second), that is about 400,000 times faster than an ordinary computer. Put another way, the IBM machine – run in conjunction with the US Department of Energy and the National Nuclear Security Administration – works at a speed roughly equivalent to every person on the planet doing 40,000 calculations per second. Computers can already perform incredibly complex tasks ranging from the detection of microscopic heart defects in unborn babies to weighing invisible black holes deep in space. By comparison a refrigerator that can order fresh milk on the Internet when it detects a carton is close to empty may not be quite as sophisticated as some manufacturers suggest. It is, however, an indication of how pervasive basic artificial intelligence is likely to become. Nearly a decade ago many of the big electronics companies set up well-funded think tanks to devise products that do not need our conscious mediation to fulfil some of our needs; networked devices making decisions on our behalf have become more embedded in daily life. But there are some significant hurdles to jump before we are fully at home with what Artur Lugmayr at Finland's Tampere University of Technology calls 'ambient intelligence'.

The big problem, some researchers say, is that computers lack 'common sense' like knowing that you can pull on a rope, but not push on one. The Massachusetts Institute of Technology-based 'Media Lab Common Sense Computing Group' is looking into ways to give computers the ability to understand and reason about the world just as well as people do. Although computers are capable of making trillions of calculations at incredible speeds, they have enormous problems with things that we often take for granted, like reading a simple story and explaining it. Although an average domestic computer set-up can accurately scan and reproduce a photo of a family birthday party, describing what the event means and to whom, leaves it dumbfounded; very small children do much better at making meaning from things. This maybe because they are encouraged to grasp common sense, as much for their own survival as anything else, from day one. It is often taken for granted, but common sense is what people agree on and which they 'sense' (in common) as their common natural understanding. Some scientists at MIT say that if computers are going to develop ambient intelligence for our benefit then, they will need a more subtle level of discernment, which people regard as common sense. For example, a self-filling, if not a self-fulfilling, fridge must alter what it orders depending on who is in the house or a smart phone which turns itself off in the cinema needs to know to turn itself back on to take a vital life and death call. To reach this point, computers will need to be programmed with massively more information about us: social knowledge of how we interact, physical knowledge of how things behave, sensory knowledge of the look, taste, smell, touch and sound of things, psychological knowledge about the way people think, and so on. Such a huge and amorphous acquisition of intelligence, much of what we call 'common sense', would be more achievable and may be ultimately dependent on computers learning to understand a natural language like ours (see case study below).

Putting aside some of the technical challenges, there are many for whom the scenario of an always on network of computers and media running in the background is problematic. A key argument against it is that convergent media technologies lead to a concentration of ownership, which accelerates cultural hegemony where the dominant ideology is reinforced at the expense of alternative ideas. Another well-documented concern is that digital media can dehumanize and alienate people. Newspapers regularly carry sensational reports of adolescents holed up in their bedrooms playing violent Internet-based computer games at the cost of traditional culture and family life. Some of those tabloid headline writers are right to say the digital media has reduced the need for person-to-person contact and is to an extent altering the definition of what it means to be human. But the florid page turning claims that digital media will lead to a generation of easily led, dysfunctional psycho killers seem a long way off the mark. Positive developments like Open Source Software, Copyright Free Knowledge and cheap global communications look just as likely to be a legacy of the digital revolution.

Where some of the concerns about the advance of digital media seem more relevant is in the realm of the Earth's biosphere. The apparent gift humans have to invent technology and media to help manage their environment is likely to become even more important. In the extremely long term there will be the need to develop systems to move people away from the solar system as the sun goes into terminal decline. More immediately, the world faces the prospect that man-made climate change needs a more informed debate and some technological solutions to negate the pollution that is causing global warming.

The media has a central role; to provide the forum for the debate, much of the content and evidence, and the two-way channels through which informed decisions can be made. But the digital media is not completely immune from being part of the problem. Beyond its role in encouraging consumption in general, media is a hungry machine that demands enormous inputs of energy and commodities for its daily survival. Adding to the pressure are discarded consumer electronics which each year make up millions of tons of potentially toxic waste in the form of old televisions, music systems and DVD players dumped when they fall out of fashion or break down. In built structural obsolescence aside, corporations and advertisers are experts at satiating the desire for the new by offering improved models to help persuade us that last year's version of something could really do with an upgrade. Less visible in this cycle of consumption is the Internet; behind its apparently green or carbon neutral surface sit resource and energy hungry computers and the power stations that help it all tick over.

It is as easy to underestimate as it is to overestimate the speed and usefulness of technological development in our desire to grasp a future free from inequality, toil, illness and conflict. But here at the beginning of the twenty-first century hundreds of millions of people live in crushing poverty, are underfed or starving with limited access to safe drinking water. The gap between the rich and poor continues to widen. As our ancient ancestors understood, technological advance and media remain our most potent tools in the challenge to reverse what should be our most pressing concerns.

Recommended reading

Bijker, W.E. (2006) Why and how technology matters, in R.E. Goodin and C. Tilley (eds) *Oxford Handbook of Contextual Political Analysis*. Oxford: Oxford University Press.

Gitelman, Lisa and Pingree, Geoffrey B. (ed.) (2003) *New Media, 1740–1915*. London: The MIT Press.

Greenfield, Adam (2006) *Everyware: The Dawning Age of Ubiquitous Computing*. Berkeley, CA: New Riders Publishing.

Case Study: Natural Language Processing (NLP)

Alexander Clark

The transformative possibilities of computers in New Media have not yet been brought to bear on the *content* of media but only on its form and delivery. The promised breakthroughs in artificial intelligence still seem as far away as they did when Stanley Kubrick set his visionary space epic in what was at the time, the far off year of 2001.

Though in computer special effects it is now possible for thousands of realistic but synthetic humans to mill about in ancient Rome, it is instructive to consider what role computers still *do not* play in computer games and movies. For example, the scriptwriting process, though using word processors rather than typewriters, still follows the same traditional outlines as before. The plots and screenplays of Hollywood films, though they may sometimes be so formulaic that we joke that a computer might have generated them, are, of course, in fact, produced by teams of writers and producers. Though there have been attempts to generate plots and indeed dialogue automatically by a computer, these have so far been rather unsuccessful. Similarly, in spite of the economic importance of the computer games industry, both in the United Kingdom and globally, its cultural impact is limited to a certain restricted demographic: the few fabled *crossover* games, such as the strategic life-simulation computer game *Sims* (Maxi 2000–), that reach beyond the traditional game players are still very much the exception.

There is a common factor: the inability of the computer to model the ambiguities and uncertainties inherent in natural language mean that the focus of the engineers and designers has been on modelling those aspects of life that are amenable to efficient computational treatment: the dynamics of a race car driven round a track, trajectories of grenades, and the other staple elements of the modern game experience. Every computer user uses a word processor from time to time, without realizing that it is a misnomer. The word processor does not process words: it treats the text that the user is editing as a sequence of uninterpretable symbols, and with the exception of spell-checking has absolutely no awareness of the fact that these letters form words and sentences in a particular language.

These restrictions are so natural and have been taken for granted for so long that we are hardly aware that they are there, but as the computerization and digitalization of our society continues, it becomes more rather than less important to identify and test those limits. It is crucial to realize the extent to which the current limitations of this technology are likely to persist in the future, and the extent to which improvements in the ability of computers to handle language, conversation, plot, social interactions, and so on are likely to feed through into the media landscape of the next 20 years.

In this Case Study, we will briefly survey *natural language processing* (NLP), and its application now and in the future to New Media, which we take to include the fields of Internet-based communications, computer games, and perhaps other forms of interactive communication and entertainment that have not yet come to pass. NLP is the field of computer science devoted to developing programs or information processing systems that can process human languages (the term 'natural' languages is intended to differentiate the field from that of formal language theory, or the theory of programming languages such as Java, Pascal, and so on). While one of the earliest applications of computers in the 1950s, it took a few years before researchers truly understood the complexity of the problem. Indeed, at that time, those working on the problem were highly optimistic that applications such as automatic translation and so on, could be produced within a very few years. Of course, as we now know, that did not happen, and it is instructive to consider why, nearly 50 years later, the only application of NLP that most computer users are familiar with is the simple spell-checker (see Kukich 1992).

Let us start by looking at a few of the problems that make language processing so hard. *Lexical ambiguity* refers to the fact that the same word can mean different things. For example, the sentences 'He put the cap on the tube of toothpaste' and 'He put the cap on', the word 'cap' means two different things. Yet, humans have no problem understanding that in the first sentence, the word cap refers to the top of a tube, and in the second it refers to a hat. This is pervasive in language and some examples are astounding in the range of possible meanings: 'rose' can be a noun, the past tense of the verb 'rise', a colour, a name, and so on. *Syntactic ambiguity* occurs when the same sentence may have two different structures: 'Carl saw the man on the hill with the telescope' can mean that Carl used the telescope to see the man or that the man was on a hill which had a telescope on it. Resolving these ambiguities requires looking at the context of the utterance: making subtle inferences based on knowledge of how the world operates and how people tend to use language. These two examples were chosen to have two plausible interpretations: in reality any sentence has hundreds of grossly implausible interpretations, but computers are not good at ruling out even the most absurd ones. For example, 'Carl drank beer with Joel', by analogy with 'Carl drank beer with bourbon', could mean that Carl drank Joel. This is ludicrous to a human, but computers, without our knowledge of what can and cannot be drunk, will consider this as a possibility. Solving these problems fully will require computers to be able to represent and reason with arbitrary facts about the world; this is not likely to happen soon.

Further problems are caused by the creativity of language use; by language change, by small errors in grammar that do not affect the comprehensibility of the utterance for a human, but cause significant problems for computers, by the use of direct speech which can include foreign languages, or phonetic spellings, by the unlimited number of proper names, by the constant stream of new technical terms that are being invented; the list is endless. Even the most trivial problems turn out to be very hard in special cases: even finding the boundaries between sentences can be difficult as the symbol '.' is used not just as a period but also as a decimal point, and as an abbreviation symbol. Applying simple rules like 'break a sentence when you have a full stop that precedes a capital letter, except when the text preceding the full stop is a known abbreviation' will work very well nearly all the time, but every once in a while will give the wrong answer.

Being rather brutal, one of the problems with NLP, since its inception in the 1950s, has always been that in general *it has not worked*: the claims made by the practitioners have always gone far beyond what has actually been achieved. Finally, however, techniques have been developed that seem to work well, and these are now being applied to a wide range of problems.

The key insight is to embrace this uncertainty: to switch from using techniques based on logic; which proceeds from one certainty to another by well-founded deduction, to using statistical modelling techniques that are capable of balancing up the plausibility or likelihood of different interpretations. These tend to be based on measuring the frequency of occurrences of features, such as sequence of words, in very large collections of text (*corpora*). These statistics can be combined, and smoothed, to provide estimates of the likelihood of different interpretations that often do not rely on deep analysis of the meaning of the utterance, but are nonetheless sufficient to resolve ambiguities (see Gazdar 1996).

These techniques have already been widely employed in several fields. For example, automatic speech recognition (ASR) is one of the technologies that will eventually transform certain parts of the user interface. Perhaps not for general office use – where practical reasons of noise and confidentiality may rule out its widespread adoption, except for special users – but in specialized applications in medicine, military, disabled, and above all, on mobile devices, whether hand-held mobile phones/appliances or in the car. The same kinds of ambiguity arise in processing speech. 'How to wreck a nice beach' and 'How to recognize speech', when pronounced naturally, are almost identical acoustically: the recognizer needs to be able to tell that one is more likely than the other (see Jurafsky and Martin 2000).

These technologies are now coming into the mainstream of New Media. It is difficult to predict in which areas these will have most impact, but there are a number of obvious candidates. One can get some insight into the way the technologies are likely to impact New Media by looking at the technologies that are now the topic of active research in academic research departments and commercial research labs, such as Google Labs, Microsoft Research, and what remains of the older generation of research laboratories such as Bell Labs and the Xerox PARC Lab.

One of the most significant current commercial applications of NLP is in machine translation, the automatic translation of text from one language to another. Very rapid progress is being made in this domain, though the results are not yet being widely deployed in ways that are visible to the consumer, for example, on the web. Fully automatic MT, that is, without copy-editing, is unlikely ever to be of very high quality, but in specific applications it will have striking effects:

- For informal conversations, such as on Internet chat networks, where misunderstandings can be clarified through dialogue.

- For real-time applications, such as the translation of weather reports, stock ticker information, and subtitles of foreign television shows.
- For browsing which documents can be selected to be translated by a human translator.

Widespread deployment of these technologies will be of enormous importance especially with the growth of Asian economies in the twenty-first century. The political and economic impact of free communication is well known, but the language barriers limit the liberalizing effect of this.

Speech-to-speech translation is another important application area. It is, however, technically even more difficult than translating written text, since there is the additional task of speech recognition. It is, however, starting to be applied in specific domains, such as doctor–patient dialogues (see Rayner et al. 2006). In this project a speech translator is being developed to allow English-speaking doctors in California to talk to patients from recent immigrant groups.

A more recent application of NLP is *sentiment analysis* (see Pang and Lee 2004). This sidesteps the detailed syntactic analysis of language, and focuses on classifying the general tone of a document, or the attitude of the author as being either positive or negative. For example, an article about a new mobile phone, or a film, may express generally favourable sentiments about it or might state that it is terrible. While it is impossible to achieve very high accuracy without understanding the text, it is surprisingly easy to achieve an acceptable standard. This is then used in a number of ways:

- A company can use sentiment analysis to analyse what consumers think of a new product. By scanning hundreds of websites, blogs and other Internet-based forums, the company can build up an accurate picture of the general impression it is having, compare it to competing products and update this on a daily basis.
- A government agency can scan discussion boards to identify posters who write positively about terrorist acts; this information can then be combined with other sources of information to produce lists of potential terrorist suspects.

The human rights implications of widespread deployment of this technology, which is currently being used by the US Department of Homeland Security, are quite serious. In the first use case, the low accuracy is not a problem, as the results of many different documents and postings will be combined, and we would expect the errors to cancel each other out. In the latter case, the individual errors will be acted upon, with potentially disastrous effects. The methods used to do the sentiment analysis ultimately combine very sophisticated pattern recognition with a very shallow analysis: some techniques currently used are not even capable of adjusting for the use of negatives or other qualifiers. Referring to a terrorist-like bin Laden as 'not a man I admire to say the least' could be enough to trigger the program as the phrase 'bin Laden' could occur very close to the positive word 'admire'. We can only hope that the use of such technologies will be transparent and with adequate safeguards to ensure that miscarriages of justice do not happen.

Web search, one of the great success stories of the web, currently uses only minimal amounts of NLP. Google, for example, uses a very small amount of *morphological analysis*. So, for example, a search for the term 'computing' will also return pages that do not contain that precise term, but only terms like 'computer' that are morphologically related. This can mean that the user will receive pages that would otherwise not have been returned to them, which improves the usefulness of the search. In English, this pre-processing step is not essential because the language has only a very limited range of inflections. In other languages, this step is absolutely vital. In Hungarian, for example, the number of possible forms of a common noun is in the hundreds, and search engines that neglect this fact will perform quite poorly. Currently, more advanced NLP is in the process of being deployed. For example, Powerset, a well-funded start-up, with significant research expertise in NLP, has undertaken to, in their own words, 'build a natural language search engine that reads and understands every sentence on the Web' (Powerset 2007). Using technology developed at the Xerox PARC Research Lab, and positioning themselves as direct competitors to Google, at least in their core search business, their goal is to use NLP both to analyse queries from the user beyond a simple list of keywords, and to analyse pages on the web to see if they are relevant to the query. One of the problems for such companies is to retrain users so that they understand that search does not just mean keyword search, so accustomed have users become to a Google-style interface.

Nonetheless, at the time of writing, there are comparatively few real applications of NLP in the New Media world. More speculatively, we can ask how these technologies are likely to impact the development of New Media in the next 10 years?

Paradoxically, one of the most technologically innovative forms of New Media, the computer games industry, is also one of the most conservative. The very short product cycles, and high costs, have driven the producers of mainstream games, such as Electronic Arts, to stabilize on a fixed set of technologies, game play mechanisms and content types. The desire to control the experience of the mainstream user, and the instability of the software, due to the very rapid development, means that the use of NLP techniques to provide a more open-ended experience is unlikely to take place in the mainstream. However, there are a number of other markets where there is likely to be adoption of these technologies in the medium term. The small genre of text-based adventure games, notably those by Infocom (1979–1989), had a very brief period of popularity. These games used a primitive parser to analyse commands that the user could type in such as 'Put the bottle in the chest'. The technological window where this was attractive compared to graphical interfaces was quite short, and the entire field more or less disappeared.

Looking forward, and anticipating that the current progress in NLP will continue, some of the possibilities in current game genres will include:

- Natural, mixed initiative dialogue with non-player characters: Currently characters in games are very rigidly scripted. The dialogue is written by a scriptwriter, and prerecorded by an actor. More natural dialogue requires a number of technological advances: speech synthesis, dialogue management and the ability to generate a slightly larger set of sentences to open up the possibilities for interaction.

- Speech-based interfaces with other computer-controlled characters. Recent game platforms make use of speech communication between players. The platforms are powerful enough to do some limited ASR: this opens up a potential avenue for speech control of, for example, other team members. Nuance, a leading ASR vendor, has a development kit that has already been used in a number of Playstation 2 games.

More interestingly, these technological breakthroughs could enable more radical forms of interactive fiction. Dynamic simulations of social interactions could allow games to start addressing the same range of topics that, for example, the nineteenth-century psychological novel did: the relationships between a husband and wife, adultery, betrayal, sexual obsession, madness, and so on.

This topic, it is safe to say, has not in the past been a central concern of computer games. It is not just that the traditional demographic, male and aged 12–25, is not overly preoccupied with obsessive examination of the minutiae of relation-ships, but rather obsession with the details of cars and guns and how heads can explode realistically (see Chapter 5).

We should also consider the possibility, not just of New Media being influenced by NLP, but of entirely new forms of media made possible by NLP. One technology that could be influential is that of having natural language dialogue. A notorious example of this was a program called Eliza (see Weizenbaum 1966), which could hold a simple conversation with a user by using a few simple tricks. Scanning the input string for keywords, using a variety of canned replies, and simple reformulations, allowed the program to fake the conversation of a psychotherapist with a surprising degree of success. What is more astonishing is how little progress has been made in this particular problem area since then. The field has been considered to be too hard for reputable researchers to work in, with a few honourable exceptions, and the field has been colonized with amateurs and hobbyists, who have done some interesting work, but using rather inefficient tools. Recent research in this area include the Companions project (see Wilks 2005), which is an ambitious attempt to produce long-term conversational companions based on the application of NLP techniques: an interesting experiment to see if one can develop a piece of software, embodied in some physical form that users will form a social relationship with. A bizarre idea initially, but no more strange than being emotionally involved with a pet like a canary; and less strange than the attachments people form with other inanimate objects like a car or a sailing boat.

This case study has only covered a small range of the field of NLP, focusing on those aspects most relevant to New Media. Inevitably, there will be surprises in store. The future development of New Media depends not just on purely cultural and economic factors, but to a great extent on technological innovation; the extent to which technologists can overcome the problems involved in the sorts of reasoning and representation needed to produce natural dialogue: and NLP will arguably have a more significant effect than many other factors. The invention of the movable type printing press was a purely technological innovation with vast cultural implications; it remains to be seen whether future innovations will have as radical an effect.

Appendix

New Media: a timeline

1941

The Z3 (one of Konrad Zuse's electromechanical 'Z machines') is invented. It was the first working machine featuring binary arithmetic, including floating point arithmetic and a measure of programmability. It is therefore regarded as one of the first computers.

1944

The Harvard Mark 1 is invented. It is a large-scale electromechanical computer with limited programmability.

1946

The US Army's Ballistics Research Laboratory ENIAC uses decimal arithmetic and is sometimes called the first general purpose electronic computer (since Konrad Zuse's Z3 used electromagnets instead of electronics).

1947

A forerunner of the video game, the 'Cathode Ray Tube Amusement Device' was conceived by Thomas T. Goldsmith Jr. and Estle Ray Mann.

1951

Vacuum tube-based computers are sold commercially.

The Xerox machine is invented.

Integrated circuit invented enabling the further miniaturization of electronic devices and computers.

1952

Intermetall unveils the first transistorized portable radio in the Düsseldorf Radio Fair.

1957

The first artificial satellite (Sputnik 1) is launched by the Soviet Union.

1958

Explorer 1 becomes the USA's first satellite.

1959

Jack Kilby and Texas Instruments received US patent #3,138,743 for miniaturized electronic circuits (also known as IC, microcircuit, microchip, silicon chip or chip).

Robert Noyce and the Fairchild Semiconductor Corporation received US patent #2,981,877 for a silicon-based integrated circuit.

1961

First commercially available integrated circuits came from the Fairchild Semiconductor Corporation. All computers then started to be made using chips instead of the individual transistors and their accompanying parts.

1962

The satellite, *Telstar*, is launched by NASA.

1966

Xerox invents the Telecopier – the first successful fax machine.

Jack Kilby invents the portable calculator.

1968

Ivan Sutherland, with the help of his student Bob Sproull, create what is widely considered to be the first virtual reality (VR) and augmented reality (AR) head-mounted display (HMD) system.

Robert Noyce founds Intel, the company responsible for the invention of the microprocessor.

1969

ARPANET is developed by the Defense Advanced Research Projects Agency of the US Department of Defense. It was the world's first operational packet switching network.

The Moon Landing – Apollo 11; Neil Armstrong walks on the moon.

1970

Sony introduces the first videocassette, the three-quarter-inch U-matic one-hour tape.

1971

The computer floppy disc is invented.

The microprocessor is invented – considered a computer on a chip.

Computer Space, the first commercially sold, coin-operated video game is launched.

John Blankenbaker builds the first personal computer, the Kenblak 1.

1972

HBO (Home Box Office) invents pay-TV service for cable.

The first video game console, the Magnavox Odyssey, is launched and the Video game *Pong* is released. Noland Bushnell, its 28-year-old inventor, goes on to found Atari.

1973

Norway and England connect to ARPANET, making the first international connection.

Xerox develops the Ethernet which will become the de facto standard for linking computers, printers and other hardware devices.

The Desktop computer is introduced by Hewlett-Packard.

1974

Products with barcodes begin appearing in US stores.

Scanners at checkout counters are able to read the codes using laser technology.

Nam June Paik, a twentieth-century South Korean-born US video artist, claims to have coined the term 'the information superhighway', that is, a route or network for the high-speed transfer of information.

1975

Microsoft is founded by Bill Gates.

First hand-held mobile phone arrives.

First major ISP (Internet service provider) CompuServe Asper established.

Xerox sells SDS to Honeywell and withdraws from computer industry.

1976

Apple home computer invented.

1977

Commodore and Tandy begin selling PCs.

North Star and Pertec introduce PCs with five-and-a-half-inch floppy discs.

Xerox releases the Xerox 9700 Electronic Printing System, the first xerographic laser printer product.

1978

The video game *Space Invaders* is released.

Texas Instruments introduces *Speak-and-Spell*, an educational toy featuring digital speech synthesis.

Pioneer develop the LaserDisc that was first used by General Motors to train Cadillac salesmen.

1979

First cellular phone communication network started in Japan.

Sony Walkman invented.

1980

The number of computers in the USA exceeds one million. Microsoft DOS version 1.0 marketed.

The originator of the Internet, Tim Berners-Lee, writes the 'Enquire Within' program. 'Enquire' has some of the same ideas as the web but was not supposed to be released to the general public.

Intelpost international electronic fax service established.

CNN 24-hour news channel goes on the air.

Wordstar is first PC word processor.

Lotus 1-2-3 spreadsheet first compact discs 1980 Sony Walkman invented.

1981

IBM PC first sold.

First laptop computers sold to public.

Computer mouse becomes a regular part of computer.

First Nintendo home video game produced.

Jim Rutt coins the term 'snail mail' to contrast traditional mail with email.

Microsoft provides software for IBM PC. The company's first international office is founded.

NASA introduces, Columbia, a reusable spacecraft.

1982

Sky Channel (first European satellite television channel) launched.

Kodak camera uses film on a disc cassette. Two hundred computers connected to the Internet worldwide.

Sony's first compact disc player (CDP–101) introduced.

1983

Time magazine names the computer as 'Man of the Year'.

First cellular phone network started in the USA.

Number of computers in the USA exceeds ten million.

Mobile phone network starts in the USA.

Bruce Bethke's short story *Cyberpunk* is published.

1984

Apple Macintosh 1 is released.

IBM PC AT is released.

William Gibson coins term 'cyberspace' in his novel *Neuromancer*.

The CD Walkman is launched.

The first PDA (personal digital assistant) – Psion Organiser, the first Camcorder and the Apple Macintosh, IBM PC AT are marketed.

The silicon microchip is developed, storing four times more data than previously possible.

The Tandy 1000 PC becomes the number 1 selling IBM PC-compatible in its first year.

A computer hacker and DIY media organization called 'Cult of the Dead Cow' (also known as cDc or cDc Communications) publishes the first 'ezine' (periodic publication distributed by email or posted on a website).

1985

Cellular telephones in cars become widespread in the USA.

CD-ROMs arrive in computers.

Pay-per-view channels open for business in the USA. Twenty per cent of US households have VCRs.

AOL – American Online is founded.

Symbolics.com becomes the first registered domain and is quickly followed by cmu.edu, purdue.edu, ucl.edu, and others.

1986

Microsoft Windows 1.0 launched.

Total computers in use in the USA exceed 30 million.

1987

The first debit card in the UK is launched.

1988

The first Internet worm (a self-replicating computer program) is detected.

Microsoft introduces its flagship office suite, Microsoft Office.

1990

The possibility of the World Wide Web is described by Tim Berners-Lee.

The Super Nintendo Entertainment System (SNES) is launched.

Microsoft introduces Windows 3.0 operating system.

1991

The first online website appears.

The European Organization for Nuclear Research announces that the World Wide Web will be free to anyone.

CNN dominates news coverage worldwide during the Gulf War.

Seventy-five per cent of US homes reported to own VCRs; 60 per cent have cable television.

The first webcam is pointed at the Trojan room coffee pot in the computer science department of Cambridge University.

The Dycam Model 1 B&W digicam is the world's first completely digital consumer camera.

1992

US cable television revenue reaches US$22 billion. TCI chair John Malone predicts '500 channel universe'.

First short message service (SMS) to a mobile phone.

1993

DVD invented by Toshiba.

V-chip proposed for television content control.

Mosaic – the first graphical Internet browser is launched.

Kodak and Apple produce first digital still image camera for consumers.

1994

US government releases control of the Internet and the World Wide Web (WWW) is born.

Justin Hall begins his online journal while a student at Swarthmore College and becomes one of the world's first 'bloggers'. Originally called 'weblogs', this was later shortened simply to 'blogs'.

First digital television service – DirecTV in the USA by satellite.

The Sony PlayStation is launched.

There are 135 million PCs worldwide.

The US government privatizes Internet management.

First advertisement on the World Wide Web for *Wired* magazine.

Canter and Siegel's *How to Make a Fortune on the Information Superhighway* is published.

Goldstein's Copyright's Highway: *The Law & Lore of Copyright from Gutenberg to the Celestial Jukebox* is published.

Interactive television is introduced in the USA.

1995

Microsoft releases its first retail version of Microsoft Windows, originally a graphical extension for its MS-DOS operating system.

Amazon.com is founded and Pierre Omidyar launches an online auction service called Auction Web, which becomes eBay.

Sony demonstrates flat-screen television set. Iomega markets zip drive.

RealAudio lets Internet users hear in near real-time.

DVD manufacturers announce the creation of a new standardized digital video disc (DVD) format, which leads to the mass production of movie DVDs.

The first cyber cafés open, which serve Internet access and café latte.

Pixar releases *Toy Story*, the first fully computer-generated animated feature film.

Microsoft introduces the Internet Explorer web browser.

Nicholas Negroponte's *Being Digital* is published.

1996

399,629 industrial robots in use in Japan (70,858 in the USA).

Total computers in use in the USA exceed 100 million.

Philips and Sony introduce WebTV boxes that connect television to the Internet.

Both @Home and Time Warner announce high-speed, cable-modem ventures in an attempt to meet consumers' growing demand for higher bandwidth.

1997

Hotmail introduces its service and becomes one of the first popular web-based email (electronic mail) offerings.

Microsoft buys WebTV for US$503 million.

The first mass-produced DAP (digital audio player) is created.

The first multi-layer video games which might be recognized today as MUDs (Multi-User Dungeon, Domain or Dimension) first appear.

1998

Hewlett-Packard releases first colour Palmtop computer.

Panasonic releases first hand-held DVD player.

Google first incorporated as a privately held company.

Compaq make the first hard drive-based DAP (digital audio player) using a 2.5 laptop drive.

The on-orbit assembly of the International Space Station (ISS) begins.

1999

Global online population reaches 150 million (over 50 per cent in the USA).

The social networking website MySpace created.

Finland's mobile phones linked to vending machines.

First WAP (wireless access point) mobile phone advertisement in Finland.

Commercial DAB (digital audio broadcasting) receivers began to be sold.

2000

'Great Dot-com Crash'. The event was marked by the spectacular failure of a group of new Internet-based companies commonly referred to as 'dot-coms'. The bursting of the 'dot-com bubble' marked the beginning of a relatively long recession in the developed world.

2001

Over 20 million subscribers on DoCoMo's i-mode network.

Designed and marketed by Apple, a brand of portable media players called the iPod is launched.

Microsoft announces the Xbox, a new video game console.

2004

The social networking website Facebook is launched.

The term 'Web. 2' gains currency following the first O'Reilly Media Web 2.0 conference.

2005

YouTube, video-sharing website (where users can upload, view and share video clips) is created.

Digital cinema projectors capable of 2K resolution are launched.

Supreme Court rules that peer-to-peer networks can be held liable for copyright infringements committed by users in *Grokster* v. *MGM* case.

2006

The 100 millionth account is created on MySpace.

Luxembourg is the first country to complete the move to digital broadcasting.

2007

The blog search engine Technorati tracks more than 112 million.

The annual *Forbes* magazine's list of The World's Billionaires ranks Bill Gates (chairman of Microsoft) as the richest person in the world from 1995 to 2007, with recent estimates putting his net worth over US$56 billion.

2012
Television digital switch over in the UK is expected to be complete.

Bibliography

Aarseth, Espen (1997) *Cybertext: Perspectives on Ergodic Literature*. Baltimore, MD: The Johns Hopkins University Press.

Aarseth, Espen (2001) Computer game studies, year one *Gamestudies, The International Journal of Computer Game Research* (www.gamestudies.org/0101/editorial.html).

Abbate, Janet (2000) *Inventing the Internet*. Cambridge, MA: The MIT Press.

Accenture, Markle Foundation and UNDP (2001) *Creating a Development Dynamic: Final Report of the Digital Opportunity Initiative*, July.

Adorno, Theodor W. ([1941] 1994) On popular music, in John Storey (ed.) *Cultural Theory and Popular Culture*. New York and London: Harvester/Wheatsheaf.

Alderman, John (2002) *Sonic Boom: Napster, P2P and the Future of Music*. London: 4th Estate.

Althusser, Louis (1971) *Lenin and Philosophy and Other Essays*. London: NLB.

Anderson, Chris (2004) The long tail, *Wired*, 12: 10.

Anderson, Chris (2006) *The Long Tail: Why the Future of Business Is Selling Less of More*. London: Hyperion.

Anderson, Craig A., Gentile, Douglas A. and Buckley, Katherine E. (2007), *Violent Video Game Effects on Children and Adolescents: Theory, Research, and Public Policy*. Oxford: Oxford University Press.

Anheier, Helmut, Glasius, Marlies and Kaldo, Mary (eds) (2001) *Global Civil Society*. Oxford: Oxford University Press.

Annan, Kofi (1999) Address to the *Telecom '99, The Eighth World Telecommunication Exhibition and Forum*, Geneva, 9 October. Press Release SG/SM/7164 (www.un.org/News/Press/docs/1999/19991011.sgsm7164.doc.html).

Anon (2004) Sony Walkman wakes up too late, *Advertising Age*, 75(34): 14.

Anon (2005) Online music lovers 'frustrated', *BBC News*, 25 April (www.news.bbc.co.uk/1/hi/technology/4474143.stm: accessed May 2006).

Aronson, Jonathan (2001) The communications and internet revolution, in J. Baylis (ed.) *The Globalisation of World Politics*, 2nd edn. London: Oxford University Press.

Bacevich, Andrew J. (1996) Morality and high technology, *National Interest*, 45: 37–48.

Bacevich, Andrew J. (2005) *The New American Militarism: How Americans are Seduced by War*. Oxford: Oxford University Press.

Bakardjieva, Maria (2005) *Internet Society: The Internet in Everyday Life*. London: Sage Publications.

Bakupa-Kaninda, Balufu (2003) Film in Africa, Africa in film: challenging stereotypes, *United Nations Chronicle*, online edition (www.un.org/Pubs/chronicle/2003/issue1/0103p27.html).

Barbrook, R. and Cameron, A. (1995) *The Californian Ideology*. URL (www.hrc.wmin.ac.uk/: accessed September 2000).

Barlow, John Perry ([1996] 2001) A declaration of the independence of cyberspace, in Peter Ludlow (ed.) (2001) *Crypto Anarchy, Cyberstates and Pirate Utopias*. Cambridge, MA: The MIT Press, 27–30.

Barnes, Brooke (2007) 'NBC in deal with Amazon to sell shows on the web', *The New York Times*, 5 September.

Barnes, Sue (2001) *Online Connections: Internet Interpersonal Relations*, Cresskill, NJ: Hampton Press.

Barthes, Roland ([1957] 1973), *Mythologies*. London: Vintage Classics.

Barthes, Roland (1977a) The rhetoric of the image, in R. Barthes (ed.). *Image, Music, Text* (trans. S. Heath). London: Fontana Press.

Barthes, Roland (1977b) The death of the author, in R. Barthes (ed.). *Image, Music, Text*. London: Fontana Press.

Bassett, Keith (1996) Postmodernism and the crisis of the intellectual: reflections on reflexivity, universities, and the scientific field, *Society and Space*, 14(5): 507–27.

Baudrillard, Jean (1994) *Simulacra and Simulation*, Ann Arbor, MI: The University of Michigan Press.

Baylis, John, Smith, Steve and Owens, Patricia (2001) *The Globalisation of World Politics*, 2nd edn. London: Oxford University Press.

Bearak, Barry (2002) Uncertain toll in the fog of war, *The New York Times*, 10 February.

Beier, J. Marshall (2007) Flower power: diplomacies of death, discriminacy, and daisy cutters. Paper presented at the ISA Conference, Chicago, 28 February.

Bell, Daniel (1976), *The Coming of Post-industrial Society*. New York: Basic Books.

Bell, Daniel ([1973] 2004) Post industrial Society, in F. Webster et al. *The Information Society Reader*. London: Routledge.

Bell, David (2001) *An Introduction to Cybercultures*. London: Routledge.

Bell, David and Kennedy, Barbara (eds) (2007) *The Cybercultures Reader*, 2nd edn. London: Routledge.

Benhabib, Seyla (1992) Models of public space: 'The Liberal Tradition Hannah, Arendt and Jurgen Habermas' in C. Calhoun (ed.) *Habermas and the Public Sphere*. London: The MIT Press.

Bergen, Peter L. (2002) *Holy War, Inc.* New York: Touchstone.

Berger, Guy (2001) *Configuring Convergence*. South Africa: New Media Lab.

Berk, Mike (2000) Technology: analog fetishes and digital futures, in Peter Shapiro (ed.) *Modulations: A History of Electronic Music*, pp. 181–201. New York: Caipirinha.

Berners-Lee, Tim (1999) *Weaving the Web: The Past, Present and Future of the World Wide Web by its Inventor*. London: Orion.

Berry, Richard (2006) Will the iPod kill the radio star?', *Convergence: The International Journal of Research into New Media Technologies*, 12(2): 143–62.

Best, Steven and Kellner, Douglas (1997) Entropy, chaos and organism in postmodern science, in Steven Best and Douglas Kellner (eds) *The Postmodern Turn*. New York and London: Guilford Press.

Bijker, W.E. (2006) Why and how technology matters, in R.E. Goodin and C. Tilley (eds) *Oxford Handbook of Contextual Political Analysis*. Oxford: Oxford University Press.

Bocquet, Gavin (2005) Audio commentary for *Star Wars Episode II: Attack of the Clones*, 2-disc DVD edition.

Boller, J.D. and Grusin, R. (2001) *Remediation: Understanding New Media*. London and Cambridge, MA: The MIT Press.

Bolter, Jay David and Grusin, Richard (1999) *Remediation: Understanding New Media*. Cambridge, MA: The MIT Press.

Braverman, Harry (1974) *Labour and Monopoly Capital: The Degradation of Work in the Twentieth Century*. New York: Monthly Review Press.

Briggs, Asa (1961) *The History of Broadcasting in the United Kingdom: Vol II, The Golden Age of Wireless*. Oxford: Oxford University Press.

British Telecom Report (2004) *The Digital Divide in 2025: An Independent Study Conducted for BT*, December.

Brooker, Will and Jermyn (eds) (2003) *The Audience Studies Reader*. London and New York: Routledge.

Brown, Alan and Robert G. Picard (eds) (2005) *Digital Terrestrial Television in Europe*. Mahwah, NJ: Lawrence Earlbaum Associates.

Brown, Julian (2000) *Minds, Machines, and the Multiverse: The Quest for the Quantum Computer*. New York: Simon & Schuster.

Bull, Michael (2000) *Sounding Out the City: Personal Stereos and the Management of Everyday Life*. Oxford and New York: Berg.

Bull, Michael (2001) The world according to sound: investigating the world of Walkman users, *New Media and Society*, 3(2): 179–97.

Bull, Michael (2005) No dead air! The iPod and the culture of mobile listening, *Leisure Studies*, 24(4): 343–55.

Bull, Michael (2006) Filmic cities: the aesthetic experience of the personal-stereo user, in Andy Bennett, Barry Shank and Jason Toynbee (eds) *The Popular Music Studies Reader*, pp. 148–55. London: Routledge.

Bumford, James (2005) The man who sold the war, *Rolling Stone*, 17 November.

Burgin, Victor (2004) *The Remembered Film*. London: Reaktion Books.

Burnett, Robert and Marshall, P. David (2003) *Web Theory: An Introduction*. London: Routledge.

Burns, Tom (1977) *The BBC: Public Institution and Private World*. London: Macmillan.

Calhoun, Craig (ed.) (1992) *Habermas and the Public Sphere*. London: The MIT Press.

Camaerts, B. and Carpentier, N. (eds) (2007) *Reclaiming the Media: Communication Rights and Democratic Media Roles*. Bristol, UK: Intellect.

Carvin, Andy (2000) More than just access: fitting literacy and content into the digital divide equation, *Educause Review*, 35(6).

Castaneda, Mari (2007) The complicated transition to digital television in the United States, *Television and New Media*, 8(2): 91–106.

Castells, Manuel (1999) *The Information Age: Economy, Society and Culture*. Oxford: Blackwell Publishing.

Cavallaro, Dani (2000) *Cyberpunk and Cyberculture*. London: Athlone.

Chandler, Daniel (2004a) *Semiotics: The Basics*. London and New York: Routledge.

Chandler, Daniel (2004b) *Using the Telephones* (www.aber.ac.uk/media/documents/short/phone.html: accessed 7 June).

Chesher, Chris (2007) Becoming the Milky Way: mobile phones and actor networks at a U2 concert, *Continuum*, 21: 217–25.

Chester, Jeffrey (2003) Determining our digital destiny: as broadband takes hold, we must decide how to make the technology benefit all of us, *Philadelphia Inquirer*, 2 November (www.philly.com/mld/inquirer/).

Chester, Jeffrey (2005) The death of the internet: how industry intends to kill the net as we know it, *Centre for Digital Democracy*, 4 April (www.democraticmedia.org).

Cline-Cole, Reginald and Powel, Mike (2004) ICTs, virtual colonisation and political economy, *Review of African Political Economy*, 99: 335–50.

Colas, Alejandro (2002) *International Civil Society*. Cambridge: Polity Press.

Collins, Jim (1991) Television and postmodernism, in Robert C. Allen (ed.) *Channels of Discourse, Reassembled*. London and New York: Routledge.

Conetta, Carl (2002a), *Operation Enduring Freedom: Why a Higher Rate of Civilian Bombing Casualties?* (www.comw.org./pda/0201oef.html: accessed on 13 November 2004).

Conetta, Carl (2002b) *Disappearing the Dead: Afghanistan, Iraq and the Idea of a 'New Warfare'* (www.comw.org/pda/ 0402rm9 exsum.html: accessed on 2 December 2006).

Cook, Michael (2003) *A Brief History of the Human Race*. New York. W.W. Norton and Company.

Cordesman, Anthony H. (2002) *The Lessons of Afghanistan: War, Fighting, Intelligence, and Force Transformation*. Washington, DC: CSIS Press.

Cover, Rob (2005) DVD time: temporality, audience engagement and the new TV culture of digital video, *Media International Australia*, 117: 137–47.

Cranny-Francis, Anne (2005) *MultimediaTexta and Contexts*. London: Sage Publications.

Crawford, Garry and Rutter, Jason (2006) Digital games and cultural studies, in Jason Rutter and Jo Bryce (eds) *Understanding Digital Games*. London: Sage Publications.

Creeber, Glen (1998) *Dennis Potter: Between Two Worlds, A Critical Reassessment*. London and New York: Macmillan.

Creeber, Glen (2004) Hideously white: British television, glocalisation and national identity, *Television and New Media*, 5(1).

Crisell, Andrew (1997) The BBC: from private company to national institution, in Andrew Crisell (ed.) *An Introductory History to British Broadcasting*. London and New York: Routledge.

Critical Art Ensemble (1994) *The Electronic Disturbance*. Brooklyn, NY: Autonomedia.

Cuneo, Alice Z. (2003) Apple transcends as lifestyle brand, *Advertising Age*, Midwest Region Edition, 74(50): Section 2.

Curran, James (1999) Rethinking the media as a public sphere in, P. Dahlgren and C. Sparks (1999) *Communication and Citizenship: Journalism and the Public Sphere*. London: Sage Publications.

Curtain, Tyler (2007) Promiscuous fictions, in David Bell and Barbara Kennedy (eds) *The Cybercultures Reader*, 2nd edn. London: Routledge.

Curtin, Michael (2003) From network to neo-network audiences, in Michele Hilmes (ed.) *The Television History Book*. London: BFI.

Dahlgren, Pete and Sparks, Colin (1999) *Communication and Citizenship: Journalism and the Public Sphere*. London: Routledge.

Dalessio, Dave (2007) A preliminary evaluation of the impact of unsolicited commercial mail promoting stocks, *New Media & Society*, 9(6), December.

Damarin, Suzanne (2000) The digital divide versus digital differences: principles for equitable use of technology in education, *Educational Technology*, 40(4): 17–21.

Darley, Andrew (1999) *Visual Digital Culture*. London and New York: Routledge.

Dean, Jodi (2000) Webs of conspiracy, in A. Herman (ed.) *The World Wide Web and Contemporary Cultural Theory*. London: Routledge.

Department of Defense (2001) *Department of Defense Dictionary of Military and Associated Terms*, Joint Publication 1–02, 12 April (as amended through 17 December 2003).

Der Derian, James (2002) *Virtuous War: Mapping the Military-Industrial-Media-Entertainment Network*. Oxford: Westview Press.

Dery, Mark (1994) (ed.) *Flames Wars. The Discourse of Cyberculture*. London: Duke University Press.

Dower, N. and Williams, J. (2002) *Global Citizenship: A Critical Reader*. Edinburgh: Edinburgh University Press.

Downing, John et al. (1998) *Computers for Social Change and Community Organising*. Philadelphia, PA: Haworth Press.

Dutton, William (2003) Information Society, in D.H. Johnston (ed.) *Encyclopedia of International Media and Communications*, Vol. 2. London: Academic Press.

Eagleton, Terry (1990) *The Ideology of the Aesthetic*. Oxford: Blackwell Publishing.

Ebo, Bosah (ed.) (1998) *Cyberghetto or Cybertopic: Race, Class, and Gender on the Internet*. Westport: Praeger.

Edwards, Paul (1996) *The Closed World*. Cambridge MA: The MIT Press.

Eldridge, M. and Grinter, R. (2001) Studying text messaging in teenagers. Position paper presented at the CHI 2001 Workshop #1 – *Mobile Communications: Understanding User, Adoption and Design*, Seattle.

Ellis, John (1982) *Visible Fictions: Cinema, Television, Video*. London and New York: Routledge.

Elmer, Greg (2004) *Profiling Machines: Mapping the Personal Information Economy*. Cambridge MA: The MIT Press.

Elsaesser, Thomas (1998) Digital cinema: delivery, event, time, in T. Elsaesser and K. Hoffman (eds) *Cinema Futures: Cain, Abel or Cable?* Amsterdam: Amsterdam University Press.

EMI (2007) Press release: EMI Music launches DRM-free superior sound quality downloads across its entire digital repertoire. Press release, 2 April (www.emigroup.com/Press/2007/press18.htm).

Enzensburger, Hans ([1970] 2000) Constituents of a theory of the media, in D. McQuail (ed.) *Sociology of Mass Communications*. London: Penguin.

Everett, James (2002) *Social Consequences of Internet Use: Access, Involvement and Interaction*. Cambridge: Cambridge University Press.

Fairclough, Norman (1995) *Media Discourse*. London and New York: Edward Arnold.

Farrell, Theo (2005) *The Norms of War: Cultural Beliefs and Modern Conflict*. London: Lynne Rienner.

Feltoe, Geoff (2002) *A Guide to Media Law in Zimbabwe*. Zimbabwe: Mambo Press.

Fiddler, Roger (1994) Newspapers in the electronic age, in F. Williams and J.V. Pavlik (eds) *The People's Right to Know: Media, Democracy, and the Information Highway*. London and New Jersey: Lawrence Erlbaum Associates.

Finder, Alan (2006) For some, online persona undermines a résumé, *The New York Times*, 11 June.

Fiske, John (1998) Television: polysemy and popularity, in Roger Dickinson, Ramaswani Harindranath and Olga Linné (eds) *Approaches to Audiences: A Reader*. London: Edward Arnold.

Flew, Terry (2002) *New Media: An Introduction*. Oxford: Oxford University Press.

Foroohar, Rana (2005) Your own world, *Newsweek*, 48, 26 September.

Foucault, Michel (1991) with Rabinow, Paul (ed.) *The Foucault Reader: An Introduction to Foucault's Thought*. London and New York: Penguin Books.

Fraser, Nancy (1992) Rethinking the public sphere: a contribution to the critique of actually existing democracy, in C. Calhoun (ed.) *Habermas and the Public Sphere*. London: The MIT Press.

Friedberg, Anne (2002) DVD and CD, in Dan Harries (ed.) *The New Media Book*, pp. 30–9. London: BFI.

Frith, Simon and Lee Marshall (2004) (eds) *Music and Copyright*, 2nd edn. Edinburgh: Edinburgh University Press.

Fuller, Matthew (2003) *Behind the Blip: Essays on Software Culture*. New York: Autonomedia.

Fuller, Matthew (2005) *Media Ecologies: Materialist Energies in Art and Architecture*. Cambridge, MA: The MIT Press.

Galloway, Alexander R. (2004) *Protocol: How Control Exists After Decentralization*, Cambridge, MA: The MIT Press.

Galloway, Ann (2004) Intimations of everyday life: ubiquitous computing and the city, *Cultural Studies*, 18: 384–408.

Gandy, Oscar H. Jnr. (1993) *The Panoptic Sort: The Political Economy of Personal Information*. Boulder CO: Westview Press.

Garnham, Nicholas (1992) The media and the public sphere, in C. Calhoun (ed.) *Habermas and the Public Sphere*. London: The MIT Press.

Garnham, Nicholas (2002) *Emancipation, the Media and Modernity: Arguments about the Media and Social Theory*. Oxford: Oxford University Press.

Gauntlett, David (2004) Web studies: what's new?, in David Gauntlett and Ross Horsley (eds) *Web.Studies*, 2nd edn, pp. 3–23. London: Edward Arnold.

Gauntlett, David (2007) *Creative Explorations: New Approaches to Identities and Audiences*. London: Routledge.

Gauntlett, David (2008) *Media, Gender and Identity: An Introduction*, 2nd edn. London: Routledge.

Gauntlett, David and Horsley, Ross (eds) (2004) *Web.Studies*, 2nd edn. London: Edward Arnold.

Gazdar, Gerald (1996) Paradigm merger in natural language processing, in R. Milner and I. Wand (eds) *Computing Tomorrow: Future Research Directions in Computer Science*. Cambridge: Cambridge University Press.

Gee, Paul (2003) *What Video Games Have to Teach Us About Learning and Literacy*. London and New York: Palgrave. Macmillan.

Gelernter, David (1998) *The Aesthetics of Computing*. London: Phoenix.

Gere, Charlie (2002) *Digital Culture*. London: Reaktion Books.

Gibson, William (1984) *Neuromancer*. London: Grafton.

Giddens, Anthony (1991) *Modernity and Self-identity: Self and Society in the Late Modern Age*. Cambridge: Polity Press.

Giles, Jim (2005) Internet encyclopaedias go head to head, *Nature*, 438: 900–01 (www.nature.com/nature/journal/ v438/n7070/full/438900a.html).

Gillmor, Dan (2006) *We the Media: Grassroots Journalism by the People, for the People*. Sebastopol: O'Reilly.

Gramsci, Antonio (1971) Selections from the Prision Notebook, edited and translated by Quintin Hoare & Goffrey Nowell Smith, Lawrence and Wishart, London.

Gray, Chris H. (1997) *Postmodern War: The New Politics of Conflict*. London: Routledge.

Gurak, Laura J. (2000) Internet studies in the twenty-first century, in David Gauntlett and Ross Horsley (eds) *Web.Studies*, 2nd edn. London and New York: Edward Arnold.

Gye, Lisa (2007) Picture this: the impact of mobile camera phones on personal photographic practices, *Continuum*, 21(2): 279–88.

Habermas, Jürgen (1989) *The Structural Transformation of the Public Sphere: An Inquiry into a Category of Bourgeois Society*. Cambridge: Polity Press.

Hacker, Kenneth and van Dijk, Jan (eds) (2000) *Digital Democracy*. London: Sage Publications.

Haldane, Maureen (2007) Interactivity and the digital white board: weaving the fabric of learning, *Learning, Media and Technology*, 32(3).

Hall, Stuart (1973) Encoding and decoding in television discourse, CCCS Stencilled Paper no. 7; also in During, Simon (ed.) (1993) *The Cultural Studies Reader*, London and New York: Routledge.

Hall, Stuart (1995) Formations of modernity: introduction, in Stuart Hall, David Held, Don Hubert and Kenneth Thompson (eds) *Modernity: An Introduction to Modern Societies*, Cambridge: Polity Press.

Hamelink, Cees (2000) *The Ethics of Cyberspace*. London: Sage Publications.

Hamelink, Cees (2003) Human rights for the information society, in B. Girard and S. O'siochru (eds) *Communicating in the Information Society*. Geneva: UNRISD.

Haraway, Donna (1991) *A Cyborg Manifesto: Science, Technology, and Socialist-Feminism in the Late Twentieth Century*. London and New York: Routledge.

Harries, Dan (2002) Watching the internet, in Dan Harries (ed.) *The New Media Book*, pp. 171–82. London: British Film Institute.

Harries, Dan (ed.) (2002) *The New Media Book*. London: British Film Institute.

Hartley, John (1999) *The Uses of Television*. London and New York: Routledge.

Hartley, John (2002) *Communication, Cultural and Media Studies: The Key Concepts*. London and New York: Routledge.

Harvey, David (1990) *The Condition of Postmodernity*. Cambridge, MA and Oxford, UK: Blackwell.

Hassan, Robert (2004) *Media, Politics and the Network Society*. Milton Keynes: Open University Press.

Haywood, Trevor (1998) Global networks and the myth of equality: trickle down or trickle away?, in B. D. Loader (ed.) *Cyberspace Divide: Equality, Agency and Policy In the Information Society*. London: Routledge.

HDP (2003) *Millennium Development Goals: A Compact Among Nations to End Human Poverty*, July.

Hegghammer, Thomas (2006a) Global Jihadism after the Iraq War, *Middle East Journal*, 60(1).

Hegghammer, Thomas (2006b) *Al-Qaida Statements 2003–2004* (www.ffi.no: accessed on 3 July 2006).

Helman, Pablo (2005) Audio commentary for *Star Wars Episode II: Attack of the Clones*, 2-disc DVD edition.

Herold, Marc (2002) Afghan killing fields, *The Guardian*, 12 February.

Herring, George C. (1986) *America's Longest War: The United States and Vietnam, 1950–1975*. New York: Alfred A. Knopf.

Hersh, Seymour M. (2004) Torture at Abu Ghraib, *The New Yorker*, 10 May.

Hertog, Herta (1941) On borrowed experience: an analysis of listening to daytime sketches, *Studies in Philosophy and Social Science*, IX(1): 65–95.

Hillis, Ken, Petit, Michael and Epley, Nathan (eds) (2006) *Everyday eBay: Culture, Collecting, and Desire*. New York: Routledge.

Hoffman, Donna and Thomas, Novak (2000) The growing digital divide: implications for an open research agenda, in B. Kahin and E. Brynjolffson (eds) *Understanding the Digital Economy*. Cambidge, MA: Massachusetts Institute of Technology.

Holderness, Mike (1998) Who are the world's information poor?, in B.D. Loader *Cyberspace Divide: Equality, Agency and Policy in the Information Society*. London: Routledge.

Holmes, David (1997) *Virtual Politics*. London, Thousand Oaks, CA: Sage Publications.

Holub, Robert (1991) *Jurgen Habermas: Critique of the Public Sphere*. London: Routledge.

Hosokawa, Shuhei (1984) The Walkman effect, *Popular Music*, 4: 165–80.

Hulme, Michael and Peters, Sue (2001) Me, Myself and My Mobile Phone (www.michaelhulme.co.uk/pdf/papers/HulmePeters.pdf).

Human Rights Watch (2002) Fatally flawed: cluster bombs and their use by the United States in Afghanistan, 14(7): 40–4 (www.hrw.org/reports/2002/us-afghanistan/: accessed 20 April 2006).

Huyssen, Andreas (1986) *After the Great Divide: Modernism, Mass Culture and Postmodernism, (Theories of Representation and Difference)*. Indiana, IN: Indiana University Press.

IFPI (International Federation of the Phonographic Industry) (2007) *IFPI 2007: Digital Music Report* (www.ifpi.org/content/library/digital-music-report-2007.pdf: accessed May 2007).

Ignatieff, Michael (2000) *Virtual War: Kosovo and Beyond*. London: Chatto and Windus.

Ignatieff, Michael (2004a) The terrorist as auteur, *The New York Times*, 15 November.

Ignatieff, Michael (2004b), *Battle without blood*, (www.salon.com/books/int/2000/05/04/ignatieff: accessed 2 April 2004).

Inman, Philip (2006) When your iPod isn't all that it's cracked up to be, *The Guardian*, Money Section, 30 September, p. 6.

Internet World Statistics (2007) Available at www.InternetWorldStats.com.

Isaacs, Arnold R. (1997) *Vietnam Shadows: The War, Its Ghosts, and its Legacy*. Baltimore, MD: Johns Hopkins University Press.

Jameson, Fredric (1991) *Postmodernism or, the Cultural Logic of Late Capitalism*. London and New York: Verso.

Jaschik, Scott (2007) A stand against Wikipedia, *Inside Higher Ed*, 26 January (www.insidehighered.com/news/2007/01/26/wiki).

Jenkins, Henry (1992) *Textual Poachers: Television Fans and Participatory Culture*. New York and London: Routledge.

Jenkins, Henry (2002) Interactive audiences?, in D. Harries (ed.) *The New Media Book*, pp. 157–70. London: British Film Institute.

Jenkins, Henry (2006a) *Convergence Culture: Where Old Media and New Media Collide*. New York and London: New York University Press.

Jenkins, Henry (2006b) *Fans, Bloggers and Gamers: Essays on Participatory Culture*. New York: New York University Press.

Jenks, Charles (1984) *The Language of Post-modern Architecture*. London: Academy Editions.

Jennings, David (2007) *Net, Blogs and Rock 'N' Roll*. London and Boston: Nicholas Brealey Publishing.

Jensen, Mike (2001)*The Rise of Telecentres and Cyber cafes in Africa* (www.acacia.org.za/jensen_articles.htm).

Jenson, Mike (2002) *The African Internet: A Status Report*, African Internet Connectivity, September (www3.sn.apc.org/africa).

Johnson, Derek (2007) Inviting audiences in: the spatial reorganisation of production and consumption in 'TV III', *New Review of Film and Television Studies*, 5(1): 61–80.

Jurafsky, Daniel and Martin, James H. (2000) *Speech and Language Processing: An Introduction to Natural Language Processing, Computational Linguistics, and Speech Recognition*. Cambridge, MA: The MIT Press.

Kahn, Paul W. (2002) The paradox of riskless warfare, *Philosophy and Public Policy Quarterly*, 22(3): 7.

Kapomaa, Timo (2000) *Speaking Mobile: The City in your Pocket* (www.tkk.fi/Yksikot/YTK/julkaisu/mobile.html).

Kavada, Anastasia (2005) Exploring the role of the internet in the movement for alternative globalisation: the case of the Paris 2003 European Social Forum, *Westminster Papers in Communication and Culture*, 2(1): 72–95.

Keane, John (2001) Global civil society?, in H. Anheier et al. (eds). (2001) *Global Civil Society*. Oxford: Oxford University Press.

Keane, John (2003) *Global Civil Society*? Cambridge: Polity Press.

Keane, John ([1995] 2004), Structural transformations of the public sphere, in F. Webster et al. (eds) *The Information Society Reader*. London: Routledge.

Kellner, Douglas and Kahn, Richard (2004) New media and internet activism: from the Battle of Seattle to blogging, *New Media and Society*, 6(1): 87–95.

Kelly, Kieran (2007) The development of the Apple iPod, in Jamie Sexton (ed.) *Music, Sound and Multimedia: From the Live to the Virtual*, pp. 188–200. Edinburgh: Edinburgh University Press.

Kemper, Victor (2005) interviewed for 'Here We Go Again': The Digital Cinema Revolution Begins. Web documentary included on the *Star Wars Episode II: Attack of the Clones*, 2-disc DVD edition.

Kennedy, David (2006) *Of war and law*. Princeton, NJ: Princeton University Press.

Kent, Stephen L. (2001) *The Ultimate History of Video Games: From Pong to Pokemon – The Story Behind the Craze That Touched Our Lives and Changed the World*. Roseville, CA: Prima Publishing.

Kent, Steven L. (2002) *The Ultimate History of Video Games*. Rocklin, CA: Prima Life.

King, Geoff and Kryzwinska, Tanja (2006) *Tomb Raiders and Space Invaders: Video Game Forms and Contexts*. London and New York: I.B. Tauris.

Kompare, Derek (2006) Publishing flow: DVD vox sets and the reconception of television, *Television and New Media*, 7(4): 335–60.

Kücklich, Julian (2006) Literary theory and digital games, in Jason Rutter and Jo Bryce (eds) *Understanding Digital Games*. London: Sage Publications.

Kukich, K. (1992) Techniques for automatically correcting words in text, *ACM Computing Surveys*, 24(4): 377–439.

Landow, George (2001) Hypertext and critical theory, in D. Trend (ed.) *Reading Digital Culture*. Oxford: Blackwell Publishing.

Latham, Robert (ed.) (2003) *Bombs and Bandwidth: The Emerging Relationship between Information Technology and Security*. New York: The New Press.

Laughey, Dan (2007) Music media in young people's lives, in Jamie Sexton (ed.) *Music, Sound and Multimedia: From the Live to the Virtual*, pp. 172–87. Edinburgh: Edinburgh University Press.

Lessig, Lawrence (1999) *Code and Other Laws of Cyberspace*. New York: Basic Books.

Levinson, Paul (1999) *Digital McLuhan: A Guide to the Information Millennium*. London and New York: Routledge.

Lévy, Pierre (1997) *Collective Intelligence: Mankind's Emerging World in Cyberspace.* Cambridge, MA: Massachusetts Perseus Books.

Lewis, Bernard (2001) The revolt of Islam, *The New Yorker*, 19 November.

Lister, Martin, Dovey, Jon, Giddings, Seth, Grant, Iain and Kelly, Kieran (2003) *New Media: A Critical Introduction.* London and New York: Routledge.

Loader, Brian (1998) *Cyberspace Divide: Equality, Agency and Policy in the Information Society.* London: Routledge.

Lofgre, K. and Smith, C. (1999) *Political Parties, Democracy and the New Information and Communication Technologies: Theorising the Relationships.* Glasgow: Centre for Research on Public Management and Organisation and Institute of Political Science.

Lowenthal, Leo (1949) (with Norbert Guttermann), *Prophets of Deceit*, New York: Harper.

Lucas, George (2005a) interviewed for State of the Art: The Previsualisation of Episode II: Documentary included on the *Star Wars Episode II: Attack of the Clones*, 2-disc DVD edition.

Lucas, George (2005b) interviewed for We Didn't Go to the Desert to Get a Suntan: Location Shooting Around the World. Web documentary included on the *Star Wars Episode II: Attack of the Clones*, 2-disc DVD edition.

Lucasfilm (2002) *Star Wars Episode II: Attack of the Clones:* production notes (www.cinema.com/articles/854/star-wars-episode-ii-attack-of-the-clones-production-notes.phtml).

Lyon, David (1994) *The Electronic Eye: The Rise of Surveillance Society.* Cambridge: Polity Press.

Lyotard, Jean-François (1984) *The Postmodern Condition: A Report on Knowledge*, trans. G. Bennington and B. Massumi. Manchester: Manchester University Press.

MacKay, Hugh (1997) *Consumption and Everyday Life: Culture, Media and Identities.* London: Open University/Sage Publications.

Mandel, Michael (2004) *How America Gets Away with Murder.* London: Pluto Press.

Mann, Michael (1988) *States, War and Capitalism: Studies in Political Sociology.* Oxford: Blackwell.

Manovich, Lev (2002) *The Language of New Media.* Cambridge, MA and London: The MIT Press.

Marge, Elridge (2001) *Studying Text Messaging Teenagers* (www. oakland.edu/~gapotts/rht160.doc).

Marge, Eldridge and Grinter, Rebecca (2001) *The Mobile Phone as a Globalising Icon* (www.oakland.edu/~gapotts/rht160.doc).

Markgraff, Desiree (2005) *Digital Africa: Filmmaking in South Africa*, Channel 4 film website (www.channel4.com/film/reviews/feature.jsp?id=147915&page=3).

Marks, Paul (2007) Knowledge to the people, interview with Jimmy Wales, *New Scientist*, 3 February, pp. 44–45.

Marshall, P. David (2004) *New Media Cultures*. London: Edward Arnold.

Marshall, P. David (2006) New Media – new self: the changing power of celebrity, in P. David Marshall (ed.) *The Celebrity Culture Reader*, pp. 634–44. London and New York: Routledge.

Masuda, Yoneji ([1990] 2004) Image of the future information society, in F. Webster et al. (eds) *The Information Society Reader*. London: Routledge.

Mayer, Fred (2005) interviewed for Here We Go Again: The Digital Cinema Revolution Begins. Web documentary included on the *Star Wars Episode II: Attack of the Clones*, 2-disc DVD edition.

McCallum, Rick (2005) interviewed for State of the Art: The Previsualisation of Episode II Documentary included on the *Star Wars Episode II: Attack of the Clones*, 2-disc DVD edition.

McChensey, Robert (1997) The communication revolution: the market and the prospect for democracy, in M. Bailie and D. Winseck (eds) *Democratising Communication? Comparative Perspectives on Information and Power*, Creskill, NJ: Hampton Press.

McCracken, Allison (2003) Audiences and the internet, in Michele Hilmes (ed.) *The Television History Book*. London: British Film Institution.

McInnes, Colin (2002) *Spectator Sport Warfare: The West and Contemporary Conflict*. London: Lynne Rienner.

McLuhan, Herbert Marshall (1962) *The Gutenberg Galaxy: The Making of Typographic Man*, 1st edn. Toronto: University of Toronto Press.

McLuhan, Herbert Marshall (1964) *Understanding Media: The Extensions of Man*, 1st edn. New York: McGraw-Hill.

McLuhan, Herbert Marshall, Fiore, Quentin and Agel, Jerome (1967) *The Medium is the Message: An Inventory of Effects with Quentin Fiore*, 1st edn. New York: Random House.

McRobbie Angela (1994) *Postmodermism and Pop Culture*. London and New York: Routledge.

Meredyth, Denise, Ewing, Scott and Thomas, Julian (2003) Introduction: divided opinions over the digital divide, *Southern Review*, 36(1).

Michel, Benoit (2003) Digital cinema key questions, *European Digital Cinema Forum*, 7 November (www.edcf.net/technical_ docs/Digital%20 Cinema%20Key%20 Questions-031107.pdf).

Middleton, Catherine A. (2007) Illusions of balance and control in an always-on environment: a case study of BlackBerry users, *Continuum*, 21(2): 165–78.

Miller, Kate (1999) Special Report, Information Rich, Information Poor: Bridging the Digital Divide, BBC, October (www.news.bbc.co.uk/2/hi/special_report).

Mouffe, Chantel (1988) Radical democracy: modern or postmodern?, in Andrew Ross (ed.) *Universal Abandon?* Minneapolis, KS: University of Minnesota Press.

Moyo, Last (2007) Digital media, globalisation and Human Rights in Zimbabwe. Unpublished thesis, University of Wales, Aberystwyth.

Münkler, Herfried (2006) *Vom Krieg zum Terror.* Zurich: VonTobel Stiftung.

Murray, Janet (1997) *Hamlet on the Holodeck: The future of Narrative in Cyberspace.* Cambridge, MA: The MIT Press.

Murray, Simone (2004) 'Celebrating the Story the Way It Is': Corporate Media and the Contested Utility of Fandom, *Continuum*, 18(1): 7–25.

Naughton, John (2001) Contested space: the internet and global civil society, in H. Anheier et al. *Global Civil Society.* Oxford: Oxford University Press.

Newman, James (2004) *Videogames.* London and New York: Routledge.

Nightingale, Virginia (2007) The camera phone and online image sharing, *Continuum*, 21(2): 289–301.

Norris, Christopher (1992) *Uncritical Theory: Postmodernism, Intellectuals and the Gulf War.* London: Lawrence & Wishart.

Norris, Pippa (2001) *Digital Divide: Civic Engagement, Information Poverty, and the Internet Worldwide.* Cambridge, MA: Cambridge University Press.

Nyíri, Kristóf (ed.) (2003) *Mobile Democracy: Essays on Society, Self and Politics.* Vienna: Passegen.

O'Reilly, Tim (2007) *What Is Web 2.0: Design Patterns and Business Models for the Next Generation of Software* (www.oreillynet.com /lpt/a/6228).

Owens, Patricia (2003) Accidents don't just happen: the liberal politics of high technology humanitarian war, *Millennium: Journal of International Studies*, 32(3): 595–616.

Paine, Jocelyn (2003) *Computers, the Singularity, and the Future of Humanity* (www.j-paine.org/singularity.html).

Pang, B. and Lee, L. (2004) A sentimental education: sentiment analysis using subjectivity summarization based on minimum cuts, *Proceedings of the Association for Computational Linguistics*, pp. 271–78. New Jersey, USA: Association for Computational Linguistics Morristown.

Panos (2004) *Completing the Revolution: The Challenge of Rural Telephony in Africa.* London: Panos.

Papacharissi, Zizi ([2002] 2004) The virtual sphere: the internet as a public sphere, in F. Webster. et al. *The Information Society Reader*. London: Routledge.

Paschal, Preston (2001) *Reshaping Communications: Technology, Information, and Social Change*. London: Sage Publications.

Paul, James (2003) Last night a mix tape saved my life, *The Guardian Friday Review*, 26 September, p.14.

Pauwels, Luc (2005) Websites as visual and multimodal cultural expressions: opportunities and issues of online hybrid media research, *Media, Culture and Society*, 27(4): 604–13.

Penman, Ian (2002) On the mic: how amplification changed the voice for good, in Rob Young (ed.) *Undercurrents: The Hidden Wiring of Modern Music*, pp. 24–34. London and New York: Continuum.

Pfanner, Eric (2007) The British like to control with their DVRs, too, *The New York Times*, 8 January.

Poster, Mark (1995) The mode of information and post modernity, in F. Webster et al. (2004) *The Information Society Reader*. London: Routledge.

Poster, Mark (1997) Cyberdemocracy: the Internet and the public sphere, in David Holmes (ed.) *Virtual Politics*. Thousand Oaks and California: Sage Publications.

Postman, Neil (1985) *Amusing Ourselves to Death: Public Discourse in the Age of Show Business*. London and New York: Methuen.

Potter, James (2001) *Media Literacy*, 2nd edn. London: Sage Publications.

Powerset (2007) *Powerset launches Powerset Labs at TechCrunch40* (www.blog.powerset.com/2007/9/17/powerset-launches-powerset-labs-at-techcrunch40: accessed April 2008).

Preston, Paschal (2001) *Reshaping Communications: Technology, Information, and Social Change*. London: Sage Publications.

Price, Monroe (1995) *Television, The Public Sphere and National Identity*. Oxford: Oxford University Press.

Prince, Stephen (2004) The emergence of filmic artifacts: cinema and cinematography in the digital era, *Film Quarterly*, 57(3): 24–33.

Quiggin, John (2006) Blogs, Wikis and creative innovation, *International Journal of Cultural Studies*, 9: 481–96.

Rayner, M. and Hockey, B.A. and Bouillon, P. (2006) *Putting Linguistics into Speech Recognition: The Regulus Grammar Compiler*. Cambridge, MA: The MIT Press.

Reed, Kristina (2007) Review of *Bioshock*, Eurogamer.net (www.eurogamer.net/article.php?article_id=81479: accessed 28/12/2007).

Reesman, Bryan (2007) For obscure DVDs, a precarious future, *New York Times*, C4, 4 March.

Reith, John (1924) *Broadcast over Britain*. London: Hodder & Stoughton.

Reith, John (1949) *Into the Wind*. London: Hodder & Stoughton.

Reynolds, Simon (2002) Post-rock, in Christoph Cox and Daniel Warner (eds) *Audio Culture*, pp. 358–61. (London and New York: Continuum) (Originally published in *The Village Voice*, 29 August 1995).

Reynolds, Simon (2007) Bring the noise: an interview with Simon Reynolds, *Fact Magazine*, 18 April (www.factmagazine.co.uk/da/53579: accessed May 2007).

Rheingold, Howard (1993) *Virtual Community: Homesteading on the Electronic Frontier*. Reading, MA: Addison-Wesley.

Richardson, Ingrid (2007) Pocket technospaces: the bodily incorporation of mobile media, *Continuum*, 21(2): 205–15.

Ritzer, George (2000) *The McDonaldization of Society*. Thousand Oaks, CA: Pine Forge Press.

Rumsfeld, Donald H. (2006) *New Realities in the Media Age: A Conversation with Donald Rumsfeld* (www.cfr.org/publication/9900/: accessed on 12 December 2006).

Rutter, Jason and Bryce, Jo (eds) (2006) *Understanding Digital Games*. London: Sage Publications.

Saward, Michael (1994) Democratic theory and indices of democratisation, in D. Beetham (ed.) *Defining and Measuring Democracy*. London: Sage Publications.

Scott, D.T. (2005) Protest e-mail as alternative media in the 2004 US Presidential Campaign, *Westminister Papers in Communication and Culture*, 2(1): 51–71.

Seiter, Ellen (1992) Semiotics, structuralism and television, in Robert C. Allen (ed.) *Channels of Discourse, Reassembled: Television and Contemporary Criticism*. London and New York: Routledge.

Servaes, J. and Carpentier, N. (2006) *Towards a Sustainable Information Society*. Eastbourne, UK: Intellect Publishing.

Servon, Lisa (2002) *Redefining the Digital Divide: Technology, Community and Public Policy*. Malden, MA: Blackwell Publishing.

Sheff, David (1994) *Game Over: How Nintendo Zapped an Industry, Captured Your Money and Enslaved Your Children*. New York: Routledge.

Sherwin, Adrian (2007) iPod Records a Magic Number, *The Times*, April 11, p. 30.

Shirky, Clay (2006) interviewed on *Imagine* (episode entitled herecomeseverybody-.co.uk), first broadcast in the UK on BBC1, 5 December.

Shirky, Clay (2008) *Here Comes Everybody: The Power of Organising Without Organisation*. London: Allen Lane.

Shubi, Ishemo (2005) Culture and historical knowledge in Africa: a calibrian approach, *Review of African Political Economy*, 99: 65–82.

SIAI (2008) available at www.singinst.org/overview/whatisthesingularity.

Silver, David (2000) Looking backwards, looking forwards: cyberculture studies 1990–2000, in David Gauntlett (ed.) *Web.Studies*, 1st edn, pp. 19–30. London: Edward Arnold.

Silver, David (2004) Internet/Cyberculture/Digital Culture/New Media/Fill-in-the-Blanks Studies, *New Media and Society*, 6: 55–64.

Slevin, James (2000) *The Internet and Society*. Cambridge: Polity Press.

Smith, Thomas W (2002) The new law of war: legitimizing hi-tech and infrastructural violence, *International Studies Quarterly*, 46: 355–74.

Souza e Silva, A. (2006) From cyber to hybrid: mobile technologies as interfaces of hybrid spaces, *Space and Culture*, 9: 261–78.

Sterne, Jonathan (2006) The mp3 as a cultural artefact, *New Media & Society*, 8(5): 825–42.

Sussex Technology Group (2001) In the company of strangers: Mobile phones and the conception of space, in Sally R. Munt (ed.) *Technospaces: Inside the New Media*, pp. 205–23. London and New York: Continuum.

Talbot, Mary (2007) *Media Discourse: Representation and Interaction*. Edinburgh: Edinburgh University Press.

Terranova, Tiziana (2004) *Network Culture: Politics for the Information Age*. London: Pluto.

Todenhofer, Juergen (2002) It's a lot easier to declare victory than to earn it, *The Chicago Tribune*, 30 June.

Toynbee, Jason (2000) *Making Popular Music: Musicians, Creativity and Institutions*. London: Edward Arnold.

Turkle, Sherry (1995) *Life on the Screen: Identity in the Age of the Internet*. New York: Simon & Schuster, Inc.

UEAS (2003) *Managing Globalisation: Selected Cross-cutting Issues: Role of the ICT in Bridging the Digital Divide in Selected Areas*, December.

UNDP (1999) *Globalization with a Human Face*, June.

UNECA (2001) *Report of the Secretary General, Information and Communication Task Force*, September.

United Nations and Social Council (2003) *Managing Globalisation: Selected Cross-cutting Issues, Rule of TCT in Bridging the Digital Divide in Selected Areas*, E/ESCAP/CMG/3 (www.urrescap.org/cmg/2003/English/CMG_3E.pdf).

UNWFP (2007) available at www.wfp.org: accessed 26 December.

Urry, John (2006) Travelling times, *European Journal of Communication*, 21(3): 357–72.

Vaidhyanathan, Siva (2003) *Copyrights and Copywrongs: The Rise of Intellectual Property and How It Threatens Intellectual Freedom*. New York: New York University Press.

Veblen, Thorstein (1995) *The Theory of the Leisure Class*. London: Penguin.

Virilio, Paul (2002) *Desert Screen: War at the Speed of Light*. London: Continuum.

Wakeford, Nina (2004) Developing methodological frameworks for studying the world wide web, in David Gauntlett and Ross Horsley (eds) *Web.Studies*, 2nd edn, pp. 34–49. London: Edward Arnold.

Waldstein, Maxim (2005) The politics of the web: the case of one newsgroup, *Media, Culture & Society*, 27(5): 739–63. London: Sage Publications.

Webster, Frank (ed.) (1997) *Theories of the Information Society*. London: Routledge.

Webster, Frank (ed.) (2004) *The Information Society Reader*. London: Routledge.

Weiser, Mark (1991) The computer for the 21st century, *Science American* (www.ubiq.com/hypertext/weiser/SciAmDraft3.html).

Weizenbaum, J. (1966) ELIZA – a computer program for the study of natural language communication between man and machine, *Communications of the ACM*, 9(1): 36–45.

Wheeler, Brian (2003) Apple emerges from the Pod, *BBC News Magazine*, 16 December (www.news.bbc.co.uk/1/hi/magazine/3321943.stm: accessed May 2007).

Wikipedia (2007) *Wikipedia: Replies to Common Objections* (www.en.wikipedia.org/w/index.php?title=Wikipedia:Replies_to_common_objections&oldid=110320112: accessed on 25 February 2007).

Wikipedia (2008) Bioshock (www.en.wikipedia.org/wiki/BioShock: accessed January 2008).

Wilks, Yorick (2005) Artificial companions, in *Machine Learning for Multimodal Interaction: First International Workshop*, MLMI 2004, Martigny, Switzerland, June 21–23 2004: Revised Selected Papers, Springer.

Wolf, Mark J.P. (2001) *The Medium of the Video Game*. Austin, TX: University of Texas Press.

Wolf, Mark J.P. (2007) *The Video Game Explosion: A History from Pong to Playstation and Beyond*. Westport, CT: Greenwood Press.

Wolf, Mark J.P. and Perron, Bernard (eds) (2003) *The Video Game Theory Reader*. New York and London: Routledge.

Wyatt, Sally et al. (eds) (2000) *Technology and In/equality: Questioning the Information Society*. London: Routledge.

Zukin, Sharon (2004) *Point of Purchase: How Shopping Changed American Culture*. New York: Routledge.

Index

2001 Space Odyssey (film), 158
Aarseth, E., 20, 82, 84
accessibility, new media
   global inequalities of, 123–9
   role of internet in enabling within
     public sphere, 141–46
Adorno, T., 13
aesthetics
   strengths and weaknesses in digital
     cinema production, 65–6
age
   variations of as barrier to equality in
     digital media usage, 127–8
Alexander, D., 76
Althusser, L., 15
American Society of Cinematographers,
   70
analogue media
   characteristics, 46
analysis, digital
   evolution and history of, 11–21
Annan, K., 129
arenas, public (concept)
   definition and evolution of concept,
     139–41
Aristide, J.B., 152
ARPANET, 30
Attack of the Clones
   case study of production using digital
     techniques, 70–75
audiences
   modernist theories of, 13–14
Bakardjieva, M., 38
Bakupa-Kaninda, B., 67
Barron, P., 56
Barthes, R., 14
Bassett, K., 5–6
Baudrillard, J., 17
Baylis, J., 125
Berger, G., 143–4
Berners-Lee, T., 31–2, 39, 45
Berry, R., 102
Bioshock (video game)
   case study of production of, 86–91
blogging, 35
Bocquet, G., 74

Brief History of the Human Race (Cook),
   157
Bull, M., 109–10, 112
Burgin, V., 117–18
business
   use of internet for, 34
cable television, 51
calendars (timeline)
   of new media developments, 170–79
Carvin, A., 123–4
case studies
   application of natural language
     processing to new media, 164–9
   digital culture characteristics of
     contemporary society, 22–9
   digital voting in Haiti, 151–56
   dynamics of digital television news
     preparation, 55–60
   implications of digital media
     representation of war, 131–38
   of *Attack of the Clones* and *Star Wars*
     production, 70–75
   production of *Bioshock* video game,
     86–91
   social networking and impact on
     self-identity, 117–21
   strengths, weaknesses and attitudes
     towards wikipedia, 40–45
   success of digital audio players,
     102–107
CDs (compact discs)
   role in digital music revolution, 95–6
Chandler, D., 14, 147
Chesher, C., 119, 120
Chester, J., 143
cinema, digital
   case study of *Star Wars* production,
     70–75
   characteristics, strengths and
     weaknesses of production process,
     61–5
   impact of development on
     independent and minority film
     production, 65–8
class, social
   variations of as barrier to equality in
     digital media usage, 127–8

THE NEW MEDIA THEORY READER

Robert Hassan and Julian Thomas (eds)

Derek Kassem, Emmanuel Mufti and John Robinson (eds)

The study of new media opens up some of the most fascinating issues in contemporary culture: questions of ownership and control over information and cultural goods; the changing experience of space and time; the political consequences of new communication technologies; and the power of users and consumers to disrupt established economic and business models.

The New Media Theory Reader brings together key readings on new media – what it is, where it came from, how it affects our lives, and how it is managed. Using work from media studies, cultural history and cultural studies, economics, law, and politics, the essays encourage readers to pay close attention to the 'new' in new media, as well as considering it as a historical phenomenon. The Reader features a general introduction as well as an editors' introduction to each thematic section, and a useful summary of each reading.

The New Media Theory Reader is an indispensable text for students on new media, technology, sociology and media studies courses.

Essays by: Andrew Barry, Benjamin R Barber, James Boyle, James Carey, Benjamin Compaine, Noam Cook, Andrew Graham, Nicola Green, Thomas Hylland Eriksen, Ian Hunter, Kevin Kelly, Heejin Lee, Lawrence Lessig, Jonathan Liebenau, Jessica Litman, Lev Manovich, Michael Marien Robert W. McChesney David E. Nye, Bruce M Owen Lyman Ray Patterson, Kevin Robins, Ithiel de Sola Pool, David Saunders, Richard Stallman, Cass R. Sunstein, Jeremy Stein, McKenzie Wark, Frank Webster, Dugald Williamson.

Contents: Extracts – Introduction – Publisher's acknowledgements – PART 1 Media transitions – PART 2 Governing new media – PART 3 Properties and commons – PART 4 Politics of new media technologies – PART 5 Time and space in the age of information – Biographical notes – Bibliography – Index.

2006 352pp

978-0-335-21710-6 (Paperback) 978-0-335-21711-3 (Hardback)

KEY ISSUES IN CRITICAL AND CULTURAL THEORY

Kate McGowan

"... the ideal book for students of cultural theory and one that is sensitively attuned to the political challenges of our times. Whether explaining dialectical materialism or the lyrics of Oasis and The Arctic Monkeys, Kate McGowan is an enlightening and entertaining guide."

Professor Stephen Regan, Durham University

From a man with electric underpants, to the indelible mark of 9/11 in a global cultural imaginary, Kate McGowan addresses the questions of cultural meaning and value which confront us all today. The book explores the often complex paradigms of critical thinking and discusses the possibilities of engaging and critiquing the cultural values that relate to our present.

Dealing directly with the issues entailed in cultural analysis, the book avoids simply looking at the eminent authors or movements in critical and cultural theory, and instead focuses on why studying culture matters to us today:

- What are the 'proper' objects of cultural study?
- What makes something 'art'?
- What can critical and cultural theory contribute to contemporary debates about ethics?
- What possibilities are opened up by theories of 'otherness' in thinking about the stranger or outsider in today's society?
- How does a culture contest its own values – in relation to race, gender, class, sexuality and a variety of faiths and abilities?

Key Issues in Critical and Cultural Theory is key reading for students studying humanities, and for those with an interest in culture, aesthetics, ethics and philosophy who want to understand how these affect the world.

Contents: Acknowledgements – Introduction – Textuality and Signification – Aesthetics – Ethics – Alterity – The Real – The Inhuman – Conclusion – Glossary – Notes – Bibliography.

2007 176pp

978-0-335-21803-5 (Paperback) 978-0-335-21804-2 (Hardback)

CRITICAL THEORIES OF MASS MEDIA

Then and Now

Paul A. Taylor and Jan Ll. Harris

'*This is a welcome critical corrective to complacent mainstream accounts of the media's cultural impact.*'

> *Prof. Slavoj Zizek, International Director of the Birkbeck Institute for the Humanities at Birkbeck, University of London*

With the exception of occasional moral panics about the coarsening of public discourse, and the impact of advertising and television violence upon children, mass media tend to be viewed as a largely neutral or benign part of contemporary life. Even when criticisms are voiced, the media chooses how and when to discuss its own inadequacies. More radical external critiques are often excluded and media theorists are frequently more optimistic than realistic about the negative aspects of mass culture.

This book reassesses this situation in the light of both early and contemporary critical scholarship and explores the intimate relationship between the mass media and the dis-empowering nature of commodity culture. The authors cast a fresh perspective on contemporary mass culture by comparing past and present critiques. They:

- Outline the key criticisms of mass culture from past critical thinkers
- Reassess past critical thought in the changed circumstances of today
- Evaluate the significance of new critical thinkers for today's mass culture

The book begins by introducing the critical insights from major theorists from the past – Walter Benjamin, Siegfried Kracauer, Theodor Adorno, Marshall McLuhan and Guy Debord. Paul Taylor and Jan Harris then apply these insights to recent provocative writers such as Jean Baudrillard and Slavoj Žižek, and discuss the links between such otherwise apparently unrelated contemporary events as the Iraqi Abu Ghraib controversy and the rise of reality television.

Critical Theories of Mass Media is a key text for students of cultural studies, communications and media studies, and sociology.

Contents: Chapter outlines – Acknowledgements – Introduction – Part 1 Then – Walter Benjamin's 'Work of Art' essay – Siegfried Kracauer's mass ornament – Theodor Adorno and the culture industry – Marshall McLuhan's understanding of media – Guy Debord's Society of the Spectacle – Part 2 Now – Introduction to Part 2 – The culture of celebrity – Banality TV: the democratization of celebrity – The politics of banality: the ob-scene as the mis-en-scène – Conclusion – Notes – Bibliography – Index.

2007 264pp

978-0-335-21811-0 (Paperback) 978-0-335-21812-7 (Hardback)

MEDIA TECHNOLOGY

Critical Perspectives

Joost van Loon

- What are media?
- Why are more and more objects being turned into media?
- How do people interconnect with the media in structuring their everyday lives?

In *Media Technology: Critical Perspectives*, Joost van Loon illustrates how throughout the course of society, different forms of media have helped to shape our perceptions, expectations and interpretations of reality.

Drawing on the work of media scholars such as Marshall McLuhan, Walter Benjamin, Roland Barthes and Raymond Williams, the author provides a theoretical analysis of the complexity of media processes. He urges the reader to challenge mainstream assumptions of media merely as instruments of communication, and shows how the matter, form, use and purpose of media technologies can affect content.

The book uses practical examples from both old and new media to help readers think through complex issues about the place of media. This helps to create a more innovative toolkit for understanding what media actually are and the basis for trying to make sense of what media actually do. It uses case studies and examples from television, radio, print, computer games and domestic appliances.

Media Technology is essential reading for undergraduate and postgraduate students on media, social theory and critical theory-related courses.

Contents: Acknowledgements – Introduction – A critical history of media technology – Alternative trajectories: Technology as culture – 'Media as extensions of wo/man': Feminist perspectives on mediation and technological embodiment – New media and networked (dis)embodiment – Conclusion: Theorizing media technology – Glossary – References – Index.

2007 192pp

978-0-335-21446-4 (Paperback) 978-0-335-21447-1 (Hardback)